WOMEN OF CRISIS II

WOMEN OF CRISIS II

"As in the first volume, the authors let the women's own words define them. The Coleses may reorganize the words, combine and condense them, surround them with explanatory notes, but never is there any sense of intrusion or deliberate shaping. These women are allowed to speak for themselves, and they do, marvelously."

Anne Tyler

"Unforgettable."

Jeff Greenfield, *The New York Times Book Review*

"This book makes the mysterious connection between the private experience of its subjects and the larger human experience that is achieved by all good biography."

Los Angeles Times

"Illuminating portraits . . . their stories delineate the larger themes of love, work, independence, and women's struggle to reconcile the three in a male-dominated society."

Psychology Today

"Fresh, utterly engrossing. The Coleses are unsurpassed at giving shape and significance to the raw material of oral history. . . . These women tell us important things."

Booklist

"Five American women, among them a Pueblo photographer and a former SNCC activist-feminist, reveal themselves in a personal yet universal way. . . . The hallmark of the Coleses approach—respect for the individual's voice—is evident in the 'documentary portraits' that make their work an everywoman chronicle."

Publishers Weekly

"Five supreme gifts are given to us by the Coleses in this most wondrous second volume of *Women of Crisis*. They are literary gifts, life gifts. To read the book is to value still again the simple life, the gifts of listening and writing, and, above all, the courage and generosity of the human heart."

Thomas Cottle, Ph.D., *The Boston Globe*

RADCLIFFE BIOGRAPHY SERIES

WOMEN OF CRISIS II

Lives of Work and Dreams

Robert Coles and Jane Hallowell Coles

A Merloyd Lawrence Book

Addison-Wesley Publishing Company, Inc.
Reading, Massachusetts   Menlo Park, California   New York
Don Mills, Ontario   Wokingham, England   Amsterdam   Bonn
Sydney   Singapore   Tokyo   Madrid   San Juan

Many of the designations used by manufacturers and sellers to distinguish their products are claimed as trademarks. Where those designations appear in this book and Addison-Wesley was aware of a trademark claim, the designations have been printed in initial capital letters (e.g., Chrysler).

Library of Congress Cataloging-in-Publication Data

Coles, Robert.
    Women of crisis II : lives of work and dreams / by Robert Coles and Jane Hallowell Coles.
        p. cm. — (Radcliffe biography series)
    "A Merloyd Lawrence book."
    ISBN 0-201-51811-2
    1. Women—United States—Biography. 2. Working class—United States. 3. Working class women—United States—Biography.
    4. United States—Social conditions. I. Coles, Jane Hallowell.
    II. Title. III. Series.
    HQ1412.C638 1990
    305.4'0973'0922—dc20   89-18558
                                                  CIP

Women of Crisis II was first published in 1980 as A Merloyd Lawrence Book by Delacorte Press/Seymour Lawrence.

Cover design by Copenhaver Cumpston
Cover photograph © Martine Franck/Magnum
Text design by MaryJane DiMassi
Set in 11-point Times Roman

ABCDEFGHIJ-MW-943210
First printing, March 1990

To the Memory of Lillian Smith
To Dorothy Day

BALM IN GILEAD
Journey of a Healer
Sara Lawrence Lightfoot

MARIA MONTESSORI
A Biography
Rita Kramer

A MIND OF HER OWN
The Life of Karen Horney
Susan Quinn

WOMEN OF CRISIS
Lives of Struggle and Hope
Robert Coles and Jane Hallowell Coles

WOMEN OF CRISIS II
Lives of Work and Dreams
Robert Coles and Jane Hallowell Coles

PUBLISHED BY DELACORTE PRESS

HELEN AND TEACHER
The Story of Helen Keller and Anne Sullivan Macy
Joseph P. Lash

BUYING THE NIGHT FLIGHT
Georgie Anne Geyer

foreword

Radcliffe College is pleased and proud to sponsor the Radcliffe Biographies, a series of lives of extraordinary American women.

Each volume of the Radcliffe Biographies serves to remind us of two of the values of biographical writing. A fine biography is first of all a work of scholarship, grounded in the virtues of diligent and scrupulous research, judicious evaluation of information, and a fresh vision of the connections between persons, places, and events.

Beyond this, fine biographies give us both a glimpse of ourselves and a reflection of the human spirit. Biography illuminates history, inspires by example, and fires the imagination to life's possibilities. Good biography can create for us lifelong models. Reading about others' experiences encourages us to persist, to face hardship, and to feel less alone. Biography tells us about choice, steadfastness, and chance.

The women whose lives are told in the Radcliffe Biographies have been teachers, adventurers, writers, scholars. The lives of some of them were hard pressed by poverty, cultural heritage, or physical handicap. Some of the women achieved fame; the victories and defeats of others have been unsung. Some of the women lived and died years ago; others are our contemporaries. We can learn from all of them something of ourselves. In sponsoring this series, Radcliffe College is responding to the renewed interest of our society in exploring and understanding the experience of women.

The Radcliffe Biographies project found its inspiration in the publication in 1971 of *Notable American Women,* a scholarly encyclopedia sponsored by Radcliffe's Schlesinger Library on the History of Women in America. We became convinced that some of the encyclopedia's essays should be expanded into full-length biographies, so that a wider audience could grasp the many contributions women have made to American life—an awareness of which is as yet by no means universal. It seemed appropriate that an institution dedicated to the higher education of women should initiate such a project, to hold a mirror up to the lives of particular women, to pay tribute to them, and so to deepen our understanding of them and of ourselves.

We have been joined in this project by two distinguished publishing houses and by a remarkable group of writers. I am grateful to them and to the editorial board—and particularly to Deane Lord, who first proposed the series, both in concept and in detail. Finally, I am happy to present this volume of the Radcliffe Biographies.

MATINA S. HORNER
President

Radcliffe College
Cambridge, Massachusetts

contents

WOMEN OF
CRISIS II

introduction

We have described in the *Children of Crisis* books, and in the first volume of *Women of Crisis,* how we established contact with the first families we visited, in Louisiana and Georgia, and how, later on, we met other families—parents quite inclined to permit their children to tell us what was on their minds, and parents also not loath, usually, to add a few adult observations, a bonus of sorts.

This second volume of *Women of Crisis* draws upon these visits with families begun twenty years ago for *Children of Crisis* and continues the narrative of a segment of that work begun in the first volume. We have not been trying to extract statements from American citizens in order to construct self-important theories. Our nation's cultural landscape—yes, from "sea to shining sea"—is already cluttered, if not badly contaminated, by a large and constantly increasing mass of "findings": the "data" of various social science research projects. Everyone's "attitudes" about everything have been, continue to be, "surveyed." We have been declared a bundle of reflexes, organisms that respond to "drives," a tangle of hidden and not-so-hidden psychopathology. We have heard our poor called "culturally deprived" and "culturally disadvantaged," our ordinary working people described as "one-dimensional," as in possession of a "false consciousness," and dozens of other not-so-friendly labels, by critics who are more sparing with themselves and their own kind. The last thing we want to do is come up with a few more pushy, overwrought, wordy generalizations about America's people, and specifically, its women, who have been getting a good deal of attention lately—not always discerning or appropriate.

We have constantly been visiting one kind of home, then another kind. In Albuquerque, as in the Mississippi Delta or the metropolitan Boston area, we moved back and forth, from black homes to white ones, from Indian homes to Anglo ones, from poor and hardly well-off homes, to comfortable ones, indeed. Within the limits of our mode of work—quite decided limits, because we spend weeks, months, with individual families, whom we try to end up knowing fairly well—we hoped to gain some sense of how different children grow up in America, and also, how their mothers and fathers and various relatives fare. We have done what might be called cross-cultural, naturalistic observation. This book remains loyal to that mode of work.

A black teacher we knew in Alabama told us this in 1965—her reaction to the burgeoning literature about blacks: "I read all those articles and reports, and I wonder what's going on. The Negro is this, and the Negro is that. Who are the Negroes those experts are talking about? What did those experts do—go and hand their questions to some people: yes or no maybe? I shouldn't be so 'defensive,' I know. But I'm afraid of this: we'll get ourselves clear of the Klan and the White Citizens Councils, and pretty soon we'll find out there's another crowd of people after us, and this new crowd won't get everything right, either, and some of what they call us may even be worse than the swear words of the red-necks.

"To me, each person is different, and that holds for our colored as well as for the white. When I hear someone describing us, all of us, as brave and courageous, I'm almost as upset as when I hear us called all the bad names we've been called here in Anniston, and everywhere else in my home state of Alabama. My daddy is a minister, and he says that every person is good and bad, though the percentages of each are different. Now, I don't like a lot of the preaching I used to hear from him; he's too kind to the white man, and he's always telling his congregation to be patient, to pray and wait for the Lord's answer. The 'answer' for us is to make our own answer—to say no to segregation and yes to our people's struggle for equality. But I'll say this: I'll stick with my father when he says that you should look at the person first, and only then should you think of his skin color or his name or his place of residence or his job or his birthplace. And what goes for 'his,' goes for 'hers.' After we've won a victory for our civil rights movement, we can start fighting for a lot of other people who don't get a good deal here in this country. These 'poor white' folk—I feel sorry for them sometimes: a diet of hate, when they themselves need better food and work and better homes, just as we do. And the women all over: black women and white women, southern belles and southern factory women and those southern women sitting at their desks typing and running the switchboards—they've got a few complaints! You'll find all kinds among all kinds, my grandmother used to say—and she couldn't read and she couldn't write, and she was the daughter of a slave!''

No doubt there are valuable ways of pulling together life's variousness into compact, suggestive statements. The point is to move from the particular person to the broader arc of humanity without violating the kind of truth that daughter of a slave knew in her bones. One old-fashioned and still rather lively, penetrating, and illuminating way of doing so is through the medium of a life-history (not to be confused with a case-history). Biographers know that through a person's story they can shed light on the stories of others, too. And novelists know that even a person imagined can do likewise—make the "real" seem closer at hand and more sharply focused: a paradox, and one of many in a world full of small as well as large ambiguities, ironies, inconsistencies, incongruities. Any psychological theory, any sociological scheme of interpretation had better do justice to all that—to the complexity of human affairs—if it is to pass the muster of a knowing daughter of a slave, and of her granddaughter. Amid all the structuring of life into "periods," "stages" of human development, with psychosocial variables and sociocultural factors, there is room for plain biographical presentation, with a vivid moment or two—stories of humor, of regret and sadness, of aspirations retained or dashed, of fears banished or never let go.

We have tried to shape what we have seen and heard into a kind of story—a life presented, with all the subdued tension and drama, the dignity, and inevitably the moments of fear and sadness, that characterize most lives. We have, so doing, compressed drastically remarks made in leisure. We have moved comments around a bit, placing statements made one time with those made another—not in order to rip words out of context, but for the sake of coherence and containment of presentation. The essential thrust is toward a reasonably accessible and suggestive "reading" of a given person's life. The writers become mediators; through them another life reaches toward the reader, and if the work has been successful, stays with the reader as a guest, a "spirit," whose mind and heart and soul have been registered upon the consciousness of distant strangers.

In the first volume of *Women of Crisis* we called upon our working experiences with five women: a black migrant worker; an Appalachian woman who had left her native soil, loved dearly, for an Ohio industrial city; a Chicana; an Eskimo woman; and a maid who attends to the demands of another woman's home. In this volume we have continued to call upon our past work, only different parts of it. We lived and worked with Pueblo and Hopi women long enough to be puzzled by them, unnerved even, challenged by them, and quite frankly, enamored of them. On the reservations we visited (north of Santa Fe, New Mexico, and in the northeast quadrant of Arizona), there were several especially strong-minded and discerning women who kept a close watch on us, and did not hesitate at certain moments to put us firmly in our place. Their view of the world was not that of the Anglo population nearby—but rather a view one might describe as wryly meditative and introspective. The Pueblos, of course, have had ample opportunity over the centuries to take the measure of Anglos. For centuries it has been New Mexico's Pueblos who have accommodated themselves adroitly to the Spanish, the Americans—all the while holding on to a particular kind of Indian sensibility. We lived quite near one Pueblo reservation north of Albuquerque. We traveled twice a week to another reservation farther north. We became especially involved with five Pueblo women whose children were guides of sorts to us—willing to take us at least part of the way into a spiritual realm rather different from the one we have learned to call our own.

In New Mexico, among the Pueblos, whom we came to know during our residence there, the contrast of moral, psychological, and again, spiritual climates became even more pronounced. Some Pueblos have traditionally held themselves back (to the utmost extent possible) from the constantly assertive, if not expansionist, presence of the Americans, and as well, such fellow Indians as the Navahos. Among the Pueblos we met, two families were unforgettable; and one woman has, for us, been a powerful teacher. From her we learned not only about "the Pueblo way," but about ourselves—what we thought of life, what we hoped for, very much feared, couldn't bear to consider, or regarded more intently, perhaps, than we realized. We have tried to bring this woman to the reader; we have drawn upon her words and thoughts, her memories and her dreams, her observations and her ruminations.

Two other portraits came out of our effort, a long and hard one, to get some sense of how ordinary working people—in factories and shops and offices—manage to come to terms with their lives. In *The Middle Americans* (1971) we tried to convey how it goes for a policeman, a gas station attendant, a fireman, a schoolteacher, a steamfitter, a druggist, a clerk—how it goes for *men* caught in the middle: not exactly poor, and certainly far from being rich, or even well off. The wives, mothers, grandmothers, sisters, daughters of the men figured in the text, and even more so in the accompanying photographs. But the predominant focus, if not bias, was masculine—reflecting the fact that American women did not yet stand up for their rights as noticeably as they have since. (The interviews that paved the way for *The Middle Americans* were, of course, done in the 1960's.) Even now, as a matter of fact, it is our impression that the women's movement has not scored the same political and ideological success among the blue- and white-collar women we have known as among their upper-middle-class contemporaries. Sometimes there has been a decided counterreaction: an insistence by women upon upholding the traditional "position" of their own sex. Here the issue of class comes in—a perception by working-class women that a number of well-to-do women are talking to themselves, rather than considering how others feel, far removed in "background," in assumptions or concerns.

In the seminars we have held with college women, we have observed constantly the distance of those women, psychologically and sociologically and culturally, from the working-class women of the country. Often it seems easier for an undergraduate, or indeed, an active member of the women's movement, to feel closer to black women in a ghetto, or Chicano women in a distant barrio, than to women living nearer at home—in a so-called streetcar suburb, or in a factory town not far away. Needless to say, any number of women activists have known the problem all along and all too well—the reluctance of many other women to see things in the way their would-be political or ideological advocates have come to regard as desirable. We felt it important to go back for additional conversations with certain working-class families— with the women who have, as a matter of fact, always talked to us the most in those families. We were, a decade ago, rather too anxious to heed the recommendations of those women. The woman who appears in Part Five of this book told us this in 1969: "We're just average housewives on this street. I don't think we have any opinions, one way or the other. All we try to do is take care of the home. If you want to know what we think here, you'll have to come on the weekend, when my husband is around. It's the men who sound off, after they have some beer in them. I'm not even curious about the news most of the time, to be honest. I have so much to do, from six in the morning to ten or eleven at night, that I can't stop to listen to those politicians, or those know-it-all commentators. Maybe it will change when my kids get older. I don't know. But right now all I dream of is sitting in the sun, listening to some soft, relaxing music!''

Actually, she became considerably more "political" a few years on, much to her own surprise. She and others very much like her make up the majority of American women—married, with or without children, of "average means," and with no more than a high school education. We've tried here to indicate some of the dilemmas such women face as they go through one day, then another. The bank teller who appears in Part Two and the self-described "typical suburban housewife" have turned out to be, in our experience, both *sui generis* and as "typical," per-haps, as anyone can be of an entire class of people. Each of us survives that tension—the particularity of our selves as against the attributes we share with others who live much as we do. We have not, we hope, tried to ignore the distinctive personal charac-teristics in the two women just mentioned. They deserve better than sociological labels such as "middle Americans," a feminine version, or women of "the lower-middle" or "middle-middle" class. They deserve better than membership in categories such as "executive woman" or "political activist" or "white-collar worker" or "housewife." The woman who has been going to a bank for years, and (while there) taking in money and handing it out, minute after minute, hours each day, five days a week, has something to tell us about her situation as a bank teller. But she also is a woman with her very own road to walk—with family, friends, and quite definitely, the men she has met. The suburban woman would be the first to admit that she isn't (who *is*, once one looks hard enough?) the completely unremarkable ("average," "ordinary," "plain") person she will sometimes claim to be. She also has a lot to tell us—about what, most likely, obtains in ranch house homes that belong to communities where factory workers and civil servants overwhelmingly predominate. But she also is a woman who has cherished reveries of her very own.

The Pueblo woman in Part Four once told us to stop asking about habits and customs and rituals and beliefs, and instead ask about the "pictures" that occasionally came across her mind. In a quite typical suburb a woman hurrying from the refrigerator to the table, thence to the washing machine, thence to the station wagon, and back to another electrical gadget, the vacuum cleaner—with a break or two at the television—is not without some of those "pictures," however different from the ones mentioned by someone standing on an Arizona mesa. "Oh, you want to hear what's on my mind!" we once heard the suburban woman who appears in Part Five say—her statement a mixture of surprise and wry self-effacement and decided pleasure, and, not least, a touch of suspicion. She would, thereafter, demur—tell us that she had no time at all to have anything on her mind. But she was annoyed with herself for saying that, and was quite willing to turn around, see herself differently, and perhaps give us, the writers and readers of this world, a bit of sanction: "I guess there's no one who doesn't have her thoughts, while she's rushing about, keeping the home in shape, and watching over the kids and getting ready for the mister's return home. I don't have much time to think. I don't read much of anything. The paper comes, but do I have a chance to read it? No! I have to admit, though—I'll daydream. In the car, I will think about how it's going for everyone in the family—myself included. I always tell myself that I shouldn't ever think of myself at all, considering all the others in the family who need attention. But I'll slip up every once in a while. Maybe we should know it about each other—that everyone has a dream or two in the heart that she carries around!"

Her dreams are part of the stuff of her life—a larger part than she would sometimes admit. So with other women more involved with the world outside the twentieth-century suburban landscape—the world of business, of finance, of advertising and com-

munications. There is no one type of "executive woman"; as
with the other women we have chosen, one thinks of the various
kindred spirits. The phrase "executive woman" costs a good
deal, because it categorizes women on the basis of the level of
employment attained—only one theme, of course, in their respective lives. Businesswomen most certainly face special problems,
and with one portrait we can only begin to suggest them. The
particular woman we have "written up" knew we were, at the
same time, talking with other women, whose lives had a rather
different momentum than hers. She was herself interested in the
contrasts she knew we were seeing. At rock bottom, however,
there are certain issues that *women* struggle with, no matter their
class or race—especially when many of today's women executives have risen rather rapidly from working-class backgrounds.
Similar experiences connect women destined eventually to be
separated by the circumstances of life. The social and economic
rise described in Part One had characteristics which even rather
poor women would find familiar: the continuing conflict between
feminist ideals and the "reality" of living with and working with
particular men.

With the increasing momentum of the women's movement in
recent years, businesses of all kinds began to look twice at their
records, their responsibilities and obligations—or maybe, alas, at
the risks entailed by discrimination on the basis of sex as well as
race. For banks an obvious move was to select a few tellers of
long service and groom them for managerial positions. The bank
teller in our book might have been one such candidate, had she
not worked in a downtown or central bank (which started hiring
women graduates of business schools nearby) and had she not,
also, through a marriage, cemented (in a strange way) her relationship to her own background. She may never have become a
bank manager, but she knew how to appraise the other two
women who, out of nowhere, it seemed, arrived upon "her"
scene. She understood them as "different" in certain respects—
but also as "fellow women."

Perhaps she has best put our case for individual portraits,

placed side by side, of women whose social and economic (as well as, naturally, personal) circumstances vary in a number of ways: "When they hired the first woman in a managerial slot, I wondered what *she* knew about banking. I'd never wondered about the *men* who kept showing up—and moving up! A woman can be dumb about women! A woman can be envious of another woman! I suppose I'm human; I'd like to be walking around, giving orders. I'd like to be a boss. But I'm not the kind who knows how to do it—give orders to others. There are plenty of women who were born without much money behind them, who could become the best bosses you'll find anywhere. Isn't that what America is supposed to be about—for men? I'm not always happy being a teller—but I'm happier when I look over there and see a woman or two sitting at those desks, even if I do get jealous sometimes, and think of myself and wish I could have been more successful. One of the women is very good to me; she keeps her eye on all of us—but I think she and I have something going. We've gone out for coffee a few times, and even though she has a few airs—you can't help picking them up where she went to school!—there's something we have in common. She told me once that one of the bank's officers told her I was 'natural material'—for a position as an officer. I told her maybe that's true, but it's not in the cards for me, even if they do need their women up front to show off how 'equal' they are! I'm a woman, and I'm a person! It takes a few years—it takes all your life!—to know that, to know something about yourself. And sometimes you find out about yourself by looking at the next person, the next woman. I told her that, and she said yes, she could see what I meant. That was the closest moment we've had, for sure!"

This woman, a person of substantial complexity, simply cannot be done justice to—not her mind, not her heart—with an approximation such as "bank teller"; nor does the phrase "bank manager" or "woman executive" encompass the variations of human experience and sensibility to be found by anyone intent on a "study." As the reader will see, this bank teller ended up seeing the world as a social and political activist might—though she did not by any means become one. Other women, too, have developed such a point of view—some of them in the course of holding down jobs such as that of a bank teller, some in the course of pursuing what gets referred to as "higher callings": the emergence of growing cadres of professional and business women. As far back as 1961, we now realize, we were rather strongly connected to certain women who were by their own description "activists." They were members of SNCC, civil rights workers—but also, *women:* black and white, southern and northern, quite well educated and not very well educated, at least in the traditional sense of the word. At that time race was the great divider—and also source of "consciousness" and of shared political protest. Yet, in 1962, in Atlanta, after one of the long, long "soul sessions" that SNCC workers took part in, we heard a black woman from Birmingham, Alabama, come up with a prophecy: "This is just the beginning. There is race—and there is sex. I'm tired of being insulted because of the color of my skin. But when those sheriffs come after us, the *women* in SNCC, they have a look in their eyes: come on, *girl,* let's stop being so serious; let's have us a good time and forget all this trouble. That's what I was told once, down in Albany [Georgia], but I've seen the telltale look on their faces for a long time—the faces of the white *men!* So, the next time around, the next battle, will be us women, black and white, against those sheriffs, and all the others, the *men* who think like them and talk like them and act like them."

For a woman, black or white, to take on those sheriffs was indeed a special occasion—given the South's long-standing insistence that women be demeaned by the pedestal. Over and over again in the early 1960's, we saw doubly lifted eyebrows, heard expressions of double surprise, resentment, anger—*women* becoming involved in a racial incident! And in the Mississippi Summer Project of 1964, we heard from certain segregationists a level of anxiety and crazy rage that was quite special—reserved for white women involved in an effort to challenge directly the most solid of all segregationist territory. Though we have repeatedly in the past written up our work with "non-violent youth" of both races and sexes (at some length in Volume One of *Children of Crisis*), we have never before tried to write specifically about the women, as women, whom we worked alongside during those years in Georgia and Alabama, Mississippi and Louisiana. One woman's story, again, is not every woman's story—not with respect to political activists any more than with respect to the other "categories" mentioned above. But threads there are—common objectives pursued, common external dangers faced, common internal difficulties faced: the fear, the anxiety that a woman on the picket line, or a woman canvassing a neighborhood, is bound to feel, even as each woman has her own way of dealing with those pressures from the outside (reality) and the inside (the mind's alarm in response to danger).

It is, for us, terribly important to have been able at least to respond to some of the strong-minded and extremely brave and determined women activists we have known—not only in the South (SNCC) but in Appalachia, where women worked for the Appalachian Volunteers (another group we became involved with), and in the Southwest, where Chicano women have struggled long and hard on behalf of migrant farm workers. One Chicana gave us the best charge possible: "Tell them about the pain and sorrow in this rich, strong country; but tell them, always, that we are not bowed, the poor, and that we are not bowed, the people they call 'minorities,' and that we are not bowed, the women who are poor and are part of *two* minorities— their race and their sex. Tell them that women are the majority who are a minority! Tell them that some of us women have said no, enough and more than enough—and will give our lives to proving ourselves women of our word! Tell them who we are! Tell them what happened to make us who we are!"

Strong words, easily dismissed as "rhetorical." And activist women have to contend with just such a line of reasoning: the arrogant condescension of those who don't like moral indignation, and know how to put it down firmly. The two women to whom we have dedicated this volume are no strangers to such criticism or dismissal. They have pursued careers as writers; but have also been outspoken champions of human equity. We first met Lillian Smith, as we mentioned in the preceding volume of *Women of Crisis,* at the beginning of the 1960's. We lived in Vinings, Georgia, she up north in Clayton, Georgia. We went back and forth, and when we weren't traveling, we were sending letters. She was a fiercely insistent advocate of the South's poor, the South's black people, the South's women—and others like them elsewhere. She was far, far ahead of her time. She was a delightfully brave, decent, compassionate, knowing woman. We were, we say it again, privileged to know her, and we take this occasion to remember her again, and thank her for the constant encouragement and support she gave us personally, and through her important, prophetic books: *Strange Fruit, Killers of the Dream, One Hour.*

Dorothy Day was also mentioned in the first volume of *Women of Crisis.* Humble woman of uncommon Christian conviction, servant of God's grace in thousands of ways over dozens of years, exemplary bridge between the spiritual and the social, the political, she was also, and not least, an American woman, whose particular struggle in that last regard has been left recorded for us—a powerful and constantly instructive autobiography: *The Long Loneliness.* We have unqualified respect for her work, and believe in the kind of religious and political stand she has taken, and have tried, in *Dorothy Day: A Radical Devotion* and *A Spectacle Unto the World: The Catholic Worker Movement,* to indicate what she and her co-workers, Christian social activists, have been trying to do, on behalf of others and in Christ's name, over these past five decades. Here, yet again, we salute her, thank her. We are grateful for her presence among us, surely a gift from on high, and grateful too for the chance to have known her.

A last word. We keep talking of "us." All this work, twenty years of it, has been done by us together. How does one separate us—until the inevitable call of fate? Each child, each family these past two decades, has had to be doubly gracious and patient and giving, if the bond between observers and informants was to be maintained. Now, we have again become a writing pair, and thoroughly enjoy the challenge. We have, together, gone back through the notebooks we jointly and separately kept. We have, together, listened to the tapes, in order to decide what to use, when, and how. We have, finally, divided up the writing by temperament and choice—the introduction and two of the portraits by one of us (R.C.) and three of the portraits by the other of us (J.H.C.) But further editing and a final written version was the result of our collaboration, so this is, again, a thoroughly shared effort. And shared, too, with our good friend and recent co-worker, Tom Davey, and with Bonnie Harris's continuing, most valuable, thoughtful, and generous support. As for the women we have tried to evoke—with affection, with admiration, with fond memories of years as their guests—we can only make the grateful avowal that students ought to make when they have been well taught, indeed.

part one

BOSSING

EVERY WEEKDAY morning Mrs. Laura Willis walks smartly out of her spacious, modern home, located by her description "far out in the country," and with a mug of black coffee in hand heads for a new Chrysler sedan. It is seven fifteen in the morning, and she is on her way to work. Before she starts the car, she sits and sips the coffee so that more than half of it is inside her: no spilling while in motion. She loves her car, loves driving, loves cutting quickly with her eyes from one scene to the next—then back to the road and its demands. She is "a morning person," she declares. She has contempt for the glib people, with their never-ending, pretentious "psychology," who talk that way: "morning person," indeed! Yet, they have a point. Before they made that point, she only knew that she could never sleep late, had never slept later than eight o'clock in her life, and was usually at her best in the hours that precede noon—thereafter, downhill all the way. For years she had always needed coffee at four o'clock, lots of coffee, and a vision of supper, merely to survive the last working hour. Until, that is, she had become "a boss." Now she could set her own hours, within reason.

Now, too, she could have that Chrysler, with its leather: "I never thought I'd drive a car like this. I used to hate expensive cars—at least the American kind. I was a bit of a snob before I learned how to become an all-out snob! I hated expensive cars because my father and mother taught me to hate them. They hated them because they had never had the money to buy them. My mother would tell me about a neighbor who suddenly made a lot of money—in 1938, of all times. The neighbor immediately started looking for a new home in another town. That took time, maybe a few weeks. But it only took a day for the neighbor to go out and buy himself a big Chrysler. My mother never forgot that car, even though it was gone, with its owner, in a month or so. She would describe it to me when she'd be telling me about the pain of struggling hard, just to get by—and the pain of failing, because there was no work for Dad a lot of the time, and he would never, ever go on relief. I remember my mother's description of that car so well that I used to think I'd seen it: two-tone, green and ivory, push-button radio, whitewall tires, and an engine that took you places fast as can be, but with practically no noise. She'd been given a ride in it once. She remembered the soft seats. She felt as though she could lie down and go to sleep, and wake up across the country, in California. I always wondered why she criticized those people for buying the car, when it was so comfortable!

"When I got older I started getting annoyed at her memories of the Depression—especially of that car. I thought she was being silly. My father said people who bought big cars were suckers, or they were show-offs. My mother finally admitted that she hated people who bought big cars because she always wanted one. She told me she had a lot of envy in her, and it got 'sour' sometimes, and turned to hate. She didn't need the courses in 'human behavior' I took at business school to figure out what her emotions were like! And here *I* am—with a Chrysler! If my mother were alive, she'd probably have no trouble telling me why I bought that car when I got my last job."

She is an executive in a communications corporation—a chain

of radio and television stations. She is a vice-president whose chief responsibility is a critically important one: she plans the advertising several stations do on behalf of their programs, and she deals with advertising executives who work for the various corporations that buy the radio and television time her company sells. At thirty-seven she has judged her life, at different moments, "strange," "a surprising success story," and "frustrating." She constantly wonders how she happened to occupy her present job. As a girl, she dreamed of being a doctor. A sister two years her elder had, at the age of thirteen, suddenly been taken ill. She became partially paralyzed, due to a hemorrhage from a congenital aneurysm of a blood vessel in the brain. She was hospitalized, and after three weeks seemed to be getting better—when another episode of bleeding took place. Several days later, she died. Laura was heartbroken. She had insisted on maintaining a vigil at the hospital, and in the course of so doing had become well acquainted with various nurses and doctors, and especially a young woman medical student who had chanced to come by. The memory of that terrible time would never leave Laura; even in her thirties she would think of that hospital ward, and what she learned about life and death—and herself, her prospects as a girl: "Sometimes I'll be driving to work, and I think to myself that if my sister hadn't become ill and died, I wouldn't be the person I am today. Maybe it's foolish to say that a single incident in your life can set its direction, but as the saying goes, 'One thing leads to another'; and the 'one thing' for me was listening to that woman medical student talk."

Laura was not only devastated by her only sister's illness; she feared that without her there would be no imaginable future life. The closer death encroached upon the family, the more terrified the daughter who wasn't sick seemed to become. She went to sleep crying and woke up crying. She suffered nightmares. She lost her appetite. She was, for a while, inconsolable. But the medical student got her going in a conversation about the blood pressure cuff—how it works and what it has to tell. And one thing did, indeed, lead to another: "Her name was Joan; I remember her telling me to call her by her first name. It was one of those strange twists of fate, because my sister's name was Joan, too—though she had always been Joannie to me. At first I wanted to know about an aneurysm: what it was and why my sister 'got' it. It took a patient person to sit with a fifth-grade girl and make everything clear. I remember that she drew me a picture of the artery, and the weak walls, and the sac, and the leak that developed, with blood coming out. Then she explained to me how the brain works, and if the blood spilled, the brain began to die. I remember her saying it to me: 'The blood is spilling on a part of your sister's brain, and she's paralyzed because of that.'

"I wanted to know why my *sister* had that 'sac'; and of course no medical student, no world-famous neurosurgeon could answer that! Not even now do the doctors fully understand why some people are born with congenital defects. The best answer came from Joan: 'Your sister had bad luck, that's all.' Somehow that satisfied me, the phrase 'bad luck.' It was like a lance, plunged into a boil so pussy you could see through the skin, it was pulled that tight! I began to feel less jittery. Every time I felt myself getting nervous, I'd say to myself that Joannie had been the victim of bad luck. Then I got sad. Before I hadn't been sad at all, just scared to death!

"I began to wake up thinking of Joan and go to sleep thinking of her. I guess she liked me, too, because one morning she asked me if I wanted to go to the hospital cafeteria and have lunch with her. I didn't wait a second to say yes! I was hungry instantly, and stayed hungry for two hours, when it was noon, and time to go meet my new friend! She was so kind to me! She became, I realized later, a different older sister—much older, very wise and protective. She told me things I've never forgotten. She told me she was the only woman in her medical school class—that very few women ever become doctors. I wondered why. I was always asking her why, and she was always telling me why! I can still hear her answer to *that* 'why'—about women and medical schools: 'prejudice.'

"It was a one-word reply, and I was lost. At first I tried to be the smart, sophisticated one; I nodded, as if to say yes, of course. But she saw the puzzled look on my face, and she went on to explain—that in many professions women are kept out because men decide who is admitted and who isn't, and the men think women can't do as good a job. I had never seen the world like that; nor had my mother, or her mother, who was alive then. I came home and told them what I'd heard, and my mother said that medicine is not a good profession for women; it's too tough, and women aren't strong enough. My grandmother was more emphatic, and became visibly upset when she talked to me. She was a staunch Presbyterian, anyway—of the old Calvinist school! She could make a child think that thunder and lightning would soon come, followed by the appearance of a stern God with definite likes and dislikes. She told me in no uncertain terms that women weren't 'made' to be doctors or lawyers; but were 'made' to be wives and mothers. Even my mother, back then, found that a little hard to take; I remember her reminding my grandmother that some women don't marry, and they become good teachers (like the one I had, then, in school!) and good nurses (like the one on the day shift in the hospital, who had been so nice to Joannie, and all of us). My grandmother nodded, but she wasn't very nice when she was corrected. She carried a grudge for hours, days. No wonder my father always took a walk when she came to visit us!''

When Laura's sister died, the medical student, Joan, came to the funeral, and thereafter remained in touch with the family, especially Laura. By the age of twelve Laura had a fairly good idea of how doctors are trained, how hospitals work, how a woman manages to hold her own in a particular kind of man's world. She also had an idea of what she wanted to do with her life: become a physician. And when her friend and mentor chose pediatrics as a specialty, Laura (now entering high school) began to picture herself taking care of the medical problems of young children. She took science courses, began to learn, firsthand, what her older friend had meant when, years before, she had used the word ''prejudice.'' Why should a ''nice, pretty girl'' want to take chemistry and physics? The guidance counselor had asked that of Laura's mother, who did not object to what had been put to her. In fact, almost word for word and with hope in her eyes, she repeated the question to Laura—hope because the mother was reasonably sure that her daughter would eventually "outgrow" what had now become regarded (by her and her husband) as an outsider's "influence" on their sole surviving child.

When Laura became outraged by the question, refused to answer it, came up with a few of her own (such as: "why should a *nice, good-looking boy* like that high school counselor end up giving advice to young people, when he could be a baseball or a hockey player?"), the mother decided to put all the cards on the table. She told Laura that she had "troubles." She told Laura that she had suffered a lot, that the entire family had suffered a lot, and that the result was "scarring": a goal in life (medicine) was really a measure of pain experienced and not forgotten. Where had the mother obtained that last notion? The guidance counselor had offered it, free of charge, as something called "insight" into something called Laura's "problem."

Laura felt like crying when she was offered such interpretive speculations. But she knew not to let that inclination take hold: "I was really beginning to grow up then. I recall thinking: my mother is a fool to swallow that idea about me. I knew that if I cried she'd only believe the guidance counselor even more! Besides, I was upset by *her*, by what she'd just said, not by some sensitive nerve being touched. They were so wrong about my friend Joan! The worst finally came out: my father took me aside—I guess my mother couldn't bring herself to say it—and told me that he thought I was 'making mistakes' because I 'looked up' to my friend 'too much!' Then he said it: I had a 'crush' on her—'a little crush'!

"I sat there and stared at him. I didn't know what to say. The poor man was upset, himself, I could see! He'd been told to go have a 'talk' with me, and he'd done his best. I decided to fight back: I told Dad that I didn't have 'a little crush,' I had a *big crush*. I'd had one ever since I first met Joan and she'd been so nice to me. I told him I thought about her almost every day, and I hoped I could copy her, and become like her—a doctor. He didn't know what to say. He began apologizing. He told me that Joan was 'a fine person,' and he didn't have anything, anything at all against her. It was just that I was so much younger, and I hadn't really done my own thinking, and so I was turning her into a hero, and I was trying all the time to copy her. I kept saying yes, that is true. He was dumbfounded. He thought he was accusing me of something, and I kept announcing, proudly, that he was absolutely correct!

"After a while he softened, and took me to him and kissed me, and told me that he knew I was bright, and he hoped I had 'a good life,' and he saw no reason why a 'woman with brains' shouldn't use them! I thanked him, and *then* I began crying—out of relief. If it was now, of course, I wouldn't thank him at all! But he had no way of knowing at the time how condescending he was being. At least he wasn't being *stupid,* though! My mother has always been a ripe one for amateur psychologists. I'm sounding like a big snob now, but I really believe that psychology is the religion of people who haven't learned enough science or philosophy, and don't go to church anymore!''

She came to that conclusion in college, where she majored in science, with a minor in the philosophy of science. She, too, was "influenced" by her friend Joan, who had developed a certain distaste for psychiatry while in medical school. For one thing, she'd been told to choose it as a profession by a teacher—a surgeon who had registered contempt for her lack of ability in his field, and so was quite prepared to consign her to what was, for him, one of the lower circles in Hell. And then, there were the fellow medical students who found it impossible to conceive of her as anything but a psychiatrist or a pediatrician. She had wanted, in retaliation, she well knew, to apply for a residency in anesthesiology or radiology—anything that hadn't been associated in the minds of others with *her, the woman* medical student. But she had also decided that enough was enough—such a decision would have entrusted to men the ultimate (her word) control over her life. She had always dreamed of healing the injuries and pain of children. She would end up doing so.

And she would end up helping her younger friend to think carefully about a career in medicine. In Laura's senior year of college she met and soon fell in love with a young man who had been an undergraduate journalist and wanted to become a lawyer. Laura had been a good student—a scholarship won, by necessity. She wondered where she would get the money to pay for her medical school education, even if she were accepted—no certainty for a woman, especially at that time. Her boyfriend had encouraged her to think of "other possibilities." She had begun to turn on him for that line of reasoning—but Joan seconded his suggestion: "She would meet me for supper, and tell me that I ought to be *very sure* of myself before I even applied to medical school. It meant years and years of hard work, and it meant taking a lot of nonsense from a lot of people who are supposed to be intelligent and sensitive, but can be impossibly arrogant and narrow-minded. Then, she began to talk about her 'personal life.' We were equals, at least. I had told her about my boyfriend, Dave, and she began remembering the boys she went out with in college, and how she, twice, was on the verge of giving up her ideas about medical school, and settling for 'home economics.' We both laughed at that idea—her figuring out menus and diets. But she stopped herself and pointed out to me that women are pushed into those courses, or in hospitals they are the dieticians and nurses, because men don't want them to be their equals. For a minute or two she stopped remembering her boyfriends and was rather proud of herself—she'd done it, despite all the obstacles. But she wanted to make me pause and think hard. She kept coming back to the troubles *I'd* face—but I felt sorry for her by the end of supper, though I didn't want to tell her that."

Laura was told about the man, a history major, and later on a historian, who had wanted to dissuade Joan from a career, in order to begin a marriage; and about another man, a medical school classmate, who had wanted to get involved, but had feared the talk, the gossip, among their fellow students, and who was short on money and couldn't imagine how he, never mind he and a wife, would last the years and years of medical training. Joan had been in love with the first man, had found herself strangely attracted to the second one, even though she had contempt for what she described as his "utter indifference" toward "the problems of society," never mind her career. He wanted her to quit school, go get a job, help support the both of them. Yet, she found the idea of yielding to his proposals attractive when she found her own journey quite burdensome.

For years she had asked herself what "the point of it all" was; she was anxious to prompt a similar kind of questioning in her younger friend Laura—the earlier along, the better. Laura responded eagerly, rather more so than had been anticipated: "I think I was waiting to be cautioned. If Joan hadn't talked with me, I probably would have begun having second thoughts on my own. I was so wrapped up in my boyfriend Dave that I began to wonder how I would ever be strong enough to have *any* career of my own, if a man could do that to me. I lost all sense of myself. I was more interested in what Dave was studying than in the courses I was taking. Besides, I hadn't taken much history or literature, and I was intrigued by the way he looked at the world— with one eye on the past, and another eye as sharp as a novelist's. He was a writer, and I loved reading what he wrote. I'd never bothered much with English composition. I was a poor speller even as a college senior, and I hadn't read a novel in several years when I started going out with Dave! I started reading what he suggested, and after a while I wasn't doing anything else. I joked with him: I was his student, his tutee. I lost all my own interests, it seemed."

She decided not to apply to medical school. She didn't want to go any further, educationally, for a while. She wanted to get a job, try to pay off some college loans, and make a little money for herself. She was full of idealism—Dave's kind. The civil rights movement was just beginning, and he had talked about its importance, its worth. She wanted to go south, but she wasn't sure what she would do there. If only she were a journalist! But she was not a writer, would never be one. She was, however, reading the newspapers more carefully than ever before, and she was thinking of new directions for herself: teaching, or work on the business side of a newspaper—with the hope that she might, one day, move over to the newsroom in some editorial capacity. When she graduated she was "going steady" with Dave, but he was not ready to get engaged. She remembers that time—another era, in many ways—with a certain incredulity: "I was like a child with him. I'd never been serious with a man before. He introduced me to sex. He introduced me to new courses, to ideas and books. We always talked about what *he* was doing, and what *he* was thinking, and what *he* thought important. He even changed the way I dressed and what I wanted to eat! He thought I was 'too formal' in my choice of clothes. He kept telling me to 'loosen up'—wear 'relaxed' clothes. He and I would go shopping, and he'd make his suggestions, and I'd go along. Then we'd go out to eat, and he'd want me to try what he ordered, and I'd go along. I was a 'meat and potatoes' person, he'd say, and I should 'stretch my appetite'; and I did. He was a great one for omelets and for all kinds of fruits and vegetables, long before the hippies and their vegetarian habits came along!

"It's not that I didn't learn a lot from him; what bothers me, even now, is the realization that I was brought up to defer to a man completely. My father always had the last word in our house. My sister and I worshiped him. My mother did, too. He was a good man: I don't mean to say he didn't earn our love. But my mother was helpless without him; it was her fault, to a large degree, that he became such a god in our home. He'd try to treat her as an equal a lot of times, but she'd have no part of it. She'd start complaining of headaches, and go lie down—leaving him to have the last word, and tell us what to do until she got better!"

She would gradually see less and less of her doctor friend Joan, who eventually (at the age of thirty-four) married an internist twenty years older, a widower with a teen-aged son and daughter. Laura went to their wedding, and found herself quite disapproving of the man. He was, she thought, gruff, self-important, petulant in his own demanding way. She couldn't understand why Joan, who was such a strong, independent person, deferred to him. She discussed her observations afterward with Dave, who had accompanied her to the wedding: "He said they were from another generation. He said we're more open with each other, and we don't boss each other around, because we're more equal." At the time I wasn't sure what he was talking about! There was no women's movement then, and he was certainly leading me around! And Joan wasn't being bossed; she was almost *asking* to be bossed. I couldn't understand why a woman who had fought so hard to be the kind of person she wanted to be would suddenly walk into that kind of marriage. And Dave had no explanation, either. That was the first time in our friendship that I began to question him. I felt a strange surge of dislike for him that evening as we talked about Joan and her husband, and compared them to us. It suddenly occurred to me that he was behaving like Joan's new husband—strutting about his apartment, full of himself! Maybe I resented him turning on my old friend. It was painful enough to hear myself being critical of a woman I'd looked up to so long! But I think that evening Joan, in her own way, had helped me more than she'd ever know, because the more Dave talked about her and her husband, the more I began to think about not only him, but myself—as a *woman*.

"In 1961 that wasn't the way we were supposed to think of ourselves: we were college graduates, or secretaries or nurses— and those were the choices most of my more *ambitious* high school friends saw for themselves in the 1950's. I can still see Dave walking up and down in his living room, telling me that Joan was a 'masochist,' and that she would always get herself into jams, because she liked them! I didn't say anything, but suddenly I thought that *I* was a 'masochist' to be sitting there and listening to him, and not walking right out of that apartment. For the first time it dawned on me that I wasn't all that different from my mother. She would always ask my father what the news 'meant,' even though she had a good head on her shoulders. And there I was, turning to Dave every other minute for advice and help in understanding what I read!

"I didn't know what to do with those thoughts, not that evening, when I was upset by Joan's wedding, never mind my own life. Dave didn't even notice that I wasn't feeling too well— further proof to me that he was so wrapped up in himself that it would take an emotional tornado to get him to look at someone else's problems other than to dismiss them with his words, like 'masochist'! That evening I decided I'd never forget the word 'masochist'; I'd make sure he would have to find another word when the time came to figure me out! I looked at the next morning's paper, and saw an advertisement for a job in a public relations firm; they wanted a college graduate to write and edit 'copy.' I didn't have the slightest idea whether I would be the kind of person they wanted; nor did I know much about advertising agencies; but it was a job, and I was a college graduate—and I hadn't talked about going there with Dave. That was what mattered to me—going off and doing something on my own. Before that evening, I would have spent a week asking Dave what to do, where to go—or being told without asking him! I felt like a new person, just cutting out that ad, and going for the interview.''

She didn't have an easy time of it when she got to the advertising agency. She was asked why she wanted such a job. She answered that she had been a science major, but she was getting more interested in writing, and this position would be a start in that direction. The interviewer was a man of about forty who smiled broadly at her autobiographical revelation, and proceeded to offer one of his own, much longer and more detailed in nature. He had always wanted to be a writer. He had published short stories in his high school periodical, his college literary magazine. When *he* got through college he had no interest in teaching; certainly not in advertising. He was going to be a novelist, "no ifs, ands or buts." He had a five-thousand-dollar inheritance from an uncle; he used it to take "a flat," and he embarked upon a long-contemplated novel. A year later it was done, and sent off to a publisher. The response was negative. Another publisher said no. A third suggested major revisions—with no promise of publication thereafter. He went "back to the drawing board." Months later he had a new manuscript, and this time it was declared "better." He had more work to do, though.

Eventually he would see a book with his name on the jacket as author—and eventually, his story, told to Laura, would come to an end: "I sat there and listened. He went on and on—and on and on! I was just beginning to think of myself as a *woman,* and here was this advertising man flooding me with the vanity and pomposity of his personality! I had a flash of understanding as I sat there and pretended to listen: he's a *man,* that's what he is—another one of *them!* Well, that's a harsh way to put it. But there was truth in it then, and there still is truth in it—the way a lot of men impose themselves on women, and the way a lot of women let themselves be pushed around. But it would take a few years before a lot of us, myself included, would begin to think about all that in a serious way—and share our ideas with each other. At the time I was a twenty-one-year-old 'kid,' full of doubts and confusion. I'd had a breakthrough in my thinking about women and men, but I didn't know what to do with it. I was scared, actually, by what was crossing my mind! I began to think I was going nuts—all the anger I felt. I sat there listening to that fool drone on and on, and I pictured him, in my mind, keeling over: dead of a heart attack! Meanwhile, I nodded and smiled!

"It seemed hours had passed when he'd finished talking about himself—in the interview that was supposed to be about *me!* And I couldn't believe it when he said that there wasn't more to *ask!* Did I have any questions? I said I didn't know what to ask—but I'd like the job. He said he'd like to give me the job, *but . . .* He didn't end the sentence, so I asked him whether I wasn't qualified. He said it was really a man's job I'd applied for. They had thought of hiring women, but it would get the secretaries upset! That's what he told me. It sounds strange now, but back then it was an everyday fact of life: no women at the management level. One or two slipped through, by accident, or by a special arrangement. But they weren't going to hire someone, a woman, off the street! I knew that I'd been a fool to come there. If I'd talked with Dave, he would have warned me—told me once more to look for a teaching job. He was determined that I end up a teacher! Anyway, I got up and left, while Mr. Novelist, whose novel didn't do well, because it was 'ahead of its time,' told me that he 'really enjoyed' talking with me, and he hoped I stuck to my guns and became a writer!''

Several days later Mr. Novelist was on the phone: did she want to meet for lunch, for a drink? She was surprised, troubled, a bit afraid—but also curious. She wanted to ask him what he had in mind, but she felt that in so doing she would be stooping to what might well be his ''crude level.'' Perhaps she would go and find out what was on his mind, she thought, as she told him that she'd have to call him back, because she was going out of town. She was telling no lie. Dave and she were driving to a lake for some camping, swimming, and canoeing. When she came back she had other matters to think about than the promised return telephone call. She wanted to break up with Dave. She had decided to do so while they were canoeing. He had wanted to canoe, and had rented one, and sat in the stern, guiding the canoe, while she paddled in the bow. When she asked if she might change places, he looked startled: did she know how? She said she didn't think it was the greatest hurdle, the greatest challenge—to guide the canoe from the stern. He told her that it was a hard job, and that there are all sorts of ''complicated strokes'' one needs to know. He had learned how to handle a canoe from his father, had only gradually felt ''competent.''

She decided to play his game. She told him calmly that he was not to worry, that she had also learned how to handle a canoe, and that there would be no problem, when she took over. He sat there, silent and glum—continuing to paddle. Then he stopped and looked to see if there was another boat in sight, or anyone looking from the shore. No, they were alone. He then told her that they could switch places, and she could paddle in the stern. But he did want to tell her of his reluctance—because ''it would look funny'' if people saw them in a canoe, she in the stern and he sitting in the bow and ''doing nothing.''

She knew what he meant, but she was determined to make him say it. She also was ''afraid'' to engage him directly in an argument: ''I thought of saying that he was underestimating me, but when I said the words to myself, they sounded weak and complaining, and I didn't want to be like that. He would have loved to hear me beg for my 'turn' at the stern of that silly canoe. I knew he wasn't even referring to me personally. He thought that no woman could really handle a canoe the way he could, or his men friends could. And even if any woman could, he was against letting her do it while others were around, because like some Chinese or Japanese man, he'd 'lose face.' I decided to be polite, but I wasn't going to give up. I waited and waited. He wasn't really going to let me do it, I could see, until I asked again—until I said I'd really like to try the stern, and come on, stop trying to prove to the world that you're a man, taking care of his weak, silly, know-nothing girl friend! Maybe I didn't have all of those words in mind at the time, but I had an angry feeling, a real angry one, that was the equivalent! I just shut up!

"He started asking *me* questions! What was wrong? Was I feeling bad? Did I have a pain somewhere? And I was a coward! I said yes, I did have a pain—a bad headache. The next thing he said was too much; he wanted to know if I was getting my period! I did get a headache then! I was ready to leap out of the canoe, swim ashore, and run as fast as I could for the road. I was ready to tip the canoe over, and hit him over the head with a paddle, in hopes he'd drown! But I said nothing, and then I felt my eyes filling up, and I couldn't stop it from happening, and I was so angry at *myself* that I wanted to disappear into the water and not come up for air! He couldn't get any more words out of me. He saw the tears. He decided that I was in pain, that I was sick. He started paddling fast. He got us to shore. He drove us back to his apartment. I had to speak then; I asked him to take me to my parents' home. He was alarmed, but I told him not to worry, I'd be fine. He put on some of his radio music, rock and roll. There was a time I'd liked it, too—but not that day. It had become *his;* everything seemed to belong to him! When I got out of that car I realized that I was through with him. I couldn't go out with him anymore. But I knew I'd have to give him a false explanation. I didn't know how to put into words what I felt about him—not even for myself. Five years later I'd know. Now

I know. But then—that was a century ago for a lot of us women. One thing I did understand, though—at the very moment I was getting out of the car: I'd never as long as I live forget what had happened in that canoe!''

She did as she knew she would; she begged off when Dave called, and eventually got her point across to him that she didn't want to see him. But she had a lot she wanted to say. She thought of writing a letter, but couldn't do so. She felt inarticulate. And he was such a wordy one—and so clever with the words he used. She decided to go talk with her old friend Joan. Surely she would both ''understand'' and help put into language what were increasingly stormy emotions. They met for lunch, and Laura soon began talking about what was happening between her and Dave. She was surprised at how hard it was, even in a conversation with Joan, to say what was on her mind. Finally, she tried to get to the heart of the matter: ''I told Joan that it wasn't 'a personality clash.' That's what she'd called it, and I had become very upset when I heard the expression. I was convinced that there was something else going on, but I fumbled for words, until I blurted out that Dave was always trying to be 'a big he-man.' Joan disagreed with me. She said he wasn't really a 'he-man,' he was 'just a man'—worried that some other man would call him 'weak' if he didn't call every shot. That was sounding more like it! We got going—and we were both surprised at the bile that came out of us!

''She talked about her husband—how he expected her to take over all the duties of a mother, as well as work—and of course, cook and see that the apartment was spotless. The children were *his,* but she had to 'organize' their lives: clothes, camp, tuition bills to be paid, invitations to spend the night checked, to see if the family visited was 'suitable,' and a million other things, like reminding them to clean up their rooms, or telling them to cut down on the noise from the record player. Why didn't the father do all that? When I asked, Joan laughed bitterly. For the first time ever, I saw her get teary. She was angry with tears, the way I'd been.

"I told her that I didn't know how to thank her enough. By sharing her own frustrations with me, she'd helped me see what was really bothering me. I was going to tell her a lot more—of my plans, and my decision to break completely with Dave, but she was quite upset, and it suddenly came to me that it was a lot easier for me, at my age, to do something about my life than for her. She was married. She probably was lonely before she met her husband. Even though she was annoyed by what she had to do at home, she still was fond of the two children. I ended up trying to cheer her, and she thanked me. But I felt it was I who should be thanking her."

Laura found herself, for a while, indecisive, preoccupied, at a loss to know what direction to pursue, with respect to a job, with respect to her living arrangements. She was out of college. She was breaking up with her boyfriend. She didn't want to live at home. But she also didn't know what she *wanted* to do. The man from the advertising agency had an idea of what *he* wanted to do. He kept calling her, and she decided to say yes—not because she relished the prospect of spending time with him, but because she wanted to "test herself," see if she could have lunch with a man and stand up to his implicit arrogance or condescension. When they met it didn't take her long to realize what she had in store: "He was full of himself, as I expected—a little more so, because he thought he was about to get another notch in his belt! I tried to be cool but pleasant—in control of myself and the situation. Oh, if I only had then the experience I've had now! But that's life, especially for a woman like me: you have to begin at the beginning with these dinosaur men, these *Tyrannosaurus rex* types in the business world, who are out to get *everything,* not just money, but power, and not just economic power, but personal power, and not just personal power, but sexual power. And who is the victim? Well, I was going to be one, at the age of twenty-one, if I didn't watch my step!

"He told me, in the first few minutes, how sorry he was not to be able to hire me; he would have enjoyed 'having me around.' He'd already given me the once-over, and now he was trying to get a stare going with me, after throwing me a few twinkling glances. I stared at him all right, but that was when I started asking him questions, one after the other! What did he think I'd do if he had me 'around' the office? Did he have lunch with every candidate for a job he had to reject? Who really did have the power to hire or fire—since he, obviously, wasn't able to follow his instincts, but had to defer to a 'company policy'? *That* got him going. He could hire anyone he wanted; he was beholden to no one, to no 'policy,' either. I had 'misconstrued' his remarks! I told him I was *terribly* sorry! He began to look at me with a different look in his eyes. They narrowed a little. I could see that I was on the right track; I'd shown him I had *my* eyes open!

"He continued talking about himself—all he'd done and wanted to do and planned to do, and where he'd gone and wanted to go and would go before he got 'too old.' When he used that expression, he gave me another one of his looks, as if to let me know that he wasn't 'too old' yet. I paid no attention. I gave him the coldest polite stare I knew how to give. I kept on asking him about himself, and he kept on talking. Finally, he looked at his watch and said it was time for him to go back to work. As we were leaving he said to me: 'I know hardly anything about you! We've been talking about *me* for two hours!' That's when I smiled and asked him another question: 'How did that happen?' He stopped in his tracks, looked at me, and then hurried on to pay the bill. I felt wonderful!''

She had brought him up sharp, and he hadn't expected it; he was intrigued, wanted more, and started calling her up. The harder she was to reach, the more persistent he became. She noted with pleasure the deterioration of his egocentricity into a plaintive questioning of her: where had she been, and what was she doing, and what did she hope to do—the very self-exposure he'd initiated during their lunch now asked of her. She was candid but restrained. He seemed insatiable in his inquiries. She began trying to get him to talk about himself on the phone, but he only wanted to ask about, talk about, her activities and aspirations. And of course, he wanted more lunches with her. She said no. She had a number of obligations; and soon she'd be leaving for a trip across the country. She was thinking of doing graduate work in education at a California college. Two days later he offered her a job—a better one, he said, than the one she'd tried to obtain a short while before. She said no. He immediately offered her a better salary, and urged her to have another lunch with him. She agreed—and felt terrible afterward. She went to see her friend Joan—prepared to tell her that she had turned into a "weak, hypocritical fraud." And she also had an ultimate self-accusation handy: she had behaved like a "whore"—agreeing to meet the man again, when she didn't like him. Did she want a job from him? Was she willing to "act like a whore" in order to get the job?

Rather soon that word came up when the two women met: "I called myself stupid; I called myself a fool; and then I called myself a cheap whore. Joan was upset, but she laughed, too. I was angry with her. I felt for a moment she wasn't taking me seriously. She saw the look of resentment on my face, and quickly explained herself. She said that every woman who has a serious interest in a career has to come to terms with men. Even in fields supposedly reserved for women—nursing or elementary school teaching—the men really have the ultimate authority: they are the principals or the superintendents, or they run the hospitals, the wards; they even supervise the education of the students. She went on and on, giving me examples. She told me of times she had at medical school, and as a young doctor. I'd never heard her talk like that: 'I've been propositioned so many times, I honestly lost count. You can go along and enjoy yourself; you can say no, but use the man's interest to help your career along; you can tell him to go to hell—it all depends on where you are, and where you want to go, and on *you,* what you feel about the man who's after you!'

"I was appalled. I thought she was joking—being gruff and cynical, but not really discussing the issue with me. I asked her to be *serious.* She said: 'I've never been more serious in my life!' Her face told me she meant what she said. I went ahead and had my say: it's being cheap and calculating to think that way; and I asked her the difference between a street whore, soliciting money, and what she said we do. Weren't we just 'dressed-up' and 'fancy' versions—prostitutes with college degrees and a veneer of respectability? Isn't there some other way to behave— stand up for what you believe in, and not let yourself get pushed around by men, or used by them?

"She had her answer ready. The world is full of liars and crooks and hypocrites and frauds; yes, even the medical world. People ingratiate themselves with those who have power, and angle for appointments, privileges, favors. What's the difference between a gambler, a numbers man, or a stockbroker who sits watching the numbers go up and down in a brokerage house? When sheriffs and city councillors and mayors and governors lie and cheat and steal, that's 'politics.' How many of them get caught? But the rest of us get caught going over the speed limit, or get called in because we made a mistake in our income taxes. We're hauled in fast. She had a long list in her head! She'd been audited by the tax people because they argued about a five-hundred-dollar deduction. She wondered how carefully the government people go over the forms of the rich and the big politicians. She said that if I can find someone who'd got up to the top who hasn't done a hundred things worse than I did when I kept my mouth shut, while that advertising man went on and on, then she'd sign over every dollar she has in her savings account to me!

"I got her point, but I didn't like it. I told her so: two wrongs don't make a right. She answered me quickly; she delivered a speech: 'I'm not giving a sermon,' she said. 'I'm not trying to tell you what ought to be in some heaven. I'm trying to tell you what *is*—what goes on every single day. If you want to try to live in some utopia, go find it. If you want to live in this world, then you've got to keep your eyes and ears open, and know what the score is!' "

There was more, much more, but Laura over the years had learned to paraphrase and shorten her friend's observations. She left that meeting in doubt, and anxious—by no means won over.

But she left, as she later would put it, "with a clearer head" than she'd carried to the lunch. She would, soon afterward, agree to another lunch with the advertising man, and accept the job offered her. She had figured out in her mind a complicated but explicit and firm moral path. She would be friendly and even openly grateful to him. He was giving her a chance to start a career. She would ignore the sexual innuendos or themes or suggestions or, ultimately, importunate requests; or, she would refuse them. She would never yield herself, but she would not walk away in a huff, or quit her job, or turn the man into an enemy—not if she had good reasons of her own to stay a friend of his, or less strongly, to keep up the semblance of goodwill.

A year later she had pulled off with astonishing success the assignment she had handed herself. She was a valued member of a leading advertising agency in New England. She was receiving a good salary, and was developing a real competence and flair at writing copy and editing what others had written. Moreover, she was enjoying her work and the life her weekly income enabled. And she had managed to shake off her anticipated problems with the man who had all too eagerly hired her—only to find herself dealing with new dilemmas: "I have good memories of that man who hired me; he had a plan up his sleeve, but he knew how to take no for an answer. I told him to leave me alone, and he did. In fact, he became a friend of mine, and a teacher. He helped train me, and he showed me dozens of shortcuts. I was as eager as I could be, and he told me to keep that way, and I did—and soon I was getting bonuses for ideas and promotions. They called me their 'prize woman.' It sounds awful now, but at the time I was really grateful.

"I'd gone through a real emotional crisis—a reaction to Dave and all his pretentious intellectual values. He was always telling me about his future as a lawyer, or a writer, or an academic—he wasn't sure which career he'd finally choose. Meanwhile, I was supposed to be a nice, underpaid schoolteacher—dependent on him for approval, for money, for position in the world: Dave's girl friend, Dave's fiancée, Dave's wife. I didn't realize how angry I was at him and at the way women are treated in our society until much later—years later. When I decided to try for that job in the advertising agency, I was feeling low, so low I thought I'd take that job, because it was the kind of job Dave had taught me to sneer at: beneath my dignity. But what dignity did I have then? I wasn't ready to ask myself that, not as ready as Joan had been. She had scared me, I now realize, into doing *something*. Maybe she'd made me so desperate that I'd forgotten all the ideas I learned in college and from people like Dave, and allowed myself to take the first thing that came along, and fly with it. That's what I did; I took off, once I was in the agency.

"The only problem was success; the better I did, the more I had to fight off the men who wanted to take me out, and in one night get serious with me. The sexual revolution hadn't quite arrived in the early 1960's, and I was no hippie, anyway; but as a reasonably attractive 'businesswoman,' they called me, I was a 'sitting duck,' one slob called me, for a lot of stupid, horny men who drank too much and were having a lot of marital problems. One of them, talented and handsome, got to me—and I guess I deserved at least fifty percent of the misery I ended up with!''

She ended up with a man who, for a while, "dominated" her; she would use that word again and again to describe what happened between them. He was five years her senior, and "on his way to the top." Everyone said that at the office, and she had no reason to doubt a collective judgment. They were "put together," Laura and Richard, on a particular account; she both impressed him with her suggestions and, apparently, prompted annoyance, competitiveness, scorn in him—all of which he was not loath to express, and all of which, it seems, she was not reluctant to experience: "I've never figured out why I was so attracted to him. I had to go see a psychiatrist, in the end—after an affair, an engagement, a marriage, and a terrible depression. Maybe I should have gone to the psychiatrist right away after I met Richard. But who lives that way—putting yourself under someone's microscope every time you meet someone? I have to admit it, though, I saw what was coming long before there was any real trouble. I wasn't dumb about psychology; I was using it every day to get people to buy things. The first time we went out was to talk about work, but I knew he had other purposes, and so did he.

"I also knew what I liked about him—the way he sized everyone up, and never seemed to apple-polish. He spoke up to, *back to,* the boss. He also treated me as if I was another employee he liked; I mean, he was gruff with me—talked with me the way he talked with the others. A few years later the psychiatrist I saw made a big deal about that: I was treated like a man, and that was what I wanted. You bet I wanted to be treated like 'one of the boys' at that agency! Everyone was treating me as if I was the surprise of the twentieth century: a woman who could think, who had an eye and an ear, who knew how to use words. One day on a confidential memo to the bosses I saw myself summed up—in Latin, no less: a *rara avis*. We had a classy staff—college degrees sewed on to everyone's suit jacket. I didn't need to show mine; I had wings, and they told the same story!

"I know it's the oldest refrain in history, but I have to say it: Richard was different, and I got hooked on that. He assumed that I was fairly smart, and we went from there. When he found out that I could keep pace with him, that I could even outdistance him, he paid me the compliment of envy. I think envy in that office was the greatest tonic of my life; no wonder I became addicted to the biggest source of it! I found myself working harder and harder—for him! I was working so that he'd see what I could do, and then *I* would see his reaction: his eyes would avoid me, and he'd start tapping his knee, as if he was a doctor trying to get his leg to kick. After a while he'd come out with it; I'd hear that I'd done a damn good job, and I made a lot of the others seem like 'imbeciles,' and he would include himself. I'd tell him to stop it, but I loved every minute! All the other men became nasty when they felt I'd done something half worthwhile. Richard had the guts to admit the truth about his feelings.

"I don't think I was nearly as honest with him! I was pretending to be an innocent, who came up with minor miracles every other week, or so. He'd ask, over and over: 'How do you *do* it?' I'd shrug my shoulders and pretend that I thought I'd done a lousy job. I guess I was a pretty good actress. He kept telling me I should stop being 'insecure,' and realize that I had 'a lot on the ball.' That would be a signal for me to pretend even more 'insecurity.' We became serious one night when he decided to play amateur shrink with me, and help me get more 'self-confidence.' I made it hard for him to 'help' me. I guess he decided sleeping with me would do the trick! And I guess I decided that I had to continue the deceit, to the point of letting him reassure me, reassure me, and finally seduce me. Did I 'want' to be seduced? Did I put on an act—let him think he was seducing me? Did I really 'need' to be reassured, even though I thought I was faking all along—pretending to be nervous and afraid and unsure of myself? Those are the questions I got asked when it was all over, and I wanted to make sure I didn't go through another such experience with a man.''

They were married two years after they'd first met. Six months before they eloped, he left the firm for a rival one. She knew how attached she was to him when she found herself yearning to follow him. She was humiliated by that desire, kept it from him, from herself, even, as best she could. She began to find sleep hard to come by—would lie awake with strange thoughts plaguing her: ''I thought I was going crazy. I would toss and turn, and all I could think of was Richard and me. I kept seeing strange scenes: he'd be lying on the road, a hit-and-run victim, or he'd be driving a car, and I'd be trying to catch up, in another car, but I couldn't. Then I'd picture us in Europe. We'd be happy, walking in London, or Paris. I had us strolling near Buckingham Palace, or the Eiffel Tower: juvenile daydreams in the middle of the night. I was afraid I'd lose this man; I was afraid that without him I wouldn't do well at work; I was afraid I'd fall through the ice and drown if I was on my own. I'd been doing *too* well, and I didn't really believe that I deserved the credit. It's easy to figure out your problems ten years later, when they're all over!''

When he left the firm, she left. She did not want to compete in business with her husband. Nor did she wish to follow him to a new company, even though overtures had been extended her. He told her of an interesting possibility—a position as a public relations officer for a major corporation. She would be more tied down, of course. She would no longer have the freedom to roam from account to account, constantly challenged by the sudden demands of a succession of worried, demanding vice-presidents who had to show (through her ingenuity) quick results in sales— or else. But she was tired of the pressures she'd managed to sustain so well, and as she kept reminding herself, she was getting married, so the time had come to slow down, prepare for a more settled life: "I was much more old-fashioned, in my heart, than I ever knew at that time, or for years afterwards. I was fighting some notion I'd inherited from my family that a woman who marries should spend her time fixing up a home—and waiting: for her husband to come home, for a child to arrive. All very conventional—and you'd think that I would have laughed at such ideas by then. I did! But there was a tug. I didn't want to give up my career, but I was afraid to pursue it too hard, now that I was married. I had to find a way of keeping going, but shifting gears enough to appease my sense of what I 'should' do—'become a good wife.' That sounds *psychological;* but I knew it all in my bones, not my head! When a psychiatrist gave me a lot of words to explain everything, I wasn't surprised, not one bit.

"I think you often find out from psychiatrists what you've known already. It helps, I suppose, to hear another person say what you've hid in your own mind—even hid from yourself. But you never completely hide those things, or at least I don't. I had my flashes of awareness back then. I remember walking to my new job, and thinking that in a year or two I might be leaving it: pregnant. I remember the phrase that crossed my mind: a good place, a place where I'll begin to 'wind down.' I'd been 'wound up' too long! I needed to relax in a company that would protect me, warm me in winter, and help me stay cool in the summer. In the advertising agency I'd been the perpetual outsider, hungry and with no place to sleep, knocking on the door, every day, pleading to be let in and taken care of. Yes, they said, we'll let you in, and give you a meal and a bed, but only for the day: you've got to produce, or else. If you come up with something, we'll be all smiles tomorrow, and there will be another big meal, and another night's sleep—but we're never going to say: welcome, come in and stay as long as you want, because we like you, and we're going to make you one of us; we're a family, and you're a member of it. I think they were willing to be a little more hospitable to one another—those men! Richard felt 'at home' there. I never did. The more they told me I'd fooled them—my 'brilliance'—the more I knew I was standing out in the snow, with my nose on the window, peeking in and waiting for someone's mercy.''

She certainly found her welcome in the new job. She was hired to ''sell'' a particular corporation to the public, and she proceeded to do so with intelligence and tact. She worked intensely, attracted the notice of the company's officials, was approached within a year with a new offer: work as an executive *in* the company, rather than as a salesman (there were no sales*persons* in 1964) *for* the company. She was tempted, but her husband advised her not to accept. He told her quite frankly that he wanted both of them ''doing the same thing.'' She pointed out that they had, in fact, gone their separate ways: her work was quite different from his. No, he replied; they were both in the same *profession*. She wondered aloud what difference *that* made. He became unusually murky; he became, in fact, somewhat mystical: they had married as a pair of ''advertising account executives,'' and if they strayed too far from each other in their respective jobs, they would be putting their union in jeopardy.

She was stunned by what seemed to be, implicitly, a threat. She told him that—said she felt they were married because they loved each other as man and woman, as one individual and another individual, rather than as two workers who had once competed, and then decided to ''combine forces.'' The phrase had been his—a ''joke'' once uttered; she refused to give it the substance of everyday life. He backed down—and, she would later realize, backed off a bit, too: "It was the first sign that there was real trouble in our marriage. He had more and more work to do— just when I had a halfway sane schedule. I'd hoped we could begin to live 'a normal life.' I'd hoped to get home and cook and turn our apartment into a home. But he always liked to go out to eat; and for the first time, he started skipping dinner with me: too much office work. I would come home, prepare a gourmet feast for us, and get his apologetic phone call. I tried each time to conceal my disappointment. I thought I heard him listening for it! When it comes to *that,* you're in trouble: suspicion is not the best cement for a marriage. And suspicion feeds on itself, until a monster has you in its grip. I was in bad trouble, but I didn't want to admit it."

She had ways of "forgetting." She plunged herself into her new work. She decorated the apartment for herself, if not for Richard. She tried to stay in closer touch with Joan. And a serious illness of her mother's took up a good deal of time. But her mind was not to be successfully deterred; it pursued her at odd moments, and finally she began to think of herself as "unhappy." In a strange way, her mother's death helped prolong the marriage. Laura's sadness had an occasion for expression. The two had never been all that close; on the contrary, they had been rather distant from each other emotionally. Laura didn't understand why she took her mother's death so hard. Her husband rallied round—and she felt that they had not been so close since they had first become acquainted. But one late-evening conversation ended that closeness. She told Richard of a question her mother had asked before she died: when would they have children? A natural, a banal question. The kind of question an advertising executive puts in the mouth of a would-be grandmother—to sell, perhaps, some item for the nursery: when the infant is born, I'll come visit, and good grandmother that I plan to be, I'll bring X or Y with me!

Richard was of no mind to let the matter drop. He turned into a prosecution attorney, then delivered his jeremiad: "I never knew that he could be like that. He went after me. What was I getting at? What did I want? What else had I talked about when I was with my mother? Why did I choose to bring up the subject of children that way? How long had I been 'harboring' my 'ideas'? Did I have an 'agenda' in my head? If so, what was it? I thought he'd gone mad. He reached for his Scotch, and drank it on ice, no water: three shots in about a half an hour, while I tried to get my point across—that my mother had put a poignant and not-very-strange question to me, and I had not been able to give her an answer. How could I, when he was the one who would have to be 'consulted'—and had not been!

"But he'd have none of my 'evasiveness.' He proceeded to hand down his decree: no children—ever. We had a bad fight. I told him I wasn't sure I wanted children myself, but I didn't like his 'imperial attitude.' He said I was throwing a phrase at him. He said I was the one who had the 'imperial attitude'; I was just another woman who had decided it was time to have a baby, and by God, I'd have my way. I discovered I had a misogynist for a husband. He'd majored in comparative literature, and he knew his kindred spirits well—Strindberg, especially. I was a typical 'headstrong' woman, and he remembered my 'type' in the plays of Strindberg he'd read. I'd never heard of Strindberg before that night! Talk about 'imperialism'—lording it over me with quotations and analogies and crazy accusations. I told him that now I really knew him, and thank God in time—because I'd never want such a man to father a child of mine. And I walked out of that apartment. I went to a hotel, and stayed there for three days. My marriage was over."

She turned to a community of fellow workers. Much is made of the coldness to be found in corporate life. But she had quite a different experience during a period of her life when she might have floundered badly, were it not for a number of warm, decent people who came to her support. They were all members of a large American corporation, but they were also men and women who became something else through their concern for each other: "I used to go to daily meetings with other young executives, and they saw I wasn't in the greatest shape. They knew my mother had died, and that was enough reason to explain the look on my face. I was the only woman in the group. They never took advantage of me when I was so down. They never treated me as weak, either. They were a nice bunch. Maybe I didn't 'threaten' them; I had my own work, and I was there, really, to help them. This was no advertising agency. But I couldn't imagine those men ever being competitive the way Richard was. They were working their way up a corporate ladder, but they were in a company that offered a warm blanket to those who gave a lot of energy and conviction in their work. Someday I'd like to write a *defense* of corporate life I've known. There are two kinds of companies: one kind consumes bright, able people as well as raw materials; an opposite kind holds its arms out and stands by you through thick and thin, if you give your best in return, and if you have a 'best' to give!''

Though Laura occasionally becomes extremely sentimental about that period of her working life, she will (at other moments) carefully qualify her remarks. She will insist that one ought not generalize from her experience to statements about corporate life. She knows that life can be "brutal" on various "company ladders" she's come to know in the course of her life. Still, "critics of the corporations" are often "complete strangers" to the particular kind of life she has come to know. And she won't relinquish the good memories—examples of what can happen in those office buildings that seem so full of fierce competition or anonymity or bureaucratic coldness. She especially will never forget Maureen: "She was my secretary, and when I first met her I was too preoccupied with my own importance to pay much attention to her. Maybe I was a snob. Maybe I didn't want to know how much alike we were—in background and in the way we thought and felt. The only difference between her and me was that I'd gone to college. Once you go to a fancy college, even on a scholarship, you're walking down a new road. A lot happens to you that otherwise wouldn't. But you still carry your old self with you— and I guess I had to get into a tough emotional jam to begin to realize that I wasn't just the rising businesswoman I'd been for five years; I was also the kind of person Maureen was—an ordinary, outgoing woman who loved to enjoy life, and not give it too much thought.

"God, I was tired of using my brain. Even the divorce had been full of clever fights with words: who owned what, and how we disentangled our property. I walked out on that! I told him to take everything except my clothes—unless he wanted them, too! If so, he could have them! Maureen gave me courage; she told me to buy a new wardrobe and look to the future. In college we learned to have contempt for people like her: no 'deep thoughts.' But she was considerate and kind and cheerful—and had been for months before I was desperate enough, needy enough, to notice. I felt like a real jerk as I thought about the way I snapped those orders to Maureen when I first came to that job. She'd been there for a year, and she tried to act like a gracious, kind hostess; I behaved like a sheriff coming to dispossess a no-good tenant. Every time I read about how men exploit women in the business world, I think of myself and Maureen—for more than a year!''

Laura and Maureen became ski buddies. They went up to various New England resorts every other weekend during the winter that followed Laura's divorce. Laura had never had a close woman friend of her own age. She found herself strangely unable to call upon Joan during her marital crisis. She turned to Maureen because work had to be (she believed) her salvation, and there Maureen was, at work every day: ''I'm no psychiatrist, but I don't see how people get through their troubles if they don't have a job that keeps them occupied. I could *never* stay home and do housework all day. I don't mean to be disparaging—I know someone has to clean the house. But once you've learned to rely upon an eight-hour (or ten- or twelve-hour!) working day, you're 'on it' for life: hooked. After Richard and I broke up I tried staying home; all I did was smoke and watch television, and I began to go nuts, quietly nuts. I noticed the liquor cabinet the way I never had before! I'm not a workaholic; but I *have* to work. Maureen was the same kind of person. She would tell me, on our way up skiing, what her life was going to be like: she'd meet the man she truly loved, she'd marry him, she'd have a kid or two— but she'd keep her job. I was such a snotty fool at first when I heard her talk like that. I would think to myself: why would she want to keep on being a *secretary?* I mean, she was building dreams for herself, so it didn't cost anything, I figured, cynic that I'd become, to dream of marrying a man who could afford to tell you: honey, you can quit taking orders from nine to five and be your own boss.

"She educated me, Maureen did; she taught me about herself and why she worked, and why she would always work; and the more I learned, the more I began to know something about my- self—what had happened to me when I was a kid growing up, and why I became the 'success' I did, but had to pay for it, I guess, with a lot of wasted time in my personal life. By the time I went to see a psychiatrist, I'd already had a lot of psychotherapy, thanks to Maureen."

She became, inevitably, Maureen's mentor, even though they were almost the same age. Laura tried hard to stop that develop- ment from taking place, but the more she tried to be on an equal footing with her friend, the more apparent it became that she *was* trying, and therefore there *was* something to be overcome. When Maureen fell in love, it was with a steamfitter—the brother of another secretary in the executive offices of the firm. When the wedding took place, Laura was her maid of honor. She re- members her struggle with herself and with others she met; others whom she wanted to be close to, and found it awkward to be close to, and was sure, one moment, she'd put utterly at ease, and was sure, the next moment, she'd made nervous: "It was just a wedding. I'd been to a wedding before! But this was dif- ferent—my closest friend, or one of my two closest friends, get- ting married. But a lot of people came up to me as if I was the Queen of England, and I'd deigned to attend a commoner's cele- bration! Maureen's cousin kept thanking me for coming. She wasn't very sarcastic, and she wasn't groveling, but I suppose she *was* thinking to herself that here's one of the bosses, and she's stopped her bossing for an afternoon and an evening, and she's out here with us. Richard used to say to me: let's go slumming. He'd picked up that expression in London, I think. I don't think Maureen's family and friends thought I'd gone slumming, but the fact that the phrase entered my head at one point must have meant something.

"As God is my witness, I didn't for a second think of myself as 'slumming'; but I kept being given respectful sidelong glances, and people were a little too nice to me. Or was I imagining things? Before Maureen got married, I would have been able to sit down with her over a beer and talk frankly about what had gone on. But there she was, getting married; and after the evening was over, she was gone—on her honeymoon. What was I to do—call her up and have a heart-to-heart on the phone? I was sad when I went home—sad because I realized there are barriers between people, stupid barriers that even a maid of honor at a wedding can't get rid of; and sad because I wasn't ever going to be as close to Maureen as I'd once been."

Her work continued to sustain her, but she was lonelier than ever before. She came to work early, sometimes at seven o'clock. She had lists of telephone calls to make, and had to wait until others were ready to receive them. She had other lists—people to write, analyses to make, decisions to consider, meetings to attend, trips to take. She kept two secretaries going. She thought of interesting ways to enhance the local and national reputation of her "firm"—sponsorship of art exhibitions, of events held in the public library, of community affairs discussion groups. And she insisted on the value of television in shaping the corporate image: a means of reaching ordinary people and conveying to them an altogether different view of business than the prevailing one—of corporations as a collective operation of greedy fat cats. With this as her excuse, she watched television programs constantly, had a set put in her office: the regular networks, educational television, the morning, afternoon, *and* evening programs. She hated to go home to an empty apartment—with no one to call, at a whim's behest, simply to chat. To call Joan or Maureen she felt she had to have a reason, even though they both would have vehemently denied this.

A year after Maureen's wedding Laura had her twenty-eighth birthday, and decided that she would never marry again. She found herself doing ''a strange thing.'' She told everyone in the office that she was taking a couple of weeks off, but told no one where she was going. She went to New York's Kennedy Airport and only on the way decided where she would be going—to London. It was the autumn, and she had no trouble buying a seat. In London she checked into a fine old hotel, and began walking to various parts of the city, day after day: Hyde Park, Regent's Park, Grosvenor Square, Piccadilly Circus, St. Paul's Church, and so on. She knew no one in the city, and she wanted to know no one. She enjoyed dining out and watching others. She was not at all lonely. She was glad to be on her own. She was glad to have no phone numbers to call. She especially enjoyed the art museums and galleries; she pretended to be rich, to be interested in buying antiques, paintings, sculpture. To the people who waited on her she talked of having her lawyer come to check up on one or another ''piece'' she contemplated buying.

She went to a few auctions, and in one case kept bidding up a painting done by a Belgian portrait painter of the nineteenth century. She was gambling—hope against hope that someone would get her off the hook with yet a higher bid. She hadn't been so excited since she went on a roller coaster as a child. Gambling at Reno or Las Vegas must be something like this, she concluded. For one tense moment she thought she'd put herself in the position of being responsible for a £10,000 purchase—the painting. She knew, intuitively, that the painting was valuable; and she could tell that three others were strongly interested in acquiring the object; and she took note of the minimum set for a successful offer. When she offered a hundred pounds over £10,000, there was silence, and the auctioneer prepared to close out the bidding. At the last possible moment, as in a movie—the car not going over the cliff, after all—one of the two men called out a hundred more pounds, and as all eyes moved to her, including those of the man she'd been competing with, the silence went uninterrupted, and she got up and walked away, feeling several dozen stares upon her back.

On the way out she began having a pursuer, a quite tall man who finally caught up with her and asked her if they might have a word. Yes. He was an American banker who happened to be in London; he knew by her accent that she was also American; he thought he could tell where she came from—"the middle Atlantic states"; and he was astonished to meet someone who also shared his interest in this artist not widely known at all in America. She reduced him to silence, confusion, and embarrassment by her blunt recitation of profound ignorance: "I told him the facts, or at least the ones that he deserved to hear—I'd been having some fun for myself. But what if I'd had to make the purchase, he asked—*then,* what would I have done? Make the purchase, I answered! I figured that I wouldn't have lost all that much—not when two others were so desperately keen to have the painting. In the picture an obviously wealthy lady was sitting on a fancy chair; she was probably a member of some salon. I figured someone in the twentieth century must be ready to spend a lot of money to be associated with that salon by owning that picture. I pulled no punches. I said that.

"Mr. Malone was the man's name, and he told me that he was intrigued by my 'psychology'—the way I appraised the interest of people in art. I wasn't especially 'intrigued' with his use of that word 'psychology'—a bit lofty of him, I thought, if not arrogant in the extreme: a put-down. So, I got a bit surly. I told him I had no 'psychology'; I was just having fun. He thought I was using more 'psychology.' I guess to evade his curiosity, I told him I was a 'professional gambler,' and that I love to buy things at auctions, especially when others are competing—a thrill. He began to understand my 'psychology'! He looked at me as if he knew the diagnosis, and wished I would go see a doctor soon, before I ruined myself. 'You might lose everything,' he said. I told him there was hardly a chance of that, because I had more money than I knew what to do with. His eyes widened—a crazy fool with lots of money. He told me that we'd have to get together back in the States, and I said yes—sure that I'd never see him again. Good-looking, I thought; a decent man who wanted to help an unfortunate fellow citizen. That's me—never one to think he may have had other reasons for an interest in me!''

Mr. Malone became a caller back in the States. Laura went out with him, and right away confessed her "joke." True, she had been acting a bit strangely—for her, *very* strangely. She had never been to Nevada, and she wouldn't know what to do even if she did go there. The relieved Mr. Malone became the suitor, George. He wanted to become the bossman. Wouldn't Laura work for the bank whose investments he handled? Banks, too, need to reach people—to get their money, but also to "improve their image." These days a "responsible capitalism" oughtn't forget to remind people of its achievements. In a war to the finish, as the "other side" sees it, the "message" that people all over the world "get" is as important as the military balance of power, which (anyway) is virtually at a permanent stalemate, due to the overwhelming destructive power both antagonists possess.

So George Malone would talk, and Laura was interested, attracted to the speaker: "He impressed me as a thoughtful man, and very decent. He didn't think only of himself; he worried about America, and the whole Western world. He read an English magazine (*The Economist*) as well as lots of American ones. He traveled not only on business, or as a tourist, but to see how other countries were dealing with their social problems. And he wanted to share his ideas with me—not teach me, or tell me what to believe, but help me (he put it) 'learn by talking and listening.' We really enjoyed our conversations; eventually, they got personal—and I learned that he'd been divorced and he had a son fourteen, and a daughter eleven, and his wife lived in Chicago, so he went back and forth a lot to see his children, and they came to him during the summers, and the three of them traveled.''

She wouldn't go work in George's bank, but she did fall in love with him, and eventually she agreed to marry him. She was thirty-one when she married for a second time, and a highly paid corporate officer: vice-president in charge of public relations. Soon enough her husband George was pressing her for a child— and she was saying no. She was also telling him that she didn't want to use his name, but her own. She'd long ago dropped her first husband's name. Laura Willis was who she was. He was hurt by her decision, and even more upset by her apparent disinterest in children. She was enraged by his insistence: wasn't it enough to have, already, a son and a daughter? Why should she interrupt work she thoroughly enjoyed to have a child—when she had no great desire to have one? Because *he* had such a desire?

He pressed to the point of acrimony, and one day, on the way to work, she came to a conclusion: "I began to have an ominous feeling that in a year or so we'd both be headed for a second divorce. I was disgusted at the prospect; I'm not religious, but I felt I was headed for a second tragedy, and that I was becoming a selfish person. I didn't agree with my husband, but I said to myself: here you are, again, in a marriage that's beginning to go bad—and what are you going to do about it? Sit on your hands and complain about *him?* Or go out and try to do something yourself to change the situation? I had never thought of going to a psychiatrist—not seriously; but this time I began to consider the possibility. It took me a few weeks to get up the courage to go. I had to overcome my objections: I believed, I still believe, that people should help *themselves*. If you get the notion in your head that every time you're in trouble, you should turn to someone else, a stranger, a doctor, and pay him to tell you 'what's wrong,' then you're going to lose your independence. I decided to go see a psychiatrist only because I was in a serious bind, *and* I'd been there before, *and* I couldn't see anything but trouble and unhappiness coming, *and* (most of all!) because to go see someone was at least something I could *do*—an act of faith in our marriage. And George saw it that way; so we agreed to shelve our discussions of who should go under what name, and how many, if any, children we should have, until I'd had a chance to figure a few things out. I was tempted to ask *him* to go see a doctor, too—but I knew in my heart that he'd be only too happy to oblige, and that told me something: that maybe he didn't need to go!"

She was told of a "good" psychiatrist, and found him to be

that—to the point that her occasionally sardonic but not mischievous or malevolent mind christened him "Dr. Good." For a few days she hesitated to go see a *man,* and sought zealously to find a woman psychiatrist. But when she obtained the name of one who went highly recommended, she found herself made anxious at the prospect of calling a *her*—and less anxious as she readied herself to call a *him.* She saw the doctor "a total of twenty times." She kept close count. She gave him, by her description, "a challenge": why couldn't she get advice from him, in an hour or so, then go think about it, and either accept or reject what was recommended? He replied that he was not in the business of giving advice—that he believed, anyway, that she would not want to take someone's "advice" on an issue so vital and personal as a marriage and the question of motherhood; and that he simply wanted to understand what her mind was "doing," how it worked, and tell her *that;* then she could decide what, if anything, she wanted to do—about her mind, and about the important questions she'd been considering.

She liked what she found to be a certain reticence, caginess, and renunciation in the man, hence her straightforward, rather than ironic, label for him: "He was good at his trade; and I respected him for it. I could joke with him, and he could laugh— and laugh at himself, at his kind of work. I told him I thought that in his profession there was a danger—the psychiatrist becomes a colossal egotist. He said yes—and asked me about the dangers *I* faced in my job. That undid me! I'd never thought of my work that way—how it might have affected my personality! I was surprised at what came to mind: that I'd become an egotist myself. I took my job very seriously; when I sold our company, I was selling myself—and a few people had said as much! They weren't criticizing me; they were saying that I really believed in what I was doing! It's no big step from believing in yourself to asking others to believe in you!

"I began to wonder out loud if it was right for me to be married, never mind have children. I really did love going to that office, *being* in that office. I had to admit to him—the doctor: I loved dictating letters and signing them and making calls and going to big-deal lunches. I guess I loved the executive life. I even got a write-up in a business magazine. Women's lib made me seem even more of an asset to our company! Actually, I didn't like the way a political movement was used by some media people to exploit women even more—a person like me becomes a star, and then gets big job and salary offers. I never fought for a movement, and I didn't want to take advantage of a movement! I refused the bonus my own company offered after the article came out, and I turned down twelve job offers. And I told Dr. Good he was right—that I was in danger of becoming an egomaniac. He told me *I* had said that, not him! Most of the time we went around and around like that. I'd tell him that he was trying to make some point, and then I'd begin to realize that *I* was making the point. Sometimes he'd make *that* point to me; but a lot of times I saw what was going on and told him what I saw. I guess that's what therapy is!

"I hadn't been able to do it alone—get into myself like that. After a while I began to think that I could, though; and I told the doctor that. He was quite good—Dr. Good! He said that if I could, fine; and if I wanted to check things out occasionally with him, fine. He said I was 'a going concern'—more than that: a 'successful person.' He said I wasn't miserable or in real mental trouble, and it was obviously up to me to work out my marriage with my husband, and endless therapy couldn't do that, but if I got into a bad spot, he'd be there. I felt relieved. I told him I wanted to 'try out' what I'd learned the past weeks—by talking with my husband, instead of reacting to him as if he was some-one threatening my life. That's how I'd felt about him—that he wanted to take me away from what I'd become and turn me into what he wanted—*his* wife and a mother of *his* children. And I didn't get any of those fears about my husband from reading the women's lib literature. I was glad that I read some of the articles when I did—articles by women about what it's like to be a woman in our society. If I'd read the stuff earlier, I would have probably dismissed it, or I would have believed it like you believe something you hear in a lecture. This way, it came out of my life, first—and then, afterwards, I saw that others were writing about things that came out of their lives. I do think, though, that when you read those articles, you should try to bring what you've read to your own life, and figure out what you're going to do about it—the way you live your life.''

She would laugh gently at her own slightly didactic approach to the confrontation of her personal affairs. She and her husband began to forge what they both felt to be workable answers for themselves. She was Laura Willis at work, Laura Malone at other times—when out with him. She teased him often: when was he going to be George Willis? Once he agreed to be exactly that, whenever he went with her to one of her company's social occasions. In fact, after a year or so, she no longer cared all that much whether she was Laura Willis or Laura Malone; she let her ''mood'' decide which name she used. She also let a ''mood'' that came upon her decide something else: ''We'd had a long talk about children. I told George I thought we should adopt a child. There are too many people in this world already! He told me that it would be nearly impossible for us to adopt a child; there aren't any to adopt—unless we were willing to bring up a black child. There was a long silence! Then he said that he wasn't pushing anything on me, but he wanted me to know that if I wanted to adopt a black child, he also did! I was stunned! First I was angry at him: it had been *his* idea to have children all along, not mine! Now we end up talking about adopting a black child! How much crazier would it get in this marriage?

''But then I stopped and thought to myself—with Dr. Good out there in the atmosphere leaning invisibly over my shoulder: we'd been two reasonable people having a serious discussion, and this was what it led to, and I wasn't being manipulated by my husband, but rather we were each finding out where we stood, what we wanted—and believed in!—and how far we'd go in facing up to the implications of our desires. I knew, now, that my husband was an honest man, and he wasn't some macho character who wanted more and more kids (sons mostly) to become extensions of himself, and to prove to the world (and himself!) what a big deal he is. I don't think I ever before had such a conversation; I was haunted for days—thinking of him and me going to an adoption agency and bringing home a black baby.''

His sincerity had touched her decisively; she felt closer to him than she ever dreamed possible. A conversation she had judged, at the time, to be half-serious at most, and certainly speculative, turned into an extremely important moment in their lives. She pictured herself with a black child: dressing it, feeding it, walking it in a carriage. She wondered whether she wished for a boy, a girl; one can choose, she reminded herself, if one is going to adopt. She wanted a girl. She would have an easier time getting along with a girl. At moments she felt puzzled by the ruminative side of her mental life—why this sudden preoccupation with a *black* child, simply because of a talk. Why not try to have her own child? She was, after all, hardly a civil rights activist. Anyway, was she the one to become involved in an interracial adoption—she, who wasn't even convinced she had the proper desire to bring up *any* child?

The bond she felt with her husband had become immeasurably strengthened. She had begun to realize how deeply suspicious she had, in fact, been of him—and as well, of all men; and she had begun to realize, also, that her complaints were not only directed at George Malone: ''I go to the doctor to *tell* him what I've been thinking about, not find out! Arrogant of me to speak like that! But he says I'm that kind of patient. I don't like that word, 'patient.' I told him another word is necessary. He asked me for a suggestion. I couldn't come up with much: visitor, friend, person. How about communicant? Well, I'm in the business of slogans; if I put my mind to it, I'd have a catchy one for him in a day or two! I've been having a more relaxed time at his office—a few visits for a checkup! I told him I was becoming a 'civil rights type.' He laughed, and said I'd always been that—always been upset by the unfairness of life. He was so right! A woman who works in a man's world and gets way up there is a woman who has seen plenty of injustice—and kept her mouth shut! What troubles me is my silence over the years. Not just silence, but willful shortsightedness. I never wanted to look closely, for fear I'd walk out on the whole scene. Now this 'women's movement' is making us all so *aware*—sometimes, I think, *too* aware, and sometimes, I think, it's about time, and the more the better.

"I don't know how I put up with my first husband. I remember office scenes when I was starting out—remarks that it seems stick in my mind, even though I thought I'd long since forgotten them. All the coffee I was asked to make—by men who wouldn't lift a finger for their own caffeine habit! Well, it's useless to go back and become bitter. I suppose I'm one of those millions of women who has taken it, taken it, taken it—and how do they put it in the southern jails?—managed to 'overcome.' But now all this restlessness! I told Dr. Good that I've got to be rid of these petty resentments. Men are half the human race, and I don't want to be fighting a battle with them all day, and half the night as well.

"My husband is a decent person; the men at the office are my friends. If I become a 'feminist,' I'll end up counting incidents, surveying attitudes, conscious and unconscious, finding fault endlessly, and soon I'll be without a job. Then I'll be even more bitter, and some life it will be! I have to find a way to be of help to other women; but also to do my job and hold a marriage together. I don't want my husband to be a stand-in for all the men I've met who are 'chauvinists.' I can't think of him as that; he's my husband, and a damn fine person. No one is without warts and blemishes. I'm not about to let politics invade my home; that's why I couldn't adopt a black child. I'd become, in a strange way, racially obsessed. Everything would center on the baby's *color*. Maybe not—I don't know; I said to the doctor: who can know about something hypothetical, about how you'd behave in the future, *if?*"

Her future began to take shape a few months later. They went to California on a joint business trip, and while there she decided that she really did want to have one (and only one) child. A friend of hers, a woman who ran an art gallery, told her of the woman who cared for her son. Laura began to visualize herself a mother, but also an executive woman. Upon her return from California she was offered an especially attractive position as a publicist for one of the major networks—with a role in programming as well. She would become a "matchmaker" of sorts: "I would connect a corporation with the best television show for its purposes. Advertising isn't as random as people believe. You oughtn't just buy a bulk of time in radio or television. It matters what product sponsors a show; it matters how a product is sold, by whom. I suppose the word is 'association'—what mental connections people make. I will also continue to have a lot to do with public television, because I won't leave my old company completely. I can help it continue its support of really good shows on the educational network."

A ·year after she had established herself in her new job, she was pregnant, by choice. She'd become angry that "it" had taken so long, and then characteristically amused at herself: "I thought that once I decided to become pregnant, I would! After a few months I was ready to go back to the pill. I began to worry. I began to feel inadequate. I spend so much time trying to do a first-rate job in the office, I couldn't believe that my body wouldn't just go right ahead and react quickly, intelligently. I'd taken my temperature daily, and figured out when I ovulated, and I have always been regular with my periods. I began to dread sex in the middle of the month—baby-making, not lovemaking. I'd come home those days and tell my husband that I'd been working all day, and here I was, with a new job at night! I got impatient and went to see a gynecologist, and he told me to relax. I went to see Dr. Good, because I knew *he* wouldn't come up with that kind of advice! And he didn't. He said the only thing he could tell me was that when a couple stops trying to have a baby, they often have one. I asked him what he meant by 'stops trying'! He laughed. He told me I'd get pregnant 'one of these days'—and then he asked me if I'd be glad when the time came, and damned if I didn't burst into tears: the only time I ever did in his office. I didn't know why I was crying. And bless that doctor, he had the tact not to ask me. There are times to let people just *be!*"

They went to California again. She decided to stop keeping track of her ovulatory cycle, of which day it was after she'd menstruated. When she became pregnant, though, she figured that California had been the place. When her daughter was born she called her a Californian—and named her after her sister and after Joan, her old friend, who had been childless. They called the child Joannie, and obtained for her an English nanny, who moved in with them to a large, old country home. Laura worried about the distance between home and office, but had always enjoyed driving, and was pleased, in fact, to have some distance between the two sides of her life: "I may be an evil person, but when I'm at work I don't think of Joannie; she's with her nanny, and that is that. I couldn't stay home and care for her. On weekends I've tried it for a day, and I get jittery. I'm good with her for a few hours, and then I wear down. I've told her nanny how I feel; she is like a nanny to me: 'Mrs. Malone, it's no great job, changing diapers and following a toddler around, and if you have a job you like, then you're lucky. I envy you, but I don't blame you for not quitting and coming home.'

"Then I began to worry that the nanny was 'bored'—so my daughter would suffer some way emotionally. Such silliness! I'm ashamed to admit that I went to see Dr. Good one time to talk about all that. He got quite tough with me! He said Americans are obsessed with their children, and worry too much about what to say to them, and how to bring them up—when to do what with them. He said he was going to use the word I hated when my gynecologist used it: relax. I said I wish I could! He said my child was *herself*—no one else's child. I shouldn't worry what experts say, and I shouldn't be asking him or anyone else about the 'right' way to do all the things that have to be done for a child. The nanny is a good, kind person; she brought up two daughters of her own, and they didn't turn out so bad. Why worry? I told him I didn't—while at work! He told me this: be glad you're at work, then, most of the day!"

She wanted no more children. She felt much better when her daughter was four, five, six—able to carry on a conversation, and demonstrate control in social situations. She could be brought into town, for lunch, for a movie or trip to a museum. Then the working schedule would give way, occasionally, to the felt requirements of a particular mother: "I love driving with Joannie in my car. She loves driving, too. She's so quiet. She stares out the window, and I can't be sure whether she's daydreaming or looking at people or the trees or the houses we pass. She asked me once when she'd have her own car. I said in exactly ten years! When we get into the city she's obviously excited. She loves the crowds, the noise; I thought she'd be scared, but no. She loves my office. She plays with the phones, the intercom. I take her to the television studios, and she's become a jaded part of that world. When I see her sitting in my chair, asking my secretary for a Coke on the intercom, and pressing the stapler on my desk, and writing on my notepaper, I wonder to myself what kind of a person she'll be in ten years, when she does have her car, or twenty years, when (I presume, I guess) she'll be through college and out in the world. Will she be like me—a businesswoman? She told her nanny once that her mother was in town, bossing people, but she'd be home in time for supper. I thought to myself that she's right. I do my share of bossing—and from the looks of Joannie's behavior in the office, she has a touch of the boss in her. But maybe she'll turn away from that, from me and my world—as I did from my mother's. I think I get more pleasure thinking about my child's future than taking care of her in the present! But I've given up giving myself a bad name for my sins. The girl is doing well, and my work may be one of the reasons she is!''

part two

MANAGING

"I DON'T KNOW how I got the name Maisie. My mother used to tell me, when I was a girl, that she had to name me Mary, because my father's older sister had that name, and she died a year before I was born. She had rheumatic fever, I think. My mother swore to herself while she was in labor with me—a long, long time!—that if she could give birth to me, she could call me what she damn well pleased, and she did. But when I would ask her 'how come Maisie,' she would smile and say it was her secret. And she would never give it away to anyone! My father once told me what he thought: 'Your mother heard the name somewhere. Maybe the woman next to her in the hospital, when she was having you, gave her the idea.' "

Maisie it has been. The name is a departure point for her, a way of talking about herself. She will be thinking of something that has happened, or may soon happen, and often enough, she falls back upon her name—as a means of explanation, of humorous comment, of self-pity, and so on. Once, visibly upset by something that had happened at work, she launched into an auto-biography of sorts, starting with her name and its possible significance to her life: "Maybe if I had been called by an ordinary name, I would have lived a more conventional life. They say the first few years are the most important. Isn't that what psychology tells us, modern psychology? Well, the first experience I had was hearing my mother say to me: 'Maisie you are, and Maisie you'll stay.' She used to tell me that—her joke on my father, but it turned out to be a joke on me!

"Oh, I'm being silly, I guess. There are no explanations to anyone's life. We wake up in the middle, sometimes, and we want to know how it all happened, and where we're going; but by that time the story is all written, and we're just waiting—a few more paragraphs, and they're no big mystery! I shouldn't talk like that! I've always *believed* in mystery—in the surprises that can catch you up. But every once in a while I begin to wonder if I've fooled myself. There's a certain kind of person who is too smart for her own good, and I'm that, I think.

"When I was in the fourth grade I had a teacher, Miss Hogan, who spent half the day telling me to 'act more like a girl.' I raised my hand too much. I spoke too much. She would give me hell in front of everyone; and the worst way—she knew it—to give me hell was to use the name Mary: 'I wish you'd stay in your seat, Mary, and stop talking to your neighbors, and stop disrupting this class.' It's been a lot of years since I last saw her, but I can hear her name, and I can see that face of hers. She gave us a little sermon, to start off each day: trust in God, and obey the law, and try your hardest, and you'll die in peace—ideas like those! And she had colossal nerve. She taught us—the girls only!—to bring her flowers in the spring. There was a field near the school, and we'd go pick wild flowers and haul them in, once or twice a week, for the vase on her desk. She didn't want any from the boys!

"She had it all figured out: boys don't have anything to do with flowers, and they can raise their hands all they want, and if they are insulted, they should speak back—even to their teacher! I remember a boy named Greg O'Donnell; he would disagree with that Miss Hogan at the drop of a hat. Once he came up to me, after school, and he gave me some advice: 'Pretend to go along with her, and swear at her under your breath.' But I couldn't do it. I couldn't be a sweet, dainty girl. I was always messing up! I was always fighting in the school yard, during recess—with boys, usually. She'd take one look at me when we came back to the classroom and she'd say I was not 'behaving,' and it was too bad, because if I would only give myself a chance, then I could be a 'pretty girl.' Once I sat there with a ruler in my hand, and I wanted to throw it at her for saying that, and I almost did. I lifted it, and I was going to let go, but I lost my nerve. I dropped it on the floor. She boomed out: '*Mary,* pick that up and bring it to me.' I guess I went a little crazy for a few minutes. I couldn't move, even though I wanted to—I wanted to oblige her. Greg leaped up and took the ruler to her. I just sat there. She stared at me; everyone in the room did. Then the bell rang. I can hear it ringing now. 'Saved by the bell,' my friends said. Greg told me later she said to him, when he brought her the ruler, that one day I'd grow up, and stop being a tomboy Maisie, and become a nice girl: Mary.''

In fact she became known, even in the fifth and sixth grades, as a ''smart girl.'' The episode just described, which she would remember all her life, was a turning point. She abandoned boys' games for books. But she could not be a quiet, demure person, the ''nice girl'' her fourth-grade teacher had wanted. In the fifth grade she had an altogether different experience, less dramatic, perhaps, but decisive: ''It was a great relief to me when I was promoted out of that fourth grade. My fifth-grade teacher was tough; she allowed no noise, no pranks. She made us settle down right away, each morning. She threatened us with the blackboard pointer: ten whacks on the hands, five on the left and five on the right, for 'disobedience.' I think my mother spoiled me. I was an only child. So, this teacher was the first person to get me under control. My father was a salesman, and he was away a lot. He was a ladies' man. I now realize he cheated on my mother a lot. She always spoke well of him, though. I remember him combing his hair, and brushing it, and putting hair tonic on it: such a to-do. I remember thinking that I'd never want to be like that—hair-conscious and looks-conscious: a 'nice girl'! That fifth-grade teacher was everything my father wasn't—gruff and casual and relaxed about the way she looked. My poor mother was always trying to fix herself up: for him, for his approval.

"Once—I must have been around ten or eleven—I asked her why she didn't stop fussing with herself. She turned and told me that a woman has to hold her husband, even if she is married to him. I remember that word 'hold'; it sometimes flashes across my mind now, years and years later. I think I knew everything I was ever going to know about men and women that moment. I wanted to ask my mother, right then and there, why, why—what's the point of holding on to someone like that? She was becoming a nothing, and I could see it—ten years old, and I could see it. He'd come home and give her a plastic smile, and put his hand through his wavy hair, caressing it, and she'd melt. He'd come home and look sour, and she'd scurry all over, trying to please him. What could she do to make him comfortable? What did he want to eat? Was there a movie he wanted to see? How about the neighbors coming over for a drink? The only thing she had to fall back on was me—and I guess I wasn't a good daughter to her even then. I didn't like the way she bowed and scraped before him. I guess the best way to put it was: I didn't like her manner. Every once in a while she'd remind me of her best moment, when she stood up to him and started calling me Maisie. But I only got angry. I wished she'd had more fight in her.

"My fifth-grade teacher was a fighter. She took no nonsense from anyone—not from us kids, and not from the other teachers. She even told the principal off. I remember the time. He came in one day and expected us all to drop everything and pay attention to *him*. She ignored him, and kept on teaching, and she made sure we ignored him by keeping us riveted to the blackboard and what she was writing. She had a way of throwing questions at us while she wrote stuff down with the chalk. I guess the principal couldn't take it after a while. He interrupted with his own question. She whirled around, and told him she'd already asked that of us, and would he please let us finish the lesson. It was history;

she was telling us about Abraham Lincoln, and how he had a debate with Stephen Douglas, and one was for leaving things be and the other was for stopping the spread of slavery. The principal said nothing. He walked over to a kid's desk, picked up the history book, flipped through the pages, slammed it down, and walked out. He shut the door hard, and we all sat there, wondering what she'd do, our tough teacher. She smiled, and told us we'd best go on, but she wanted us to know something first: there were slaves a long time ago, and slaveholders, and there still are people who look down on other people, and treat them like dirt, and expect to be obeyed, no matter what.

"I've never forgotten that moment. I tried to tell my mother what happened, later that day, but she wasn't interested. She had to go get herself a permanent. My mother got one every month or so, and each permanent gave her what today's kids call a fix; she'd be high on her hair for a day or two, and I guess she'd be *hopeful: he* might notice, and *he* might smile, and *he* might pay attention to her. I can hear those words 'pay attention' coming out of her mouth even now: 'Your father was in a good mood yesterday; he paid attention to me. But he sure is wrapped up in his problems today.' She'd never admit to being angry at him. She was forever telling me that it's hard to sell umbrellas. That was his job. Wholesale umbrellas—to all the stores in sight.''

Books took her away from her childhood; books harnessed her quick, deep mind to facts and to the lives of other people, dead or far away. She especially loved history, her fifth-grade teacher's favorite subject. And she would never forget Abraham Lincoln and what he stood for. In high school she wrote her longest, most comprehensive, and successful paper on him—a frank exercise in admiration as well as historical analysis. She found a picture of Lincoln in a backyard sale, and hung it on her bedroom wall. His heavy-lidded eyes intrigued her. What kind of a person was he? What did he truly think—and how could he have borne the evident sadness he felt, and still carry on as President of the United States, in the midst of a serious war, as Commander-in-Chief of the Union forces?

Such questions pursued her in high school, even as she had

little interest in asking about other matters: who was going out with whom, and with what seriousness? By then she was known as "the brain"—an all-too-serious student, but not the usual, compliant pedant by any means. She was outspoken. She was unpredictable. She had a way of putting others down—of asserting an intellectual and emotional independence that distinguished her from other studious youths. And she was attractive, whether she liked it or not. She recalls not at all liking it; she recalls doing everything she could to make herself unattractive: "I was blond, and the boys liked my hair; I could tell. I left it alone. I even messed it up. My mother kept pushing me: go to the beauty parlor. I said no. Finally, she asked me once too often, and I exploded. I told her that I'd never step foot in that beauty parlor; I told her I'd sooner die. Then I tore up the slip with the appointment she'd made for me. She started crying. I wished she would have fought me—at least me if not her husband! But she was not one to get angry.

"I now realize that she *was* a fighter. She would never take no for an answer. If my father didn't give her the right time of day, she'd wait and pretty herself up and keep smiling at him, and serving him, and asking what *more* she could do, and eventually she'd get from him what she wanted, what she believed was her due, the crumbs of his attention. He'd say 'thank you' to her when she brought him something at the table, and you could see her light up. She knew she was going to win that day. He was 'coming around.' That was her expression; every time I heard her use it, I got sick to my stomach. But I never dared tell her what I really thought of her. I was afraid it would kill her to hear. I now know I underestimated her. Nothing I said would have undone her. Nothing my father said ever did! She lived for her hair, and for her figure, and for what she got out of them—the smile he'd give her at supper that meant they'd have sex that night. I must have been thirteen or fourteen when I figured that out—when I connected his smile in the evening with her singing the next morning.

"She sang that song, 'On the Sunny Side of the Street'; she'd hum it over and over on certain days, while making breakfast. He'd be silent. He'd be in a *bad* mood! He'd get out of the house as fast as he could. I guess he couldn't stand her happiness. I guess he must have wanted to tell her off, but he didn't know for what. Oh, I understand all that now! She'd won; she'd gotten what she wanted out of him. She was singing a victory song; she was telling him off; she was showing him that *she* was the strong one, that she was the one who could set her course, keep to it, and get where she wanted to be. He ran because he knew he'd been outmaneuvered, outlasted. He was a show-off. She was a dumb blond who had a fox in her. I think I had a fox in me, even in high school; I realized that the more I ignored my hair and my clothes, the more interested the boys became. I had my mother in me: one way or the other I knew how to get the boys to 'pay attention.' "

She did not return those young men much regard. Nor was she especially popular in high school with her young women classmates. In fact, she was seen as a quite eccentric person. Her plain clothes and plain manners were offensive to those of her sex who at fourteen or fifteen had already begun devoting themselves to men: the coiffure, the waistline, the hemline, the shade of lipstick or fingernail polish. She wore no makeup, and she never sat around in feigned indifference or helplessness, waiting for a boy to come and start something with words. She became, in her last two years of high school, a close friend of two boys, one a bright youth headed for college, the other an athlete who dreamed of a career as a pilot in the air force. She was still the tomboy—or so her mother thought, as well as many of the high school's women. But she knew better, even then—and certainly later: "I knew I wasn't a tomboy. I didn't want to be a boy, or to hang around with boys because I liked them better than girls for company. I was never the girl who dressed in pants when all other girls were wearing skirts, and played with the boys all the time. I was shy, and I wanted friends of my own sex, but even back then, in high school during the 1940's, I knew there was something wrong with the way we were behaving—the girls in that school, and everywhere else. I remember the hate I felt for this one girl, Kathy McNulty. It's strange how you can remember someone so clearly years and years later—someone you never liked, never even talked to! She was a silly little blond who sat at her desk humming and giving sly looks to the boys. She would scrape off her fingernail polish, then put it back on. She would drop books or pencils or compasses, and look around as if she was blind—when she knew perfectly well what was right at her feet.

"Once I saw her let a book drop after she saw a certain boy come around the corner. She got her way; he picked it up. Then she smiled, and thanked him, and he walked off with her, and I wanted to run up to her and sock her one, and I wanted to sock him one, too. I got scared, because I actually followed them a little. I could feel my heart pounding, and I was flushed, I knew. She had a spell on me. I couldn't get her out of my mind. Weeks later I'd be studying or doing an errand or listening to the radio, and she'd cross my mind. I know what the psychologists would say today. They'd say I wanted to be like her. But they would be wrong. She was everything I knew I didn't want to be like. A person can remind you of that—of what you detest!

"I guess I felt sorry for that Kathy McNulty. I imagined talks with her. I would tell her that she was behaving like a silly fool; that she wasn't kidding anyone, especially the boys she flirted with and teased; that she was only earning their contempt. But she never would have given me five seconds of her precious time. No wonder I asked my friend one day if I could go into the air force with him. He said sure, and I was ready to enlist—only I wasn't old enough, and they didn't have women then, I don't think, in the air force. Maybe a few. I don't know. I just wanted to be away from people like that Kathy McNulty. She and my mother were a pair; I knew that then, and at that time we had no Ann Landers explaining the mind every day in the newspaper."

She lost control one day. She did something she would never forget, never really forgive herself for doing. She came in extremely early, and went over to Kathy McNulty's desk and opened it and took the little containers of fingernail polish and spilled them; then she closed the desk, and left the empty classroom for the school library. She returned when she knew others would have arrived, but not Kathy McNulty, who always made it her business to come in dramatically in an apparent rush—almost but not quite late. Twenty-five years later, on the occasion of her high school class spring reunion, which she did not attend, the memory of that incident persisted: "I wasn't ashamed for what I did; I was ashamed that I'd actually gone and done it! I mean, she deserved much more—a public scolding. But I knew when I watched her open that desk, and then scream, that she'd worked her way too far into my head! I remember that morning so clearly, even now. I had taken out my American history book. I was pretending to read it. I was trying hard to read it. I'd turned to the section on the Civil War. I was reading about Abraham Lincoln, and the troubles he had. I kept reading the same paragraph over and over again, and still I didn't know what I'd read. Then she came in. Then she opened her desk. I caught her in my eye just before she saw it—her usual shake of her head, to show off her long blond hair. Then she stood up. She had the whole class watching her.

"I can remember her every word: 'I don't believe it!' That's all she said. She just stood there and looked and looked and shook her head and put her hand through her hair and pulled on her dress, and pretty soon she had everyone in her little hands. They were cleaning and scrubbing for her, and they were telling her how sorry they all felt for her, and they were offering to give her their desks to use, and meanwhile she was repeating herself, every minute or two, just to keep the fires of sympathy and attention going: 'I don't believe it.' *I* couldn't believe it! I think that was the most important moment in my life! I've never been the same since then. That Kathy McNulty has been a guardian angel of mine! I guess I decided that if you can't beat them, join them! Oh, I couldn't do her act. You have to be born for that; or you have to be her kind of person. But she had taught me a lesson, and I remember later that day telling myself what the lesson was: a woman who wants to get ahead in this world of ours won't get far if she seems too independent. She has to look as if she's a little helpless, or in trouble. But she has to know what she's doing—otherwise, she'll work herself into trouble and stay there for good, like my mother did.

"But Kathy McNulty wasn't my mother. Kathy McNulty was never going to be pushed around. I guess I realized that day how much I envied her. I didn't want to be like her; but I wanted to get the same results. I hope I don't sound hardhearted. I was desperate. I wasn't calculating, I was upset. I saw all those girls getting ready to throw themselves away—anything, so long as they had a boy, as long as they would get married and not be an 'old maid.' The difference between them and Kathy McNulty was this: she knew what was happening; she saw that there was a war going on, and she wanted to win and not lose. I admired her. After that day, she became my heroine! And I never talked with her. I used to wish I'd gone up and told her what I had done. I used to wish I could become her friend. But those were idle thoughts. I knew in my heart that the best thing for me to do was keep her in my mind, and talk to her that way. As for feeling 'bad' because of what I'd done: nonsense. She loved every minute of it—all those boys around her, trying to help her, and all the girls feeling sorry for her, but wishing they were in her shoes.''

There was no sudden change in Maisie's personality after that event took place. She didn't start using fingernail polish herself. She didn't ''arrange'' her hair, nor did she take to postures of innocence, vulnerability, confusion. But she decided, quite knowingly, that she was no longer going to ignore what she often would refer to as ''the facts of life,'' by which she meant the way men and women get along in the world she was born to know. She remembers quite clearly the chain of psychological developments, the sequence of alterations in behavior, in attitude—not, it must be emphasized, the result of a plan, a schedule that had been worked out, a grand design of sorts. She recalls one early incident, and with the telling wants to emphasize the *drift* of things—the manner in which, almost but not quite unselfconsciously, a person can end up doing things differently, can end up altogether changed, while at the same time convinced deep down that there is an emotional life within that will never in the least undergo modification: ''I was walking with my friend; he was talking, as usual, about the air force. He wanted to be a pilot so bad he could taste it. He wanted to fly all over the world. He was fed up with his parents; I guess a lot of us were then. His mother was a nut, he kept telling me, and he wanted to get away from her. I knew there was something wrong with her, but I didn't know what. He said that if he was stationed in some air force base in Greenland or over in the Pacific he'd be happy—no mother, with her pain-in-the-neck talk. His father never said a word of disagreement with the mother, and that was hard for a big strong son to take.

''I didn't think about all that family trouble at the time. But I must have had something on my mind about psychology (*my* psychology!) because I told my friend that I was going to fly the coop, too—the sooner the better. And I told him his parents and my parents didn't live the kind of lives I wanted to live. He nodded, and he said 'yup,' and he said 'yup, you're right.' Then he asked me what I was going to do. I told him I didn't know, but I was doing my thinking. My father wouldn't send me to college. He said he didn't have the money, though if I was a boy I'd have been given another story. I said that if I was lucky, I'd find a job in New York City. Someplace big and far enough away, so you can start your own life and live it without interference. He asked me whether New York was far enough away, only a few hundred miles. I laughed; I said Greenland isn't far enough, if you don't change yourself.

''That's when I first realized what was happening to me. There I was, talking about things I'd had thoughts about—but they'd never come together the way they did when we were walking. I said I knew one thing: I'd never live like my mother; I'd never be the kind of person she was. He said he would never be like his father; that's why he wanted to be a pilot. I guess his father was an electrician. I told my friend he had to do more than fly away in a plane. He told me New York City wouldn't change me over-night. We were teasing each other! Suddenly I stopped and turned toward him and asked him why I didn't go to Greenland and he to New York. He asked me what *I'd* do in Greenland. I said I'd do the same thing he wanted to do—be a pilot. He thought that was very funny! I asked him why he thought I shouldn't become a pilot. He said it just wasn't possible. I re-minded him of Amelia Earhart; we'd all heard of her. He was right, though; even she couldn't have become an air force pilot then. Even now I don't think there are any woman *pilots* in the air force. We started walking again, and I told him a woman is a fool to try to copy men. And she's a fool if she's like my mother, and tries to win them over. The best a woman can do is win over them—a different thing! If she tries to push into a man's world, she'll be on their ground, and she'll lose—even if she does all right, she'll lose. She'll be outnumbered. They'll call her a tomboy—everything. The best a woman can do is decide to be a woman, but keep her eye on men, and realize what they're like!

"My friend said I was talking 'real wild.' He said he didn't get my point. I wasn't sure of my point, either. I was a kid then. But something was brewing in my head. I know that now, because I can remember so clearly what my friend and I said to each other. I told him I'd get 'a woman's job.' I said: secretary, typist, that kind of job. He said it was no fun, doing such work. I told him it was no fun selling umbrellas; that's what my father sold. And it was no fun putting wires in people's homes—what his father did. But my friend didn't like my talk about 'a woman's job'—because he told me we should *both* become pilots, and he was sure I could do better than Amelia Earhart. I wouldn't get lost and die in the Pacific Ocean! I knew then that I'd better stop talking with him about the future. I could see that he probably wouldn't be a pilot anyway, and I'd end up with a typewriter to operate, not a plane, so what was the use of dreaming. But I'd heard myself use those words 'a woman's job,' and in my opinion, I was never the same person after that. I'd connected in my mind work and sex. A lot of women won't admit to themselves that there is that connection, even though in the back of their minds they know better.

"When I finished with high school I got a job in a super-market, packing groceries. I had to stay at home; I was saving money so I could go to secretarial school. My father said he'd help out, but he was going downhill then. He had a bad ulcer. He became impossible. My mother kept telling me he was 'sick,' but he wasn't any sicker than she was for putting up with him. That year I finally found out the facts. My mother took a job housecleaning for a lawyer's family, and I had the morning off, so I could work in the market until ten at night. One day I started looking through my father's bureau, and his closet. At first there was nothing to surprise you. But I was pretty thorough! In one of his fancy cashmere sweaters—and he had no money to put me through secretarial school!—I found pictures of a woman, and some letters she wrote him. Then I went through all his clothes and it was like I'd discovered gold! He must have had ten women on the string! Maybe he'd known them, one by one, over the years. I never found out because I never said anything to him, or to my mother. To tell the truth, I wasn't even angry at my father. I think I was always angry at my *mother,* for putting up with him.

"I kept looking at those women. I wanted to know who they were! I wondered whether they were married or not. I tried to fig-ure out who they were. Only two wrote letters that told me much. One woman lived in an apartment house downtown. She was a Miss. The other woman lived in a suburb, and she was a Mrs. The first woman sounded friendlier, and she had a job I was in-trigued by—she worked in a museum. I guessed she was the director's secretary, but she called herself his assistant. I went to the museum one day, when I had time off. I went to the direc-tor's office. There were three women outside, two typing and one on the phone—and I didn't know what to do. I walked by, then got cold feet, and kept walking. Then I went to look at the pic-tures, but I couldn't really pay any attention to them because all I could think of was that woman whose letters I'd read. She was the only one who hadn't given my father a picture of herself—or, if she had, it wasn't with the four letters in his shirt, and none of the three women in the museum looked like any of my father's *other* girl friends!

"After about ten minutes of tiptoeing and sneaking around and pretending to be on my way someplace, I almost stumbled into one of the women. She was coming out of the reception area, probably on her way to a coffee break or the ladies' room. I thought she recognized me. She seemed to be staring at me. I was fumbling for words in my mouth. I was about to ask her: Are you . . . But she moved away, and I was afraid to follow her. I left the museum right away. I went home and I kept thinking to myself that there must be a way I could figure out which one of those three women was my father's girl friend.

"I waited for another time when I had the house to myself, and I read those letters carefully, and sure enough, she mentioned my father's black hair, and she said she loved it, and even though everyone wants to be a blond, and she's one, she always wished she had hair the color of his. I thought she was being stupid—but, I thought to myself, having an affair with my father was stupid, too. I couldn't remember the hair color of any of those three women in the museum. Maybe they were *all* blond! But I went back, and I looked, and my heart began to go faster when I realized that two were brunettes and one was blond, and she was the one who'd gotten up and walked right by me the other time. But I was really nervous, and I didn't think I could do it—go up to her and introduce myself. I walked by, and I tried to get a good look at her without being noticed. She was a fancy dresser. She seemed to have a necklace, and she had big earrings. Her hair was long. She was typing away, and she didn't look up, so I stood still and stared, but one of the other women saw me and I saw her staring at me, and I was afraid she'd come over and say something. I was really afraid, I guess, that she'd point me out to my father's girl friend—but that was a foolish thought!

"I kept on trying to think of how to introduce myself: 'Hello, I'm Maisie, and you know my father'; or 'I'd like to talk with you for a minute, because we know someone in common, I think.' But nothing seemed the right thing to say. I kept hoping she'd come out, like last time, but she didn't, and it was after lunch. I decided to go home, but I couldn't get myself on the bus. I had the whole day off, so I decided to go back and look at the pictures. This time I tried hard, and I remember seeing some nude women, and wondering why they let those painters use them that way. There didn't seem to be any pictures of men lying around! I had a chip on my shoulder, even then! Or maybe I was learning the score! I went in a courtyard and sat there. I had my paper, and I read it, and then I sat and wondered what I was doing there in the first place. The few people nearby—they were old women. I could tell by their accents, they were rich. They talked about parties they'd gone to and parties they were planning to go to. There wasn't a man in sight. I reminded myself that men work during weekdays. I remember thinking to myself that I'd like to bring my friend over, and let him see that if he had his air force, I had my museum; but I thought to myself that I'd take the air force any day! Finally, I heard an alarm go off—or I thought that it was that. I saw people leaving, and I realized it was five o'clock. Everyone else was getting out of work, and these people were going home after drinking coffee and tea and looking at pictures. I wondered who was cooking the food for all the families of all those women!

"I hurried to get out, and I stood there waiting. I figured the employees would come out after the visitors. After a while I saw her—but she was with someone. I didn't know what to do. I stood there and waited, to see where they were going. They both walked toward the bus stop, so I hurried to get over there, and be with them, in case a bus came. On my way over I saw that the other woman was saying good-bye and walking. I was relieved; but I also was scared, because now there was nothing to prevent me from going right up to her and starting to talk. I just kept walking, and the next thing I knew I was right beside her, and I could see her blond hair up close, and her face. She wasn't all that pretty, I decided. I looked to see if a bus was coming: none in sight. I stood there trying to figure out what words to use.

Then I must have realized that you never can plan words in advance; you just have to plunge in! So, I did; I went right up to her, and looked at her, and said: 'I beg your pardon, but I think we know someone in common.'

"She looked at me as if to say she was sure that wasn't true. First her eyes got wider, then she gave me a quick once-over, then she glared at me, but she didn't say a word. I think I expected her to cooperate, by asking who it was I meant. When she didn't, and when I saw the look in her face, I got mad as hell. I just gave it to her; I mentioned my father's name, and I said it real loud. She whirled around; she must have thought Dad was coming toward us from behind her! But he wasn't there. She glared at me again. I didn't say a word. Then she started talking: 'Who are you?' she asked me. I was tempted to say nothing— give her some of her own silent treatment. But I couldn't hold out. I told her. I said my father is the one we both know.

"She was surprised. I could see it. She didn't know what to say. She looked me up and down, stared at my face, and then I guess she decided I looked enough like him to be his daughter. So, she said we should go take a walk. I said yes, and we started out. She asked me how I knew she knew my father. I told her. She didn't pretend, and I didn't. Then I asked her how she got to know him in the first place. She said he'd picked her up. They were in a drugstore, and he was standing beside her, and he just started talking with her. Then he asked her if she wanted to go have some coffee. She said yes; and then one thing led to another. After a while she spotted a restaurant and asked me if I wanted to stop and get something to eat. It was suppertime, and I thought of my mother. She expected me home for supper on my days off, unless I told her in advance that I was going out, and I hadn't. I really wanted to stay with that woman and find out more, but I felt bad about my mother, and as I stood there, trying to decide, I began to hate my father. The hate must have spilled over, because I blurted out that I didn't want to talk with her anymore, and I was going home. She looked at me as if I was crazy, and I guess I *was*, because I suddenly took off. I just started walking away, real fast. She knew enough not to follow me.''

If the two women had spent more time together, come to know each other, Maisie might have put the matter to rest—by making much of it, thereby ridding herself of its hold on her, or by gaining some wry distance on it, right off: salesmen have their girl friends, and here is one of them, and after a meal or two, a few hours together, I know her a bit, and that way, understand my father somewhat better. For Maisie such psychological possibilities were foreclosed by her abrupt departure—and even more so by what she chose to do thereafter: nourish in her mind a moral or cautionary tale of sorts. The woman in her father's life became a steadfast figure in Maisie's life. Within minutes of leaving her, Maisie had begun to construct a mythic story: the sad, abused woman who will never escape her fate as a mistress to one two-timer after another. The woman's features, for Maisie, began to sag. The woman's hair, for Maisie, lost its vitality, fell awkwardly, and tellingly, over the forehead. The woman's posture became increasingly poor, a reflection, naturally, of what she had become and would always be.

Such dramatic emotional usurpation of reality doesn't get seen, at the time, for what it is. A young woman meets another woman, not all that much her senior, under difficult circumstances, and after a few tense moments they talk openly. Then they hastily separate—and that is that. Years afterward, Maisie would understand and speak of the significance such a brief walk with a woman turned out to have for her: "I can't imagine what kind of person I'd be now, if I hadn't tried to see that woman. She changed me, even though I never saw her again. First there was the girl in class, Kathy McNulty, and then there was that woman. I never think of her as having a name! I pushed her name out of my mind. I didn't go home that night for supper, even though I told the woman that was why I had to go. I just got lost in a trance, you could say. I took the bus home, but I got off near the high school, and I walked over to the football field, and I climbed the stands and I sat there. Now, so many years later, I can see myself: hunched over and looking at the wood of the stands—the grain, the letters carved out. I must have been so lost in my thoughts that the only relief I could find was to get even *more* lost—in that wood.''

She got up soon thereafter and walked toward home. But half-way along she veered off, and got lost in a long night voyage. The streetlights, the homes, the passing cars disappeared. She became oblivious to her own body's movements. She was living another woman's life, as a means of beginning to live her own: ''I pictured her talking with my father. He was leaving her for another mistress. She was crying. He told her not to get so worked up. That was my father, through and through: he pretended he never could understand why anyone got upset by anything! He pretended to be Mr. Cool. No wonder he got a big ulcer. No wonder they had to take out half his stomach.''

But Maisie wanted to go further—pursue a particular woman's life. She wanted to live out that life, follow its trajectory in hopes of finding one for herself; ''I made her into my closest friend! That's strange to do that, I know. But I guess people are stranger than they let on! Whenever I've had to decide something, I've thought of that woman. In my mind, she'll be standing on the street, just as she was that day, but she'll be talking to me—telling me not to be like her, not to make her mistake, not to let a man like my father get me and ruin me.''

She has begun to reveal the nature of her long-held daydreams, the way she had altered reality: ''I'm not sure that woman was really on her way to nowhere! I don't know her *real* life! In my mind she was an attractive woman who had suddenly become old and tired. But I now realize she was about twenty-four or twenty-five. She was probably full of pep. But why was she going out with my father, almost twice her age? Why did she write him those love letters? She must have come from a nice family. She wrote good letters. And there she was, working in that museum. I wouldn't know what to do in a museum! Nor would my father, when he was taking her out!

''My father wasn't a good father, and he wasn't a good husband, either, and he had been fooling around for years with one woman after another. How did he get a grip on this nice young woman? She wrote him as if she was fifty-five, and she'd loved him all her life, and it was cruel that they couldn't be together all the time. There she was, with her life just beginning, but turning herself into some old man's pastime! I was sure that after they'd break up she'd be heartbroken, and she'd probably find some other man who wouldn't be any nicer to her. He'd be some salesman, too—or maybe someone she met in the museum. She'd end up giving the best years of her life to these no-good, lying men; and she'd feel sorry for herself, because they left her, one after the other. All she'd have at the end is her memories, and they'd be bad memories, but she'd have tricked herself into thinking they were good memories. That's the worst way to end your life.''

Maisie began to build her own life as an answer to that *doppelgänger* of sorts she had imagined for herself. She decided to try to get a job as a teller in a bank. She was sure that, in so doing, she would learn how to save and invest money. Her father had always spent every penny he made, a good share of it on himself. Her mother had always told her that she dreaded an incapacitating illness in her husband—there would be no savings to draw upon. Nor did the mother imagine herself able to go out and work: ''My mother was a complete failure as a woman, I guess I'd have to say. If she'd been more like Kathy McNulty, she would have got my father to do more for her. Instead, she was his servant. Meanwhile, he was always cheating on her. But would she admit that? Would she go out and get a job, and build her own life? When I was old enough to be in school all day, she cleaned up once, then again, then a third time. She had that house shining as if it was on display. She'd be waiting, all day she'd be waiting—for me, then for him. She'd make a day's activity out of shopping. And there was church! I can't go to church, even now, without thinking of her—all those prayers, all the turning of the beads, and the novenas she'd get herself worked up about. That was the way she put thick clouds between herself and what was really going on. She'd say that 'it's all in God's hands.'

"Even when I was ten or eleven years old I knew that God had other things to do than take care of my mother in case her husband walked out on her! She'd pray to God as though He were her Big Buddy! Meanwhile her own husband would be pulling the wool over her eyes; and she'd tell me what a *good* man my father is, and I must respect him, the way the Lord said we should. When I went to the bank for an interview, and the man asked me why I wanted to be a teller, I felt like saying that I wanted to be near some money, for a few hours each day, because I never saw any at home, and my mother didn't either. But I said no such thing. I came up with some poppycock—about good working conditions and meeting interesting people, and he smiled. I was never sure whether he was a fool and believed me, or a hypocrite who knew we both were pretending!''

She got the job. She became a teller in the same bank her father used. Not that she worked at the branch he frequented. She wanted to work in the heart of the city; she had made that request during her interview. The bank official who interviewed her had assumed that she simply was attracted to the glamour of the downtown business world. She had, in fact, other reasons for her request: "I had pictured trouble in my mind. What if I saw my father come into that bank—with one of his girl friends, with *her,* the woman I'd met! What if he came in alone, and I was the teller who had no one waiting in line, and I had to wait on him! Then, I'd finally find out about his 'business affairs.' He was always talking about his 'business affairs,' as if he was Henry Ford or one of the Rockefellers. Well, he never talked to us about his *other* affairs. But I had found out about those affairs, and for a long time I wanted to tell my mother. I would have enjoyed seeing her get angry, and shouting at him to get out of her life. I knew, though, she'd never do that, no matter what I told her. I knew that if I told her the truth, it would be like hitting her in the face—and then she'd lower her head, and maybe cry a little, but in a few minutes she'd be looking up, and making her excuses for him, and apologizing for herself. She could turn anyone's crime into her own!

"If I had worked in our neighborhood branch bank, I'd have found out about more of my father's lies to us. Now a teller can find out about any customer's balance. But at that time there was more independence for the district branches; we didn't have all the banks linked up with computers and video screens and automatic phone connections. I didn't want to be away from home because I loved the idea of seeing a lot of stockbrokers and politicians. I was afraid I'd lose my job if the day came that my father came into the place I was working. For my mother's sake I could always keep quiet at home. But at work I might go berserk if I caught him in a lie—a financial lie. But I probably would have been paralyzed by fear. I was scared of him for a long while. He was a big, heavy man, and even though he was always telling everyone not to get upset, and not letting on that he was upset, either, I had memories of his tempers. I was a baby, a small girl, and he'd pound his fists on the table and throw glasses into the fireplace. I could remember them—smashed. I could remember my mother cleaning up the big pieces with her hands, and sweeping the splinters into a tray. We had no vacuum cleaner then."

Maisie's work as a teller became the mainstay of her life. All people, to a degree, "become" what they "do." We sleep, more or less, for a third of our lives. We work, most of us, for another third of our adult lives. And a good part of the remaining time is significantly affected by the job we have. Psychiatrists have given a lot of attention to the way family life bears down on us emotionally—and rightly so. But a working life leaves its strong imprint on us, too. Our dreams, our occasional nightmares, our daydreams, our hopes and worries and fears, our loyalties and animosities, are constantly being influenced, if not shaped outright, by the work we do—what kind, with whom, under which set of circumstances. The pay, the respect earned, or denied, and the recognition won, or missed—those "factors" become for particular individuals a sense of ongoing personal satisfaction, or a sense of unremitting pain and disappointment, or some set of feelings in between: the forbearance that goes with a continuing need to bow before the world's "necessities." Often it is hard for a person to talk about what he or she is in the midst of "living out," but there are (as existentialist philosophers have known) those "true moments" when for one reason or another a person becomes more self-observant, more reflective.

For Maisie the bank became a world, and as a teller she could be an observer, as well as an underpaid, overworked person— who was able, even so, to appreciate the dilemma she faced as yet another "white-collar" working woman: "I just barely got through high school. I could have done better, but I knew I'd never be going to college. I had a mixed-up family life, and I wanted to get away from it. My parents never set high sights for me. I was a girl, not a boy. I remember once, in the sixth or seventh grade, hearing my mother say to my father that if I was a boy, she'd really push me in my schoolwork, but a girl, it's different. She was right, it *is* different!

"At the bank I don't have time, most of the day, to think about all that—my childhood, or the wrongs of this world. I stand there and take in money and hand out money. Some mornings I wake up and I swear I've been dreaming about money, and the first thing that comes into my mind is money! I'll think of a bundle of twenties, or of some change that has to be made, or a check that looks as if it's got a lot of rubber in it, and will bounce to the ceiling. Then I put on the television, and they're talking about money, money, money—even early in the morning: buy this, save with that, try something out, and you'll profit, avoid something else and you won't lose. Then they'll give you the news, and there's more money talk. Someone tried to rob a bank. Someone saved the people millions or billions, or he wasted the same amount, says his enemy.

"Maybe it's just that I work in a bank, and I'm sensitive to the subject, but I wonder, every once in a while, whether we *have* to live in a society where money means so much. 'Money talks,' you hear; and it isn't just that people respect you if you're rich— it's the fact that people don't seem to know how to talk from the heart. They use money to speak with each other. You know where I got that idea—from a man who came up to me one day in the bank. He wanted to break a twenty. I said sure. I handed him the two tens he said he wanted. All of a sudden he looks at me and asks me if I'm married, if I have children. I guess he hadn't seen my left hand when he decided to say something to me. Of course, I thought he was a wise guy, out for a fast pickup. I didn't say a word to him. I shook my head, to answer his questions. Then he told me what was on his mind: he was going to give one of the ten-dollar bills to his daughter. It was her birthday, and that's what he decided to give her. I smiled; I was relieved that he wasn't going to bother me, and I was glad for his daughter. My father was never that generous to me when I was a kid! But the guy had more to say: he told me that he had a hard time talking with his kids. He had a boy and two girls. He can always go play baseball with the boy, but the girls are 'a mystery' to him, so 'I leave them,' he said, 'to their mother.'

"I didn't know what to do then. I felt like telling him to cut it out—and go try, go really try to talk with those daughters of his. But I'm a bank teller, not someone writing an 'advice' column for the papers. So I said it's too bad, and that got him going. It was a slow period, and there was no one behind him, so I had to put up with it: women are a big mystery, all of us, not just his daughters. Then I thought he was trying a trick—to get me into a loaded conversation, so he could ask me out. But sometimes a person in my line of work becomes too suspicious. You spend all your day trying to anticipate bad checks and cheaters and people who add wrong or subtract wrong, and in the back of your mind there's always the chance that some kook or crook will want to rob you or even kill you—it's happened twice in the bank since I've been there—so you forget that a lot of people are just like yourself, trying to live the best way they can, and not always as successful at it as they'd like to be. That poor guy, after he told me more (what he could pack into a couple of minutes, until a woman came along with a check to cash!), I realized that he wasn't the right kind of man to be the father of girls—and that was why he gave ten-dollar bills to his daughters, and that's probably the message they got from him.''

She rather enjoyed brief meetings such as that one. For the rest of the day, in between customers, she thought of the talkative, all-too-open man, and pictured him putting a ten-dollar bill, as he told her he would, into a large birthday card. She wished she had made a suggestion to him—that he write a note to his daughter, rather than rely upon a product of mass-production sentimentality. But she changed her mind on that score. On her coffee break she decided that the man who had trouble figuring out women in general, and his daughters in particular, was not a man to put on paper matters of the heart. She was glad, too, that she didn't come up with a specific suggestion, because she feared the man would then have been ''encouraged'' to come back—and who knows, bring more of his difficulties to her attention.

She was no amateur psychotherapist, but she did have her ''regulars,'' and they added what she called ''a little spice'' to the day's work. In an introspective mood she could go into the symbolic significance of her work—the meaning that a trip to the bank has for many of us: ''When I first started working I was all business: I didn't even look at the customers. I took their money, their checks, their withdrawal requests, and I did what needed to be done. Then I was on to the next customer. I was very good at glancing at people when I knew they weren't going to be glancing back. I could *feel* when their eyes were off me! I could *feel* when they were too busy counting their money or signing something or arranging their papers neatly to pay any attention to me or anyone else. Then I'd give them a quick look—sometimes. But I began to realize, even in the beginning, that a lot of customers want to talk with you. Not just say hello and thank you, but talk with you—especially downtown, when they feel a little loose, not as close to all their problems as they are back home in the residential parts of the city, or in the suburbs.

''After a few months I got tired of being so efficient. I was working so hard that even the manager told me, one day, to 'take it easy.' He said he'd been watching me, and I worked through

lines of customers faster than any other teller, and twice as fast as
some. He said he'd taken a course on the psychology of business
administration, something like that, and he learned that there are
'types' of workers, and I belong to the 'type' that is super-
efficient, and often it's because there's something the person is
running away from, so work becomes a safety valve, or an escape. I didn't say anything. It's not my business to talk back to
him, I thought. He's so smart; or he thinks he is. All he wanted
me to do was look surprised, and then look as if I'd just found
out the big secret of the universe, and then look as if my life
would now be different, and then look as if I owed him the
biggest debt anyone could imagine. I couldn't give him any of
those looks, so I gave him a blank stare. I guess he decided that I
was a pathetic creature who could profit from his wisdom.

"Then he asked me to sit down. That's when I decided I was
going to lose my job. I guess I got tense, and it showed. He was
watching me as if he'd just caught me with his fishing rod, after
waiting all afternoon. I was already wondering what I'd do
next—what kind of job. Through my head there came a flash: go
south, way south, and get a job as a waitress. Then he started in
again. He told me I was doing a *very* good job. He said my
'demeanor' was one hundred percent. He asked me if I was
always so prompt and courteous. I didn't know how to answer
that. I couldn't say that when I come home, I'm so tired I have to
sit and stare into the tube—it doesn't matter what's on—just to
let my feet rest, and my head get off the subject of cashing
checks, and besides, there's no one to be 'prompt and courteous'
to when you're living alone in a small apartment.

"After a few seconds of my silence, he decided I was scared.
He told me to relax. I didn't know how to do that. If he'd left me
alone, I would have relaxed in a second. He tried to make
friendly chat—thinking I was too dumb, I guess, to see what he
was up to! Wasn't it a nice day. Well, it *was*—until then! Didn't
the bank's Christmas decorations look good. Well, they *did*—until he started in with his 'personal attention.' That's what he
started telling me he wanted to give to 'each and every employee'

who was under him—lots and lots of personal attention. Of course, with my suspicious mind, I was beginning to think that he didn't want to fire me, he wanted to proposition me. But I was wrong on both counts. He went into a long lecture on how people should do their work: they should take each minute as it comes, and not try to think ahead too much. For instance, if there's a long line waiting before you, and you're doing your level best as a teller, then you shouldn't get upset, and you shouldn't work so hard and fast that you start making mistakes. You should just remind yourself that you're there to do the best job you possibly can, and that's how it is. That's just empty talk, I thought to myself. I'd seen him start to panic when there was a crowd in the bank, and there weren't more teller stations to open up. He'd look as if he'd whip anyone who took time out to sneeze, never mind tell herself not to get 'upset'!

"Finally, he got to his 'main point.' He told me for the second time that I was 'a little nervous.' He didn't want to 'pry into' my 'affairs,' but he did want me to know that he had 'a good ear,' and if the time ever came that I 'want to talk,' he'd be glad to listen. Over my dead body, I thought—but I knew I couldn't even hint with a look how I felt. I decided to smile—give him a real big, phony smile, the kind my father gave store owners when he was softening them up for a large order. I even thought of my father as I broke my cheeks and opened my mouth and lowered my eyes, as though (gee whiz!) I'd come upon my first friend, and praise to the Father, the Son, and the Holy Ghost! He melted, and I was grateful to the Lord. I said to myself: Thank God.

"I knew I'd be sent back to work, pronto. He'd been right in his opinion; I'd showed him that, so there was no point going any further! That's when he reminded me not to try to 'run from anything' and instead, to 'face' what was going on. Well, I said to myself, I'd like to run from you, starting right now, and before I'd start, I'd face you, all right, and tell you what's on my mind. But I said nothing. A bank teller is someone who keeps her mouth shut, and listens to supervisors like him—or customers who have a lot of money troubles and want to let off a little steam when making a deposit, or drawing out money from the bank.''

The man who was so attentive to her "problems" was soon enough on his way upward. She began to see that his talk hadn't been meant for her, really. His talk was a reflex—an outpouring of good behavior, proof of how well he'd learned his lessons. Above him was someone else, a man who prided himself on having intelligent, well-trained assistants, familiar with all the advanced business and psychological "techniques." And, of course, there was someone above him, too—layers and layers of authority. Maisie would sometimes wonder who actually owned the bank. She would ask herself that question from time to time as she did her work, but come up with no satisfactory answer. Her fellow tellers would answer the question, she realized, the same way she would, if asked by them: the rich people, who have plenty of money, and need a place to store it! Yet, there were so many hundreds of plain, ordinary men and women who came up to her stall, day in and day out. They weren't rich. They were struggling hard to make ends meet, as do most people, all the time. She would think about that kind of issue, now and then—the matter of a few who have, and many who don't have. She was certain, for instance, after she'd worked in the bank for a year or two, that she could spot the people who were having financial troubles from the ones who weren't—and not by the way they dressed. There was something in their gait, or maybe it was an expression they wore on their faces. She could spot the "rich ones" who only looked poor. She could spot the very well-dressed ones who were in lots of trouble—maybe, near broke. She could spot the conscientious ones, the "worriers" who spend half their lives balancing their checkbooks and adding up how much they have, and how much they owe, and how much they'll make in X years and Y years, and what their retirement income will be, down to the last cent.

"Money runs more lives than anyone knows," she would insist, and then do the necessary amplifying and qualifying: "I get to know a lot of the people; they joke with me and call themselves my 'customers.' They tell me how they go from week to week, always worrying about a bill or a payment they have to make. Or the ones with more money—they will tell you that they're saving for something big, or they're going to make sure that their children never have to think about money. I joked with one lawyer; I said to him he could set up the trusts for his kids, and he could put money in accounts for them, but he can't get rid of himself: he's the one who's doing it for them, and they'll always know that. I was thinking of my own father; even if he had given me some money, I don't think I could have enjoyed it. I'd have wanted to give it away, or spend it fast.

"Most of the people I see in the bank tell me that they live from paycheck to paycheck. The rich ones have 'goals'—they're out to make this much, or salt away that much. It's all the same—money becomes the reason you keep going. One of the richest men in the city comes and jokes with us; I guess he's a stockholder in the bank. He comes over to us tellers and asks us how we're doing. There's nothing snobbish about him. Then he'll say that we're as important as the grocer or the priest, because people live from meal to meal, and they need religion, or there'd be nothing higher to believe in—and they need us, because without us there'd be chaos, and there wouldn't be work, because there'd be no pay. It's all too much for me, to think big like that!

"One thing I know: there are more important things in this life than making money. A lot of people are looking for someone to trust, to love. That's harder to find than a job and a paycheck. Most people go to work, but look at all the trouble they have at home. Look at the divorces—all over, to the left and the right. Look at the marriages that seem to be in good shape—but underneath, it's a different story, as I well know from my parents, and how they were together. I think it's loneliness that people are afraid of; loneliness and becoming poor, and going hungry. The combination is the worst. Maybe a lot of people become 'money-warts' (we call them that; it comes from the expression 'worry-wart,' I think) because they'd rather have something else on their minds than the personal troubles they're having. They can't be happy, so they try to get rich—or not become poor. That's my small interpretation of psychology, I guess!''

She makes that last assertion with obvious but unnecessary modesty. She was by no means unaware of the connection between her view of human nature and the particular psychological struggles of her life. Until she was thirty-one, she went out only casually with men. She might have been, by her own description, more attractive than she allowed herself to be. Even so, she was never homely, and she was never without someone who wanted to take her out. But she seemed, in the clutch, unavailable. She found that she might like a man "in the beginning," but as "it got more serious," she grew less and less interested, or to be exact, more and more distrustful. She occasionally slept with a man, but never carried on "a real affair." She did have her preferences, but they were not enough to carry her very far toward a lasting friendship, never mind the experience of love: "All during my twenties I was a bank teller, and nothing else. That's the sum of it, I'd have to say. No wonder they were so pleased with me at work. My mind didn't daydream as much as it would have if I'd been in love and planning to leave and get married! My friends from high school got married, one after the other, and then they started having children. But I saw the troubles they had, and soon the divorces started happening. I can't say I envied my friends. I was building up my bankbook; and I was getting advice at the bank about the stock market, so I went into it, and pretty soon I could look myself in the mirror and say I wasn't the poorest person I knew! I would flirt with the stockholders and lawyers I met, and they'd want to take me out, but I never let myself get involved with them. I wasn't going to become like that girl friend of my father's. I kept thinking of her—or Kathy McNulty.

"I would often think of the two of them when I'd go out to lunch with some businessman, or for a drink with him after work. Kathy taught me to think of what I can get out of a man, rather than to be taken advantage of. That sounds bad, I know. It sounds cheap. But what's on the mind of the man when he's with you? Those businessmen who took me out were mostly married, or they were divorced. They didn't want to get to know *me;* they would always associate me with my job, I knew that: a bank teller, and so 'beneath' them! I never fooled myself! I never put on airs to myself! Those men thought they could start with a sandwich and coffee, or a drink, and end up in bed; and after a while, good-bye sweetie, and on to the next one. Meanwhile, I'm supposed to be flattered that the man I'm in bed with has a Buick or a Cadillac, and he wears a fancy suit, and he has a lot of Standard Oil stocks, and IBM, and the rest of those blue-chip ones, and he gets tips on good bargains in Wall Street. Nothing doing! Not for me! I get their tips, but they don't get me—that was my slogan. Then I'd have my talk to myself when I was home cooking supper: thanks, Kathy, for teaching me how never to lose. And I'd think of that girl friend of my father's: how many times did she let herself be tricked?''

When she was twenty-eight she moved to a rather nice apartment in the city; she could walk to work. Her old friends considered her a ''businesswoman.'' She had a small income from her investments, and she consistently reinvested the interest. She had received several pay increases since she started working as a teller. But her career in the bank had, mostly, preceded the 1970's and the arrival in American life of an important ''women's movement.'' She had, on her thirtieth birthday, just about written off the chance of significant change, personal or professional, in her life: ''I was as happy as I knew how to be. A few times I'd met a man I liked—one was a policeman, another was an automobile mechanic. I went out with them a little longer, and I was on the brink of getting serious, but something turned sour each time, and it was in me; it was my fault. The mechanic was a nice man. He'd been hurt a lot; he'd been in an accident with his wife—they'd just been married. She died. I felt sorry for him. I think I did trust him. I don't know what was the matter with me. I apologized to him. I told him I wasn't the marrying kind, but I wasn't the kind who sleeps around.

''After I broke with him, I decided I was going to be an old maid, and I was even happy at the thought. I figured I was a loner, and so what! I didn't have any close girl friends—just a few women I knew from high school days, all married. I'd go to their homes for a Sunday lunch. I had one girl friend who was a teller with me in the bank, but she went and got married, and she never wanted to see the bank again. They settled way out; her husband is a carpenter, and he grew up in the country. I spoke to her on the phone, but I didn't see her much; it was a real effort to get out there, and with a baby (which she had in six months after getting married!) she wasn't able to come into town. But I didn't mind. I was happy with my routine. And I was making enough from my salary and my investments to live a comfortable life. Since I never spent much, I never needed much money. When my father tried to borrow money from me, he learned what I thought of him! That was a big moment for me—to tell him off! And I made sure my mother heard, from me, what I said. She burst into tears, but I caught a little smile on her face at the same time—sun on a rainy day, I thought to myself when I got home!''

Having had her say as a daughter, and made her way as a worker, Maisie began the fourth decade of her life relaxed and at peace with herself. Her feet were becoming a problem—all that standing up. Time could be a problem, too. But she was not as bored as she knew other tellers become. Perhaps too much of her life depended on her job for dissatisfaction with it to set in: "I think you get fed up with something when you think it's possible to do something else; that's my opinion. What other life did I have, then? Was I supposed to go on welfare or unemployment and sit home and eat and watch television? Sure, it's hard, standing there all day, stamping checks and breaking bills and handing out money and making sure you take in as much as the customer says he's putting in, and making sure you don't become Santa Claus by handing out more than the right amount. Sure, I see numbers all my life. Sure, it's not 'interesting work.' I heard someone on a television show talk about 'interesting work.' That's a laugh! Whose work is 'interesting'? The people over me—they're juggling numbers, too. I'm not saying I wouldn't want to be in their shoes, but I'm lucky not to be in worse shoes, I know that.

"In the morning I feel glad to be out of the apartment, and with people; I joke with the tellers next to me, and with a lot of the customers. Coffee break is pleasant. Lunch—I enjoy myself with a good bite to eat, sometimes with a friend from work. By afternoon I'm tired, but there's a pride you feel each day when you leave work: you've earned your day's pay. That's important, not to be a burden to anyone; to me, it has always meant a lot that I make a living. I'd hate to think of what would happen to this country if people stopped trying to carry their own load—if people started feeling sorry for themselves all the time, and asking everyone else to do things for them. I'm for being independent. If my corns bother me, and I get tired in the afternoon, and I wish I was lying on a beach in Florida, soaking up the sun, then tough luck!"

But a year or so later she would have a somewhat different point of view—at least with respect to one other human being. At the age of thirty-one she met a young man, eight years her junior, who had graduated from high school, been accepted at a major university as a future engineering major, then failed to matriculate for financial reasons. He got a job as an automobile mechanic and tried to save money, but had given much of his salary, week after week, to his parents—a disabled father, a mother with younger children to feed and clothe. She had met him through a girl friend, the same woman who had, a few years earlier, introduced her to the first auto mechanic she went out with. She had immediately liked his appearance and manner; but there was something else, as well—and in retrospect, she was able to see that from their first date she was hopelessly "involved," if not in love: "He seemed so friendly, but he wasn't a smoothie; I know that type so well! He was like a boy I thought, a grown-up boy. He didn't seem to care about money. He didn't stare at the check to see if the waitress added it up right. He gave her a big tip, I noticed; but he didn't do it to impress me or her. He slid it under· a cup, and it was only because I wanted to find out how much he left that I did. I guess I discovered, being with him, how money-conscious I'd become, without even realizing it! I found myself looking at him and thinking to myself that I'd never met anyone like that before. He seemed to worry about everyone except himself: his father, his mother, his younger brothers and sisters, an aunt who went in and out of the hospital with bad arthritis. And as if that wasn't enough, he was on the side of all the poor—the minority groups. I told him I didn't know much about them, the colored and the Indians out West. But he seemed to know everything about their troubles.

"He said he read the paper from beginning to end every night, including the editorial page; and he watched the evening news on television. And on a Saturday he'd go to the library and sit and read for an hour or two. He was a superior person, and I guess I just fell for him. When we said good-night, he didn't just grab me and start making out. He told me he'd enjoyed meeting me, and wanted to see me again. He was a real gentleman, and for the first time in my life a man actually entered my head—so that all I could think of, after he'd left, was him. They noticed at work, too; they joked with me, and told me I must be in love, because I had stars in my eyes and I would sing off and on, and they'd catch me daydreaming in between customers."

One date followed another, and soon Maisie was prepared to own up; she began telling her friends at work that they were right, that she'd met a man, Donald by name, and they were going out a lot, and she "really liked" him. When asked for a description of him, however, she would become somewhat guarded. Later on she would be able to understand why: "At the time I thought I was just being the shy, bashful girl who doesn't want to brag, and isn't used to talking about her many boy-friends, and doesn't know what to say, anyway—other than that he's nice, and it's great to go out with him. But I remember that even then it would flash through my mind that if I told some of the businessmen I knew, or the bank manager, or the assistant manager, what Donald thought—his ideas on politics and on the country, and how it should be run—they wouldn't be as happy with him as I was! When they asked me what sort of person he was, I'd say that he was a good person. He was; he is. But he isn't their kind of person.''

After two months of dating Donald, Maisie was convinced that she wanted to marry him. He told her that he loved her, but with each week the burdens he carried became more explicit to her. Half his paycheck went to his family. He lived at his parents' home. He visited his aunt twice a week, and often left her a ten-dollar bill. She had been close to him as a child, when his mother was having one baby after another. She had, herself, suffered several miscarriages, then lost her husband to a fatal coronary attack. As he kept reminding Maisie, during the early weeks of their romance, the aunt was a member of his family. But his ''family'' was even larger than that. He had some friends from high school who had one problem or another, and he worried on their behalf, tried to be of what help he could. Often he went drinking with them, and ended up buying their beers. And as the civil rights movement got under way, he was one of the few white workingmen in his city who was willing to respond to an appeal for ''bodies,'' to be put ''on the line'' against certain prevailing political, social, and educational traditions.

Because she dared not take on Donald's family or friends, Maisie began to register complaints, early on, against his larger, ideological interests, and with some success. The mere fact that she had taken the initiative in making a protest showed her (and him) how close they had become. But the intensity of the argument that ensued also became a warning to her, and an occasion for a deeper kind of introspection than even she, a rather inward-looking person, had ever felt the desire to pursue: ''I began to realize that I was over my head—that's how I put it to myself. I could either stay with him, or try to get away as fast as possible. I'd only known him a couple of months, but that was a longer time than I'd ever gone out with anyone. I guess I was getting jealous. I was becoming possessive. I wanted him to worry about me and no one else. I didn't realize how *good* he was. Maybe in a bank you don't see the good side of people; you see the greedy side, the frightened side.

"I was so used to talking with people who were afraid the bill collector was after them, or who wanted to be the richest person in the world, that I forgot something: some people are different. I didn't believe Donald when he first told me, but later I realized he was telling the truth: he had only been in a bank about two or three times when he met me. He cashed his check at a neighborhood store. He parceled parts of it out to his family. He put the cash on his bureau; and he gradually used it up during the week. If more people were like him, I'd never have got a job at the bank, because there wouldn't be any bank! I told him about interest, and he laughed. He never has any cash left, he reminded me, by the end of the week. Then he said that even if he did have a lot of money, he wasn't sure it should make money, just sitting in a bank account. At that point I gave up and asked if please, I couldn't go home, because I had a headache. I didn't have one when I said I did, but on the way home I developed one, a big one.

"This man was making me feel that I was in the rackets; that the bank was a house of sin; that I had sold my soul to the devil! But when I was alone with myself, I began to agree with him, in a way—because there are a lot of selfish people in this world, and they want to get all they can for themselves, and they don't care what they do, so long as they end up where they want to be, on top of everyone else. Hasn't my manager said for years that this system is based on competition, and the one who can run the fastest wins the race, and in business it's got to be like that, because we're not a charitable organization, and we have to place our money with the people who are the toughest fighters, and the people who are soft are going to have to stay on the bottom! That's about it, word for word: the message I'd lived with, to the point I didn't even think twice about it all—until Donald entered my life."

For a long while she thought of little else: him and him and him. She wanted to marry him. He told her he loved her, but he was in no rush for marriage. He had so many responsibilities, and also, dreams. He wanted to go to college; he also wanted to help those many others who were worse off, by far, than he. Within six months of their friendship, and affair, Maisie had become "a confidante" for Donald. She herself knew the possible risks in that development: "I wanted him to go to college. I wanted him to make something of himself. I began to resent all those people he worried about. I even began to resent his family. They weren't bad people; they weren't like my father—dishonest and selfish. But they were taking, all the time taking from Donald. What would happen to *him,* that's what worried me—not what would happen to *them.* I tried to keep quiet for a long time—to hold my opinions to myself. But you get closer and closer to someone, and he tells you everything on his mind, and you want to hear everything he tells you, and you can't keep your tongue in check every minute.

"One day he was telling me about this one's troubles and that one's, and everyone's, it seemed; I couldn't take it any longer, so I exploded. I said: what about *you,* Donald, what about *your* troubles? Then he looked at me as if I was a terrible sinner. What problems did *he* have, compared to all the people he'd mentioned. So, I exploded even more. I said: everyone has problems, the rich and the poor, the colored and the white, the Americans and the Russians, or the people way off—in those African countries. I said: if you spend all your time worrying about the problems of too many other people, then you'll end up not doing a damned thing for them, and pretty soon, it'll be *you* that has a pretty bad problem yourself. I said: a person has to look out for himself, too; you can't just go around looking out for everyone else—or you'll become a servant to the whole world, and what will you have to offer those people? Nothing, because you've been neglecting yourself and that means you're talking big about being generous, but you don't have anything to give away. If you're going to help people, you have to have the money to give them, and that means you have to give a little consideration to yourself.

"Well, he was upset with me. He said he loved me and wanted us to be together, but he thought I should leave the bank! When I asked him why, he answered that I was being 'corrupted' there. I

told him I didn't even know what he meant. He said I was helping a bunch of bankers make a lot of money, and they were doing
it by using other people's money, not earning it through their
own work. That was our first fight, and it was a big one! I told
him that we *work* at the bank, the manager and the assistant manager and the tellers. I told him there have to be banks. Where
would you put your money? Not everyone is like him! I told him
he was sounding like someone who doesn't like society, and if
we got rid of banks, then there soon would be chaos, and then
there'd be more suffering. But he stuck to his guns, and he tried
to persuade me with all his knowledge, from those library
books—until my head was buzzing. And would you believe it,
the day after we had that argument, he asked me if I could lend
him some money, because his mother had bad teeth, and she
needed to have them out! Of course, I gave him all he needed. I
went further, actually. I told him I had this money I'd saved, and
it was his, if he needed it."

Her love for him was strong, but at work she would sometimes
get tired, as had always been the case, and then she found her
heart assailed by bitterness. She never doubted Donald's sincerity, but she had no use for some of the people who had obtained
from him (she believed) an undeserved sympathy. A black man
would come into the bank, and Maisie would be friendly to him.
Afterward she would think to herself that he was "the kind of
colored person who doesn't want charity, and works for a living." Then an image of nameless, countless other blacks would
gnaw at her, and she would notice that her feet were hurting, and
she would find herself more "businesslike," less interested in
"making conversation" with the customers. Once, in the midst
of a reverie, she heard someone coughing—to tell her he was
standing there with his mixed collection of checks and cash. It
was a "regular," and she said hello, but a bit distantly. He
looked at her keenly, then wanted to know—his voice solici-
tous—whether she was all right. Why yes, of course she was all
right. Why was he asking? She seemed flushed, that was all—and
maybe lost in thought. After the customer left she became per-

plexed; she stood still and tried to figure out what had been going through her mind while the man also stood, for ten or fifteen seconds no doubt, waiting to be noticed and helped. Yes, it was the poor, the people on welfare, the "minority groups"; she'd been thinking of them, and as she realized that they were the objects of her mind's attention, she felt her face get full and hot. Very soon, a headache began.

A year after Donald had entered her life, she told her friends and her parents that she was engaged. She also announced that her future husband wanted to be an engineer, and was going back to college, so that he could finish his education and become one. She didn't dare tell him what she was telling others. She was hoping he'd go back, hoping he'd stay in school, hoping he'd become an engineer. And she was prepared to do more than hope; she had told him that she would pay for his education. Why not? She had saved the money. She loved him. He was intelligent and not without ambition. Why not? He would more than earn back the investment in time; and it would be a much better life— living with an engineer rather than an automobile mechanic. Why not?

She kept doing that with herself, telling herself something, then emphasizing its significance with a rhetorical, exclamatory question, addressed in silence to herself. For several months they talked about his "future." They were talking about the "future" of both of them, but neither was prepared to make such an acknowledgment for a while. It took their second heated argument for that matter to come to the surface: "I tried to be encouraging to him. I tried so hard that I began to put on weight! I mean, I would tell him what a good and smart person he is, and I'd say that he deserves a better life than he has, and since he once did set his sights higher, they shouldn't come down just because his parents aren't well, and he hasn't got the money. I told him I'd lend him the money; I'd *give* him the money. I told him the world needs people like him, and it would be a good thing *I* was doing, to help him out, because I'd be contributing to society, and isn't that what he always says we all should do, the best we can! But as much as I said what I did, and tried to lift him up, he would come back with his talk about how lucky he was to be healthy, and to have a good family, and to have any job at all, and to make enough money so he isn't hungry, nor his family.

"Hungry. I got so tired of hearing about all the hungry people in the world; and I got so worn down trying to build him up. I got pretty hungry myself! I'd want to fill myself up with a big steak. But then he would tell me how lucky we are to have the best food in the world. I'd try to make a joke of it; I'd say that we might as well build ourselves up, if we're going to try to help others, especially if we're going to worry about ninety percent of the world—the number of hungry people he keeps quoting to me. But he didn't think I was being funny; so I just got hungrier and hungrier!''

It took a year of discussion, but finally Donald did decide to start college—and get married. By the time he agreed to start a career as a student, he was twenty-five, she nearly thirty-three. She felt that it was *she* who was enrolling, because he'd fought so hard not to do so. But he had become extremely attached to her, and over time, willing to do as she suggested. They got married with no one but a friend of his and the friend's wife as escorts. Maisie would have no part of a family affair, because of her cool attitude toward her own parents. Donald's parents were, as always, ailing; they were glad to be informed in advance, and not piqued by the arrangement of a virtual elopement. Donald moved into Maisie's apartment, and soon the long spell of study was on its way.

For Maisie it was a promising period; she had an exceedingly long view of life: "I came in one day to work with a marriage ring on. I decided to tell no one; just to wait and see who would notice, after how long. Almost the whole day passed, and nothing happened. At three I had to go talk with the manager about a big check that was being cashed, and as I put it before him, he looked at my hand that was on the desk, and he said: 'What's that?' I told him. He said he didn't know I was engaged. I said I wasn't; I was married. He asked me about Donald—all the usual questions. I had to be careful about my answers, because I didn't want to say that if he heard Donald talk, the FBI would be called in! I noticed that when I was talking with the manager, I began to sympathize with Donald's ideas. I resented being asked what he did, and whether he had a good job, with good pay, and if he could take care of me. I felt like saying to the manager that money isn't everything in the world, and you don't only judge people by how much they make, or what kind of work they do, or where they live. But you also learn in this world to button up your mouth, and keep it buttoned up, at certain times. Besides, if I got fresh and lost my job, where *would* Donald and I live, and what kind of work would we both be doing? I suppose he can always go back to being an auto mechanic. But he likes the studies he's doing."

Her husband not only liked his studies; for a while he seemed ready to commit his entire life to them. He became interested in philosophy, and started taking courses ("The Philosophy of Science") which were not necessary for the career he originally had in mind, and indeed, were even considered by his adviser to be "a luxury." That description prompted the stormiest argument between the two. In a terrible moment, later regretted, Maisie asked: "Who's paying for that 'luxury' course?" He left. He came back a half an hour later. She apologized. He said he wanted to quit school and go back to his "own people." She insisted that he had every right to be where he was, and she had every intention of helping him stay there because she believed in him. Anyhow, she reminded him, they had decided not to have children, more her decision than his, and so what else ought they do with the money she had saved and invested for a decade?

She would be proud of herself to her last day, she always reminded herself, for what she had managed to say to her husband that fateful and quite frightening evening: "I was afraid that our marriage was over before it had really had a chance. I guess I felt really bad for what I'd said, and I was scared that he'd never really trust me again, or be able to believe what I said. I hadn't realized until then how much he'd changed me. I was so busy trying to change him! I grew up in a home where my mother was beaten down, and glad to crawl before her husband; and he was a no-good person. I found out that he'd been lying to her all through their marriage. I guess I'd learned not to trust people! I told Donald that. I told him all about the letters I'd found, and the woman I followed, my father's girl friend. I even told him about Kathy McNulty—how she taught me to get smart, and not get stepped all over. That's why I gave up on marriage, even before I turned twenty-five, never mind thirty. I never wanted to live through a repeat of the marriage I'd known as a child. That's why I don't want to have kids. I'm getting older, and he has to go through all that education, and even if he didn't, I have such bad memories of my mother being at home, and me with her, and the heaviness in that house, the loneliness she had in her, and the sadness. She'd cry, and I could never figure out why. I know I couldn't stop work and stay at home, and sit there all day—even with a baby near me.

"I told Donald all that. I told him everything I could think of—all that crosses my crazy head while standing there taking the dough in and handing the dough out! I told him that I didn't make this world, and that I'd suffered in it, too—just like others he mentions suffer. Maybe I'm not starving to death, but I work damn hard, five days a week—up at six, and home at six, and lots of hours in between standing, always standing, and keeping my eyes on the columns, the debit and the credit, because if I make a mistake, it's my money, not the bank's that pays for it!

"I told Donald that I shouldn't have thrown the money up to him. It was wrong of me. But can't he see that maybe I'm a 'victim,' too? He's always talking about the poor people here and there and all over the world. Maybe I've become my own kind of 'victim.' Maybe money has gone to my head—just like he says it has gone to everyone else's head. Maybe it's gone to *his* head, too. If you fight something, the way he does, you're under its control. I told him that; I told him that the only chance we both have is for him to finish his schooling, and try to be a *good* engineer; try to help others get ahead, just as he got ahead. If God gives you intelligence, you should use it. But I agree with him, you shouldn't take advantage of your abilities in such a way that you abuse other people—take advantage of *them*. Most of all I told Donald that he had to see that if I could help him, I was helping *us;* and to be selfish, I was helping myself—because maybe it was through him that my money was being used for a good reason, and not just sitting there, like a miser's gold. And besides, I was working, through him, for some of the things he believes in.''

They were quickly reconciled, but Maisie continued to have her moments of resentment—perhaps, she observed, because she had ''to go out into the world and fight it every day,'' whereas her husband ''spent a lot of his time at home, reading and day-dreaming.'' She had indeed avoided her mother's predicament, but given the way her husband would continue to be, even after he graduated from college, she sometimes wondered about her own situation as the ''breadwinner'' in a particular household: ''It's for life, my job, and I get low sometimes, but whose life doesn't have its ups and downs. I'm managing, as the teller next to me says, when I ask her how she is doing. Then she'll sigh, and we'll go take a break. I go home, and that's a break, too. I start a new life, with a different world, for sure: my husband and his friends and all their ideas. I've learned to manage that, too— and still get up at six and show up for work on time.''

part three
FIGHTING

We want to tell the reader, right off, that in this particular portrait we have decided to keep ourselves at a farther distance than is usually the case. There are, we believe, good reasons for us to help along the momentum of the personal narratives we have presented in this book and its predecessor. We have been drawing upon years of work done with individuals not always inclined to organize their thoughts and words in such a way that a reader (rather than a regular, hence familiar, visitor) can recognize the prevailing themes of their respective life-stories. Put differently, many of the women we have come to know, both poor and well-to-do, have had no special reason to make exceedingly long, uninterrupted statements—declarations of purpose and intent, avowals of activist commitment, assertions of ideological faith. Our task with respect to these women has been not only that of listener and observer, but also that of narrator, whose aim it is to construct, out of themes only gradually or intermittently revealed, a certain co-

herence, to point up the significance of each life-history.

But in our years spent in Louisiana, Mississippi, Alabama, and Georgia, we met a number of civil rights activists who were extraordinarily outspoken. They worked with SNCC, as did we. They rode the freedom buses to Montgomery and Jackson in 1961. They picketed building after building—state, county, city, or private—to protest all aspects of segregation. They lived in the various "freedom houses" which, finally, by the end of 1964 changed Mississippi irrevocably. And about half of them, we would estimate, were women. Lillian Smith told us that such SNCC women had their own "double burden" to bear. We would, soon enough, realize the dimensions of that burden—be told of it by several brilliant and hardy spirits. And we would be told what we were told in no uncertain terms—with a compelling clarity, a directness, a lively forcefulness that required, we would later understand, no clarifications or interruptions by us; no extensive editing, either; no remarks meant to shift focus, make a summary, or offer a qualification, a demurrer; no authorial presence. These were women teachers of a special kind, and the best way to understand these years and their stories is to retire to the back of the class and let one of them give us her lesson.

IT SEEMS a long time since I lived with my parents in Pittsburgh—well, to be honest, Sewickley. I suppose it's a bit presumptuous of me to talk about "a long time." I'm not *that* old! But I feel as if I've been living another life since I went south to live and work. Sometimes I look at myself in the mirror and talk to myself and say to myself: you're Sue, the same Sue who grew up in that great, big, comfortable house up North, and had such a nice, nice childhood; but you're a different person now—the Sue who sometimes can't even picture that very house, and has almost forgotten what her parents and her sister and her brother look like.

I'm exaggerating, of course! I know perfectly well what each member of my family looks like—including my rich, reactionary grandparents on my mother's side, and my nervously conservative grandparents on my father's side! I see them all from time to time, so why the melodrama on my part! But the meetings are painful, and I suppose I want to forget them—mostly. I have to forget them. That's shrink talk, I guess; and I don't like it. Even my mother's father, who's a banker, and hates psychiatrists, once decided I needed "a doctor," and had the nerve to come up to me and say so! I told him he might try one, and if he did, then I would. He turned away from me. If I could get a man like that to start questioning himself, I'd be on first base, headed for second.

When I was seven or eight, I can remember my parents trying to squelch my interest in baseball. I was a *girl!* My brother was the one who should be interested in baseball. But he wasn't. He collected rocks and stamps. He was shy and distrustful. I was a "tomboy"—they all said. I would be furious when I heard the word: the stupidity of name-calling, I knew even then. Sue is this; Sue is that; Sue is not doing what she should be doing, and she is doing what she shouldn't be doing. And where did they all get those ideas—those stereotypes? They would never have pulled out guns and shot at "colored people," as they got called in my home; but my father and mother had fixed prejudices about everyone in the slightest different from them (by ancestry, race, or class) and they also had the narrowest ideas about what their own children should do—should be like. They managed to get me away from baseball by giving me a horse, and getting me involved with riding lessons. I loved my horse—until it came to me, one day, that I'd been conned! Well, I still loved the horse—Godfrey was its name. But a lot of the time poor Godfrey had to listen to my gripes about life!

I had a dream when I was seven or eight that I'll never forget; I've had it several times in my life—a "recurring dream," a friend of mine, a psychology graduate student, called it. I was riding Godfrey, and we were having a great time, cantering across my favorite field. Suddenly the field disappeared, and I was on a narrow path. I kept cantering, but I was a little nervous, because I didn't know the land. Maybe there were holes in the ground, or logs in the way. Maybe we'd come to some water or rocks; Godfrey hated both. But quickly we saw ahead another field, and it was where baseball was played. I spotted the bases! I was really happy! I rode Godfrey around and around the bases, and I kept on shouting "home run," as we passed the home plate! Then I looked and saw that there were some stands behind the home plate, and no one was there—except for my mother and father and my brother! I looked at them for a long time. I stopped the horse and kept looking at them. Then I kicked Godfrey hard, and we cantered away—back to the path and the other field. That was the end of the dream.

It's hard for my friends to believe this, but when I *first* had that dream I was able to figure it out. I didn't even know what psychology was. I wasn't trying to psych myself out! I was just a kid like all the other rich, lucky, spoiled kids in Sewickley. But I'd tried a little too hard, a little too often, to stick with my dungarees; and I'd wanted a little too often to play baseball—wanted to do it so badly that I can still feel the taste in my mouth. The dream made me realize, for the first time, that I wasn't as lucky as I'd been told I was; that I was a *girl,* and that I'd have to "shape up," as my grandfather used to put it, and learn to be *his* kind of girl—or else; no baseball, but all the riding I wanted!

My parents were caught in the middle. I used to feel sorry for them; I used to think they were having as rough a time as I was. My mother once called me into her sewing room; I was ten, I think. She wanted to have a "heart-to-heart" with me. If I close my eyes, I can see that room, with every detail. She was sitting in a Windsor chair, a rocker. She had just been knitting. She put her needles down on that old cherry table of hers; it's been handed down for a century or two! I was getting older—that's what she opened up with. I joked with her; I said that every day we all get older. She said yes—but when the days turn into years, then it's *time to talk.* Those last three words—her way of getting down to business, and no fooling around!

I stood there—damned if I was going to say a word! But I knew what was coming. First I was invited to sit down in her wing chair, another heirloom. Then I heard a story about Gramma, and how she loved to sit in that chair and read, and how she mostly dozed in it, her head leaning, always, on the right "wing." Well, she *was* a right-winger. I knew that even then, when I was only ten years old. I knew she hated Roosevelt, and hated Truman, and didn't like "liberal Republicans." Her great hero, at least in the last years of her life, was Robert Taft. She thought he'd get rid of the bureaucrats. They were, she was sure, all over the place; and they were out to take her money away. She had a lot to lose, so they must have been pretty greedy, if she was right. I'd asked her once, when I was eight or nine, what a "bureaucrat" was. I thought of men dressed in black capes, with pitchforks in their hands, and maybe sticks of dynamite tucked under their black sash belts. But she told me they were small men in dark suits who sat at desks all day, doing nothing, mostly. Yet, they were paid "fat salaries." I thought that was a pretty good deal. Then I remembered a remark my mother had made about her mother—that she had two men going over her dividends and bank accounts all the time, and that she'd never held a job in her life, because she thought it was a waste of time to work. I pictured them, sitting at desks. My grandmother liked to garden, and she liked to ride and she liked to sit and read Roman history and English history. And she liked to do her reading at her desk. I asked my mother if Gramma was a bureaucrat, or if the two men who worked for her were bureaucrats—because they all three spent a lot of hours at their desks. My mother laughed, and dared me to ask her mother that question. When my mother realized I was all set to do just that, she pulled me aside and said no: leave Gramma alone. Why? She was getting very old.

I was getting old! Ten, going on twenty or thirty! What did I want to do—spend the rest of my life in dungarees? Keep on reading about baseball on the sly? Build one tree fort after another "with the boys"? My mother was smiling as we talked about *her* mother, but I saw the hard look in the eyes. I remember looking away from them. I fastened on her needles, instead—one for each of her eyes! I was too young at the time to connect those needles with Madame Defarge in *A Tale of Two Cities;* but when I read that novel, I remember thinking of my mother's knitting needles—and of that afternoon. It was cloudy, and quite warm and humid for an early October day. The leaves were turning. I know for sure, because she changed the subject because of my silence. She started one of her soliloquies: the trees start out as shoots, mere twigs in size. Then they grow. The leaves start out as buds, and then they grow and become large and green, and then they get old and die, just as our grandparents were then doing: two in the hospital at the same time, and one just out! The best thing that happened that afternoon was the thunder! A clap of it interrupted my mother, and she stopped the sermon. I looked out the window and hoped for another, and then another blast of sound. I think I may have wished for some lightning to strike! Later I would realize what was wrong with me: I had a lot of "aggression" stored up inside my head. I needed to "talk" with someone!

That's what it came to: I was only ten, but my mother was dropping hints: if I didn't keep a tidier room; and if I didn't start "behaving more grown-up"; and if I didn't stop disobeying her; and if I didn't take better care of myself—then she'd have to go looking for someone I could "talk with." I told her my friend Dave was someone I could talk with; and my friend Jim; and my friend Daisy (her real name was Deborah). But my mother didn't like any of them. She described us as four "rowdies"!

On the other hand, I knew that she didn't always agree with her own parents; and that she and my father didn't get along all that well; and, most important I now can see, I knew that she secretly got some fun out of watching my various antics—especially my rebelliousness. She would tell me I had to change my ways, but she also would tell me I was strong-minded, and she hoped I would stay like that later on. (I guess I haven't disappointed her!) And though she kept warning me that I had better shape up, learn how to study better and "carry" myself better, she also told me how she hated to go to a lot of formal dinner parties, and she only went because she had to—her mother insisted, or Daddy insisted.

And sometimes (she admitted) she caught herself dreaming of the summers she used to spend out West in Montana, on a ranch. Her uncle owned it, and she loved him better than her own parents. He had left Pittsburgh as a young man, and never once returned. I went out West for the first time when he died. I was only thirteen, but I remember the funeral even now. My mother cried so hard I was afraid she'd get sick. On the way back she told me how much she loved her Uncle Ben, and how much she loved those summers she'd spent with him. She wanted me to know that she was not "stuffy"; that she still had some "hell" in her; that she connected me in her mind with her uncle, and we were both her "favorite people"; that she was sure I'd always be my own "true self." Of course, she immediately added that people have to make their "adjustments," and there's no two ways about it!

I stood there nodding away. She gave me a real close look. She said nothing for about ten or twenty seconds. Then she told me that she could "read" me—that I was doing the same old thing, letting words come in and then go out of my mind. I nodded at that, too! I didn't realize what I'd done until I'd done it! I'd intended to mollify her one more time with an up-and-down movement of my head, but instead—as she hastened to point out!—I'd agreed with her critical judgment. But she didn't press her advantage! She smiled at me! She told me I looked fidgety—and hungry. I should go get a peanut-butter-and-jelly sandwich. I told her I didn't want one. I told her I'd wait for the maid to make me one.

The maid was my buddy. She'd been with us since I was little, and she would stay with us until I left for college. She died in her room in our house. My mother came to the dining room table and rang for her one morning, and got no reply. She went into the kitchen, and Martha wasn't there. My mother decided to be a martyr. Rather than go wake Martha, she began to prepare her own breakfast—expecting to go no further than the pouring of juice, or turning the knob of the stove in order to heat up the water for coffee. But Martha didn't show up, and my mother couldn't hear her moving about, doing the laundry or whatever. She went up to Martha's room, knocked, waited, knocked, waited; and finally, opened the door and saw her, slumped over the bed, on her stomach, her feet dangling. She was obviously dead. The doctor said she'd been dead most of the night. He said it was a "good" way to go. My mother called me up at college, and before she told me I knew the news. By then I was nineteen, and able to anticipate just about everything my mother had to say.

I don't mean to be condescending; it's just that she has always been "predictable"; that's her word, applied to herself—with a bittersweet smile, to let me know that she's both proud of herself and disappointed in herself! When I picked up the phone and heard the crack in my mother's voice but realized she wasn't *too* upset—as she would be if one of "us" had died!—I thought to myself: it's Martha, something has happened to her. But I didn't expect the news I got! My mother said, in a flat voice: "Martha died." Nothing else! I didn't say a word. I couldn't cry—at least not then. I said "oh," and then I told my mother I had to go to a class. She apologized for calling! I guess she thought that it was wrong of her to interrupt my college schedule with a bad telephone call! She said she should have written me a letter—told me that way. I repeated that I had to go, and I hung up. I sat down and cried and cried. I didn't go to any classes that day.

When I was six or seven, Martha was the one I looked up to. I had a nurse until I went to kindergarten. I remember her, but not fondly. She was always pulling me; I didn't walk fast enough for her. She would make me change my clothes because I was "dirty," or I'd gotten a "spot" on something, or I was going to visit someone—or someone was coming to visit us. I'd drag my feet, but she was persistent. Not nasty. Not the bullying or two-faced governess of fiction. Just a woman who had given her life to spoiled, rich brats like me! The one line of hers I really hated went like this: "Sue, you must learn to behave like a proper woman!" I'd asked her why. She'd either give me the same old tired explanation—about what's *right* and *wrong*—or she'd not answer at all. It was her silence that must have intrigued me, because I asked her once if she was *afraid* to talk. She shouted no, and left the room. I don't remember the incident, but Martha did, and she told me about it several times.

The nurse quit when I was ready for school; my mother wanted her to stay, but she liked younger children, younger *girls*. She didn't really enjoy taking care of my brother; and I think she'd been made nervous by my jumpy, outspoken manner! Martha used to say that she almost quit herself, especially when I was about eight or nine. I would ask embarrassing questions of her, and my parents were nearby—within hearing distance. I don't recall a lot of things I said or asked, but *she* did, and the one example she would bring up—later, when I was fourteen or fifteen—was this: she had told me to put on a dress, and I said no, my corduroys were fine, and she said no they weren't, because my mother had said I was not to go out to lunch with her, wearing pants. I guess I stood my ground. Martha told me over and over again to do what my mother wanted. Then I asked her what *she* thought. I got no answer. Then I asked her if she'd let me answer for her. She didn't answer, so I did. I told her that she disagreed with my mother. I told her she realized that my mother didn't even agree with herself! She was just following everyone else's lead! Martha apparently told me to hush, or else she'd quit. I got scared. It was the only time she ever threatened to leave. I was more attached to her, at the time, than I ever knew.

My parents were always going out: dinner parties and receptions and concerts and God knows what. Before they went, we'd be taken to them in the early evening—dolls for their inspection. I was always the cause of an uproar on those occasions. I'd make it my business to mess up my appearance before I was brought in, or I'd say exactly the wrong thing—especially if there was company. When I was eleven—it was in the wintertime, I know, because there was talk of a blizzard—a college roommate of my father's was spending the weekend with my parents, and I was brought in to say good-night. My brother was sick with the flu. The man kept asking my parents about him. Then he started asking *me* about him. I must have sensed that he didn't give a damn about me. When he asked me what my brother's favorite game was, I told him "playing with dolls!"

My father glared at me, and told me to leave the room. I didn't move, though. My mother tried to get me out of the jam. She said I was only fooling, and she said my brother loved soccer and baseball, and could ice-skate very well, and was a great swimmer for his age, and was learning how to ski. But I guess I wasn't interested in being saved, because I added my two cents again; I said my brother Gary did do all those things, but still, he had his dolls. That's when Martha was called in, and she took me away. The next day my mother told Martha to ask me why I did what I did. I explained that I meant by dolls Gary's teddy bear, and his other animals. He was only seven or eight then, and he *did* like those animals a lot. But though I said what I did to Martha, I knew I'd been deliberately mischievous. And so did she.

When I'd finished with my phony excuses and explanations, she told me off. She said she was on my side; she knew why I did what I did. But she added that she'd always thought I was pretty smart—until that moment. Then she said nothing more. Of course, I was caught! I had to hear more. I asked for an explanation. She pretended to be busy. I asked again. "Never mind," she said. I was furious. I thought of throwing a tantrum, but I'd never done that with her. Anyway, I was getting too old for that—and I wanted to win her over, not drive her away in fear or anger. So, I just clammed up. I tried to ignore her. She loved to talk with me, so she was frustrated. In a few minutes she was telling me all—a lesson I'll never forget: that I was like her, a weak person, as compared to the strong people—my parents and grandparents and all the grown-ups called their friends; and that a weak person has to know how to survive, or else she'll be worse off than "weak," she'll be "a nothing." She said that in her case it meant that she'd lose her job, be out on the street, have no place to live or to work. In my case it meant that I'd be punished and punished until I lost all my nerve, all my confidence, and I'd end up being—just what she'd said, "a nothing."

I've thought of that expression for years, in those moments when I've seen bosses of all kinds pushing around the weak ones Martha referred to back then. She was urging guile on me. She was telling me what Gandhi told his people—that if you're going to be free, you have to use your heads, your will, as well as your bodies. You have to spot the oppressor's weaknesses. You have to know your own weaknesses, too. But maybe that's not a fair comparison—Gandhi and Martha. She was no apostle of non-violence. She was a shrewd "housekeeper" (my mother called her) who did the best she could to hold on to the only life she felt able to imagine, or obtain, for herself. She just happened that one evening to identify herself, her situation, with mine. And because she did so, she revealed something to me I would never forget, and would certainly remember when I got involved in social action, when I joined the civil rights movement: that inside the apparently "passive" or "nonpolitical" person, the so-called "uneducated proletariat," there is plenty of political savvy—a kind of observing intelligence about how the world works, and what one can get away with, and what one can't in a million years (it seems) get away with.

When I became a teen-ager I "changed," and my parents were as happy as could be: I'd come to my senses. I guess I took Martha's advice: choose your moment of confrontation carefully! Actually, I wasn't conscious at the time of any decision to act one way, or act the other way. I gave up fighting my family because I was scared; I was becoming a woman, and I didn't know what to do—except flee from that fact (I now can see) by becoming an obedient, studious "girl." Instead of going to parties and getting involved in a rich, suburban "rat pack," I stayed home, opened up every book in sight, and told anyone who called (or my parents, who had their agendas for me) that I had exams coming. And in the summers I fled to the West, where I could ride and hike and swim and not worry about what my "peers" were doing, and what the "social calendars" had waiting for my kind of person.

After a while my mother began to tell me that she was worried about me all over again! A few years before she'd been saying that I was "wild," and I needed "discipline," and I was a "rebel"; now she took me aside and asked me why I wasn't having more "fun." I knew I'd never win an argument with her. She never argued, anyway. She said what passed through her mind, and banked on civility to protect her from serious or strenuous disagreement. All I did was say I *was* having fun—learning. She laughed and said she'd always been a mediocre student. I told her I would be one—if I didn't sit down and concentrate. She told me I looked tired right after I said that! I told her that I felt great, just great. She ignored me: "Sue, you should go get a checkup."

"Mother," I said, "I don't need a checkup. How about *you?* Are you sure you're feeling fine?"

"Oh, I'm in great shape," she insisted.

But she gave me a quick glare, as if to say that she had her limits, all right; and I was about to exceed them. Then she changed the subject drastically: what did I want for Christmas? I told her: a big Webster's or an Oxford dictionary. She didn't say another thing to me! She said she had to "run." That's my mother's favorite expression—when she wants to put an end to something she doesn't like one bit! I sat there and watched her "hurry." Two months later I found my two-volume Oxford dictionary under the tree.

It was tough turning sixteen. I refused the party my parents wanted to give for me, and the parties they wanted me to attend. I told them I had a lot of work. I told them I wanted to go to a good eastern college, so I had to get the highest grades. And finally I told them I wanted to be a biologist, so I really had to stick with the books. They were both stunned. A *biologist!* My father wanted to know what *kind* of biologist. My mother said I was "going through a stage." She gave me the longest speech of her life, I'm sure. To paraphrase: "Sue, dear [always a hint, in that expression, of her anger!], I don't want to interfere in your life. I'm sure you know what you're doing. I'm sure you've given a lot of thought to your plans. But a mother has to have her say, too! You're wearing yourself down with work, and you're becoming a hermit. All work and no play makes Jack a dull boy. [I should have screamed that I was *Jill,* and I wasn't missing a trick!] We're not against your wish to do well, and go East to school. We're just for some balance. You're out of balance, and we want you in balance."

It went on and on; I just haven't the stomach to remind myself of her trite phrases. "Balance" was the key word, though. She used to use it on herself—when she'd gained a few extra pounds. She was "out of balance," and needed to "get back in balance." All her euphemisms! Her evasions! I used to listen and think of sarcastic replies—never spoken, though. And my father: he wasn't afraid to be blunt—coarse and brutal, in his own polished way! He'd give me, his daughter, a sly, appraising look—the kind of look he gave every woman he met. Then he'd come up with *his* comments—that I was not only "tired," as my mother said, but I was becoming jittery, unfriendly—and chubby. I needed exercise. I needed to get out of my room, and go *do* something, not just sit and read. Didn't they have compulsory athletic programs in the colleges and universities? Shouldn't someone going into biology think of her own biology? Then, zeroing in like a panther: if I could forget my books and my worries about the future, and just relax and have a good time and get out of my room, out of the whole house, I'd probably feel better about myself, and I'd start losing weight, and I'd look better, and the boys would pay more attention to me, and then I'd enjoy going out, and I wouldn't "need" to lock myself up in my room and do "all that studying."

My father always had the makings of a psychologist! He also had the kind of arrogance a lot of psychologists have! He was a Mr. Know-It-All from way back. He learned how to have an answer for everything from his father. And, like some psychologists and psychiatrists I met when I was older, my father wasn't really interested in what other people had to say, though he claimed he was. He sat and waited for the right moment to make *his* statements. I was never sure he had really heard me. I was always sure that he knew exactly what he had to say before he even caught sight of me. But he at least pretended to listen to my brother. And that's a long story in my life: my father and my brother—and my mother and my brother, too!

I hate shrink talk. I knew what the "family dynamics" in our house were all about years before I ever took a psychology course in college. I used to hear my father call my brother "Junior," and talk with him about money and the family and the responsibilities he'd have—and baseball!—and I had enough intelligence to compare what went on between them with what I'd experienced as the daughter of the family. And I'd seen my mother's pride and deference when she called my brother "Son." She never called me "Daughter," of course! But I'm not sending out signals of "sibling rivalry" or "penis envy"; I'm just remembering the disgust I felt toward two reasonably intelligent people who never cared about any of their children enough to stop and ask themselves what a boy or a girl will think of the kind of behavior they showed us. My younger sister—what choice did she have? Since I stood up to my parents, she could only be their "darling little pet"—exactly what my mother and father took to calling her when she was about four or five. They've never stopped treating her that way—a cute feline creature to pat and feel cozy with every once in a while. My brother—small wonder that he became just what my father always called him: Junior. He's a rather strikingly exact duplication of "the old man." And me: by the time I left Sewickley for Radcliffe, I was ready to get a new passport and say I belonged to the Martians, or the people who lived on Pluto—the further the distance from home, the better!

When I landed in Cambridge, I began to have second thoughts. I say "landed" because I really did feel as if I came from another planet during those first weeks in Cambridge. (We were at *Radcliffe,* then; it's *Harvard* now, for women.) I was homesick— *me!*—for a few days. I didn't really want to go back to Pittsburgh, but at least I knew how to deal with that life back home. Cambridge was strange and scary, and after I stopped thinking about what I'd left, I began wishing I'd gone someplace else— Smith, where I'd be in the country, or Barnard, where I'd be able to go visit my aunt and uncle and cousins, who lived on the East Side of Manhattan, or one of the small midwestern colleges I'd thought of attending. But after a while I began to get used to my little section of Harvard and Cambridge—the biology lab, the language lab, the classrooms and lecture halls, the libraries and stores and the people I met. I was shy, though. I'd asked for a single—a mistake. They put me, fortunately, with one room-mate—an Italian girl from Staten Island, New York. That's the way I thought of her when I first met her: Gloria Santosuosso, whose father came from Naples, and who lived in an apartment house, and who had a long, long name I couldn't reliably spell without looking at it, for a few months. I was more my parents' daughter than I knew at the time. I was a snotty, sullen, sarcastic kid who was always watching others and coming to critical or cynical conclusions about them. Not my roommate; Gloria talked while I listened, and she smiled while I peered or turned away to my private thoughts, and she was generous with her money (and she had very little) while I was a stingy one. I can't think back to those days without a deep feeling of shame!

Gloria was a therapist. I guess I could say that—as a serious joke! She showed me another world: hers. But she also showed me myself. I'd talk with her, and then begin to realize what kind of person I was. It's one thing to be critical of your parents, your grandparents; it's another thing to see, through another person, how much of your own life has been shaped by the very family people you fancy yourself observing at a distance, with a critic's sharp eye. The money business was the hardest for me: Gloria always ready to spend her last cent for me or someone else, whereas I (who thought I didn't "care" about something as crass as money) never seemed able to have any or (when I did have some) cough it up for a friend.

For a while I kidded myself: I had this trust, this trust officer, and so I was "ignorant" about money. But I didn't ask the man for much—on the excuse, I would eventually realize, that he would say no. But he would have sent me the few dollars I needed to pick up a few restaurant bills, or movie tickets; *I* was the one who got anxious about "treating." I was even a little anxious about treating myself! It was Gloria who kept suggesting we go out. She was working for her money—cleaning other peo-ple's rooms, putting away other people's books in the library. And she had a scholarship, too. She had to keep her grades up.

Even so, she liked an occasional good time. Meanwhile, I found myself with awful thoughts: how can she work so hard, and then spend her money so fast! Or this: how can she be so calm about her studies, when she might not be able to come back to school if she doesn't get a certain level of grades? Underneath such thoughtfulness on my part, such concern for my roommate, was a really obnoxious condescension. I expected Gloria to be a drudge, a workhorse. Wasn't she getting a scholarship? Didn't that require her to slave away—to earn the approval of her betters: my parents and others like them, who gave generously to Harvard, besides paying the tuition in full, and lots of other expenses that go with college life?

The day came when Gloria got in trouble. I'd been "right" all along: she *was* a spendthrift! She was in bad debt. She'd borrowed money. Then her father fell dead on the street in New York of a stroke. And she decided to go home and be with her mother. It was the spring of our sophomore year, and I couldn't understand how she could do it. She was the youngest child. She had two married sisters who lived near their mother. She had three brothers who weren't far away—and a brother still at home. I kept telling her she was throwing away her life. She was throwing away all her hard-earned school victories—and wasting all the money she'd worked for and used to pay those big college bills. When I heard that she hadn't paid them all completely, and that she was worrying about *that,* too, I offered to lend her money. But she wouldn't take me up on my suggestion—and when I found myself relieved, I began to hate myself with such intensity I fell back in my studies and thought of dropping out myself. I decided that I was a really bad person—"vile" was the word I'd use as I wrote notes to myself: a journal I kept for a year or two. The excerpts, even now, are hard to take, though I have a good deal of distance on them, and realize that college students often go through such soul-searching. Not that I want to let myself off the hook through psychology. I deserved the critical going-over I gave myself!

When Gloria left, she left a part of herself with me. I don't know how else to put it. I'd never known someone like her—from her background. Her loyalty to her family, rather than to herself, confused me, amazed me, made me envious. I began to look closely at myself, because she, as a person, had *confronted* me. Later, when I'd be doing a lot of confronting myself—in the civil rights movement—I'd think of Gloria. I'd wish that somehow I could work my way into the minds of those southern segregationists the way she worked her way into my mind. But that was a ridiculous hope. And it was unfair to think of Gloria as a propagandist or an advocate of something. She was herself—and no saint. She was, I suppose, an excuse for personal change in me—though I hate to be so cold-hearted and "instrumental" (as the philosophers or psychologists would put it) in my thinking. I didn't get to know her as well as I might have. That was the point: I was stingy with my emotions as well as my cash. After she left, I was obsessed with her—a distant, shadowy figure who pointed a finger at me, critically, during my last two years at college, and also pointed a way for me, a direction. I'm becoming a bit melodramatic here, but that was how I felt at the time. I was full of that "turmoil" those people in "human development" write about!

I did go to Staten Island to visit Gloria during my junior year. The first time, I was on my way to Europe. The second time, I was on my way back from Europe. In the late fall of my senior year I made a special trip down to New York and we met in Manhattan. She seemed to have no desire to return to Cambridge. Once again, I learned about myself by being with her. Cambridge had now become my life. How could she be so indifferent to the place? How could she be "happy" in Staten Island, taking care of her mother, visiting her sisters, working in a law office, part-time, as a *secretary?* What a *waste,* I thought. I wanted to save her. I told her I'd been given a lot of extra money, and wouldn't she let me give some of it to her, so she could come back to school? No, she didn't want to return. Harvard wasn't for her. Even if there was no family reason for her to stay, she would remain where she was.

"older" myself! But, to be honest, and I think, to be fair, *she* was beginning to feel sorry for herself, and envious of me. She even said so—in a joking way, always. But the humor was bittersweet; her eyes were the clue. She wandered away with them, for a brief moment, every once in a while—into her own "thoughts." Then she'd come back, and apologize.

Only one time did she tell me, without making light of it, how she felt. She was pregnant for the fourth time in seven years, and I was deeply involved by then in the civil rights movement, and had come to New York for a fund-raiser, and called her just to say hello. I hadn't expected to see her. I was all tied up with people I had to see, and I had to fly back to Atlanta the evening of the day I'd called. But she asked me, *please,* to meet for lunch, and the emphasis she put on that word "please" made a point I couldn't overlook. I got scared, as a matter of fact. I'd never known her, even once, to be in that position—asking for someone's help.

Between the call and the meeting Gloria composed herself. She was under real control, I could see—as if she decided she had to go one way or the other: let go, and pour something out; or keep a close watch on herself every second. I knew she was in some trouble by the way she sat and tried to get me to talk, and by the tight, sad way she looked. But I was afraid to ask her what was wrong; and I was—once again!—selfish. I was so full of my own life, and so glad at last to have a kind of life I could respect and feel to be useful, that I didn't have the desire to listen to someone tell me about her life—which I knew was less interesting, more humdrum. That sounds worse than it should. I was all keyed up. I was in another world. To leave that world and have a two-hour lunch with someone who was far, far away from me psychologically at the time was difficult. And Gloria didn't want to break the barrier between us—until the very end, when it was too late.

We said good-bye. I was walking away—glad to be leaving, because my mind was already back in Atlanta. She caught me by the arm, looked right into my eyes, and said she hoped we won in the South. I could see tears, and I felt close to her and grateful for her support. Those were tumultuous days, the early 1960's. Lots of people cried for us then. But in a second I could see that she wasn't shedding her tears for Georgia and Alabama and Mississippi. She was upset for personal reasons. She said one sentence to me, and told me she had to go: "Sue, when you've won down there, come back here and help us out—the housewives all over the place!" I didn't even know what she meant, for a while. I was actually angry at her. What nerve—to equate being a Staten Island housewife, who lived in a nice, single-family house, with all the gadgets she could want, to being a black, living in a broken-down cabin in rural Georgia, where I'd worked, or the Delta of Mississippi, where I was going to work. I was full of self-righteousness on the plane; and the same smugness I'd always had. I was disappointed in Gloria. I felt she was no longer a friend of mine. As usual, I was wrapped up in my own preconceptions and problems, and unwilling to understand where she was coming from, what she was really telling me.

I guess, to grow up a little, I needed more time down South, and I got that time, lots of it! The Freedom Rides took place in my senior year; I remember reading about them, but not thinking at the time that I'd ever be involved in something so far off and removed from my own concerns. Around that time I was thinking of going to Europe after graduation, and living there for a while, maybe in London. I had a friend in the dormitory whose father ran a bank in England, and I knew I could get a job through him. It was that friend, ironically, who helped get me involved with the civil rights movement. She was fighting *her* father. She was taking a lot of economics courses, and she'd decided that she was a socialist, and her father an exploiter, if there ever was one: an international banker! It all sounds so naive in retrospect—the bunch of us, going through our little "identity crises"!

That friend, Mary, didn't last long as a socialist; she quit her radical position by the time she graduated, and it turned out that she was the one who went to London—where she studied antiques and paintings in some course, and became a certified museum curator, and married one, too. She's still there—"permanently abroad," she said once in the "class notes," though she hedges her bets by coming home to see her mother's family on the North Shore of Boston every few years.

But it's not for me to bad-mouth Mary. God knows, she was patient with me back then in the dormitory—explaining the different economic systems, and showing me how important "class" is. For me the word used to mean "in good taste," something like that: a classy place to eat, or she has real class. I suppose such a use tells something—an irony!—about my class! Mary made sure I got to look at myself in a new way—a rich girl who had everything, even though she'd never earned a penny by her own efforts. And Mary made me think of others—not only the poor people all over the world, but a lot of our classmates: their backgrounds, their futures—based on what was possible for them, as compared to us.

It struck hard when I realized that the grades we all got, the amount of work we all did at Harvard, weren't as important as we thought at the time. Mary and I were rich, and that was what really mattered. Sure, there were lots of Harvard men and women who started out poor, or not so poor, and would manage through sweat and brains to rise up the ladder. But they were a handful; for every one of them, there are thousands and thousands of Americans who have to struggle hard just to get by, or struggle hard just to stay alive. Meanwhile, Mary and I had the whole world at our fingertips, and we'd never earned the right to be in that position. Pure luck. Nothing more. As Mary used to say— then!—it wasn't "just"; it was "unfair."

There was a rally in the Yard on behalf of the Freedom Riders, and Mary suggested I go to it with her. It's hard to remember my frame of mind at the time. I didn't really know who the Freedom Riders were. To be honest, I didn't know where they were coming from, going to—or even why. I think I could have answered a *quiz* about the South, in a history or government class; I mean, I knew that there was something called segregation, and it meant that blacks and whites had to stay apart in schools or restaurants or movie houses. But I'd never given the matter any great thought. We didn't have black people work for us in Pittsburgh—only whites, and only Protestant, I'm doubly ashamed to admit. Once I was lying in bed in that Freedom House I helped start in Canton, Mississippi, and suddenly I remembered something I'd completely forgotten for years and years: my grandmother telling my mother never to have "a colored person" work in the house, because "the colored people" are unreliable and lazy; and never to have a Catholic, because they're superstitious, and the children would "catch it"!

My mother wasn't in the least annoyed by the advice she was getting. In fact, I recall her telling my grandmother that she already knew all that. I also recall asking my mother, later, who "the colored" were, and who Catholics were. She told me they were different people than us; they weren't educated, and they weren't as smart. I asked her why, and she told me she didn't know, and no one else did. God made them that way—and of course, I knew, He had made us "our way": that is, the very best possible people.

When we went to the rally I was quite uncomfortable. Maybe in the back of my head I was reminded of what I'd heard my mother and grandmother say. I felt nervous; I was scared, actually. I wanted to leave. I'd never before seen so many "colored people" in one place! I asked Mary if we could go—as if I was a child of hers. She said I should leave, if I wanted to, and she'd see me back in the dorm. I couldn't walk out, though. I felt like a coward. I felt cheap. I felt spoiled and callous. I asked myself how it could be that I was so ignorant, and there I was, almost ready to graduate from college. But I also knew I felt shy and awkward. I didn't know what to say or do. I guess I felt, that moment, the way black people feel over and over again—in a strange, uncomfortable, vaguely dangerous, and exposed position.

I left. I moved gradually toward the rear, and then bolted into the night. It was something, coming to my senses a few minutes later: I was running! I had to *tell* myself to stop. I spoke to myself: Sue, you're in Cambridge and there's no one after you, and there's no one you're keeping waiting, and you have nothing pressing to do. I stopped for some cars, and then began walking, rather than running. And I thought. I never before in my life thought so much! I thought and thought. I started out by calling myself a few names: blind, insensitive, narrow. Then I imagined the life ahead of me: large, beautifully furnished homes, lots of travel, country clubs, garden shows, antique auctions—my mother's life. Is that what a Harvard education was all about—a few years spent reading, taking exams, fooling around, meeting eligible men and making friends from a pool of eligible women? A few years of "polish"—so I'd be able to go to England and know some Shakespeare, and go to Dublin and know who Joyce and Yeats were, and go to Paris and name-drop about Proust or Debussy's music, which I'd just been listening to in a course and hadn't liked one bit!

I was in a bad state, and I knew that if I shared my thoughts with my friends, except for Mary, they'd tell me I was being "silly," or I was being too "down" on myself, or I should go see a shrink and he'd help me out. Since I was too ashamed of myself to talk with Mary, there was no one, really. Finally, because I'd wake up low, real low, and find myself crying a lot, but not knowing why, I *did* go see a shrink.

It was like adding oil to a fire—the visits to that doctor. He was a man of about forty, I'd say, and if ever there was someone in love with himself, and enjoying his every word and gesture, he was the person. He would wipe invisible dust off his trousers. He would button his J. Press jacket, then unbutton it. He'd ask me the predictable questions, and sit there, silent and full of his self-important "neutrality." I disliked him when I first saw him, and after three visits to him I was ready to sign a Mafia contract to wipe him out. But the anger I feel now toward him, and all the others like him, wasn't so easy for me to express then, though I knew I had it. I just clammed up. I said less and less. He sat there, apparently unconcerned. Once he asked me if I was "blocked." I didn't know what to say. I said nothing. By the third "session" I'd decided that this man was a flunky—a flunky for Harvard, and for my parents, and for anyone who wanted a guy around to make you stop and question yourself until you no longer have the slightest kind of disagreement with the status quo.

My first real political ideas of my own were in that office with him—the realization that I was struggling with one kind of "conflict," and he was seeing it as something quite different. I mean, when I *did* get going a bit, he'd always try to bring me back to Pittsburgh and what happened to me as a kid. There I was, sad for others, and sad about my own apparent inability to help those others out, and true, sad about my earlier life, but because it had made *me,* as well as the blacks, a victim of prejudice and hate and provinciality; and there *he* was, adjusting his striped ties, and giving himself pats on the knee or the ankle, and buttoning and unbuttoning those expensive pieces of Shetland wool, or whatever, and thinking the obvious thoughts: her mother, her father, her complex—a rivalry, an attachment, a reaction of jealousy or aggression, the stuff I'd heard the psychology professors talk about.

I know, I know: I had a "resistance." The doctor told me that on my fourth and last visit. I spoke up, at last. I told him yes, I did. I told him I'd been doing a lot of thinking, and I knew why I was upset at that rally. He asked me what I'd "discovered." I said I'd discovered that I was a pretty sheltered person, and that I didn't want to be so anymore. He said "yes." Then I turned the tables on him. I asked him what he thought about segregation, and the Freedom Rides. I asked him if he had gone to the rally (I knew the answer in advance). He didn't answer me. If it had been any other situation, I would have been entitled to call him rude. He tried to change the subject. He ignored my questions and started asking one of his own: Had I ever been "openly angry" with my parents? I told him yes. I told him that if I asked a question of them, and they didn't even try to answer it, or explain why they weren't going to answer it, I'd be pretty angry at them, and I'd tell them off, loud and clear!

He then gave me what he thought was his *coup de grâce:* I was "full of rage" and that was why I felt "depressed," and the way for me to get over the "feelings" I had was to "talk about them." When he'd had his say—at last!—I sat there, quiet myself. I had no intention, I knew then and there, of coming back. I was going to get up and walk out, but I knew I was supposed to stay there longer, and *I* didn't want to be rude. I decided to sit and sit and sit, and wait for him to make the next move. It took courage, if I have to say so; it took more strength than I thought I had—to be silent and silent and silent, while a doctor sits there and stares right at you, waiting for you to open your mouth, and of course, stumble again; and of course, prove him right again! A minute can seem like twenty-four hours, at least, under those circumstances.

After a few minutes, he fidgeted. I sat perfectly still, holding on to every muscle in my body for dear life, from my vocal cords to my thighs and calves and ankles. Then he broke down. He asked me what I was thinking. I told him what popped into my mind after he'd asked; I told him that I was thinking about the Freedom Riders, and the Negro people I'd seen at the rally, and I'd been thinking of a lot of other people, all over the world, who didn't have the good deal I had; and I'd been thinking of what I could do to be of help to them. Incredibly, when I finished, he was ready for me—no pause at all: if I had such a "good deal," why was I "unhappy," and why did I come to the clinic looking for a psychiatrist in the first place?

I was hit between the eyes. I didn't know what to say. I said nothing. Then he asked me why I wasn't answering him. I told him, in a burst of anger, that I wasn't answering him because I was thinking about what he said! God, the arrogance! I could see that he was moving in, trying to win an argument. I could also see that no matter what I said, he'd use it for his own purposes. And I could see that he could call me any name he'd like—with his psychiatric vocabulary. Eventually, I dared ask him what he thought *he* ought do about the way Negroes live in the South. And he told me; he said that there wasn't *anything* that he could do. He said that he was on the side of the Negroes. He was sure they "deserve better." But it was "their fight," not his. And he wondered why I was making it mine!

I had an answer. I said I was against injustice in my own country. I said I had been given a lot by America, and I wanted to show my gratitude by helping others. I was stealing those words from Mary, but for the first time they really meant something to me. When I'd made my brief speech, he told me that I'd been given a lot by my *parents,* but maybe I didn't feel I'd been given *enough!* His face beamed with his triumphant interpretation. He waited for me to worm my way clear. I felt trapped in a foul-smelling swamp. Wherever I turned he'd be there with his net! And if I struggled with him, he'd call me "sick." I just sat there, silent. And he continued talking, oddly enough. I realize now that he thought I was defeated; I was ready, at last, to hear him out. He told me, like a lecturer, that I was suspicious of him, because I knew, "deep down," that the more we talked, he and I, the more I'd reveal of myself, and it's always unpleasant to face the painful truth about one's "inner feelings." He went on to say that I was, really, trying to run away—not only from *his* truth, but from my own problems, and the possibility that I'd find out what they were. I was going on a "ride" of my own—but not to "freedom." I was trying to "evade" what was troubling me.

For a moment, I was convinced that he was absolutely right. I slumped back in my chair, and thought to myself that I was going to become a patient—his patient, if he'd have me. I drew a blank on what my "problems" were, but I knew I got impatient or resentful sometimes at home. Maybe I did have a "complex" about my mother, and my father—all that family trouble we'd talk about, occasionally, in polite and guarded ways in the dorm. But something came out of me; that's the only way, to this day, I know to describe what happened: I opened my mouth and said to him: "No matter what's wrong with me, they said a few weeks ago at the rally that they needed us, they needed young white volunteers, they needed troops to help fight their war, and if we believed in their cause, we should sign up." That was what I was going to do. Maybe I was, as he implied, a neurotic. Maybe I was in a lot of trouble with my "conflicts." Even so, there were those people down South, and they *did* need the help of outsiders, especially white people, and that was what I was going to do, try to be of help; and maybe, if I was lucky, I'd even come out a little better person myself.

I was ready, by then, to sit there and talk with him forever. But he glanced at his watch, and said we had to end. Did I want to see him next week? I abandoned myself to impulse; I let my mouth talk without my brain telling it what to say. I moved toward the door, and heard myself tell him that I wanted to "think," and I'd call him for an appointment. But even on the elevator going down, I knew I wouldn't call, I wouldn't return. I knew I was going to go South. I knew what I was going to try to do—and I knew that, in a strange way, that doctor had been more helpful to me than I'd ever dreamed he'd be, and I'm sure, more helpful than he believed he'd been!

I waited to finish college. I wasn't *that* converted to "the cause." I remember the graduation as if it took place yesterday. My mother and father were very upset, because I'd told them, finally, of my "plans." They'd been pestering me for months to come up with something "good." They'd been offering me trips. They'd been asking me questions. I knew I could never tell them to their faces; I knew I couldn't even tell them on the telephone. I wrote them. A very simple letter it was: Dear Mother and Dad, I'm going to be living in the South, in Georgia, for a while. I'm going to be involved with SNCC, the Student Nonviolent Coordinating Committee. It's struggling on behalf of the Negroes. I'll be trying to help Negroes register to vote. I'll tell you more when I see you—soon. Love, Sue.

That was all I could say. I thought that the idea of voting registration wouldn't bother them. Who could be against that and call himself—call *herself*—an American? My mother! She was furious. I'd expected heat from Dad; but I knew he'd drink his way into acquiescence. I'd expected curiosity from Mother, and her sly manipulations, through suggestions and hints and offers that amount to bribes. I didn't expect her to shout at me—and call me "in danger of becoming a radical." I didn't think she knew what a "radical" was! Actually, she didn't know; but she *did* know how to use the word—how to insult and smear and register her own dumb smugness. She called me up and sounded off. I kept silent. I kept repeating that I was going, I was going; I was going to help more Americans to vote, and that was what the country is all about—democracy. She wasn't interested in a word I had to say. She wanted me to know that I was "treading thin ice." She was on the shore, hollering at me in the hope I'd quickly turn around and rush to her country club arms.

It was the one and only time I'd ever hear my mother become *political!* It was the one and only time she shed her veneer of indifference to the social problems of the world outside her cozy, protected life. In a way I was touched and impressed. Years later I would begin to understand what she had been showing both of us that evening on the phone—her anger at a life that kept her from ever before or afterwards expressing a strong, unequivocal position on anything that mattered very much. I'd roused her to a look inward, and she didn't like what she saw. She was telling me what she'd learned to accept—an un-Christian life! She, who used to tell me about how "good" and "kind" and "generous" Jesus Christ had been, was not about to risk losing everything by living like Him! She couldn't believe I had it in me to start down that road myself—call it a Christian road, call it a radical road, call it anything that indicates a dissent from the greed that rich people like her must know, somewhere inside themselves, won't earn them credits when the day of reckoning with St. Peter or Christ Himself takes place!

At the graduation Mother was quiet and composed. You'd have thought she'd never had that phone conversation with me. You'd have thought I hadn't even told her where I was going the next week. It was incredible—the way we all decided to "pretend." We had our lovely meals in lovely restaurants; we wore our fine clothes; we met and enjoyed people like ourselves—and as for the others around, different from ourselves, we smiled at them or said our hellos. It was much later that I would think back and realize that "segregation" isn't only racial in nature, or confined to the South! Even when my parents left, they were either trying to fake it, or whistle in the dark. Not a word about my "plans"! They said good-bye. They told me they hoped I liked the car they'd given me for graduation, and that I could fit my belongings in it without too much trouble, and that, of course, I should "keep in touch." I said yes, I'd call them soon. But I didn't. I wouldn't talk with them for a long, long time. I'd write occasionally. The South did a lot to me—and to all of us in SNCC. The South made me write a lot. I discovered a lot about myself by keeping a diary. I would write home, too; that was the only thread I could keep from breaking between "them" and me. And they became that for me, a "them."

The drive South was terrifying. I was alone and, finally, scared. I didn't know what to expect. All I had was an office address in Atlanta, and the name of one person, whom I'd never met. I didn't know if she was black or white: Alice Jefferson. The farther south I got, the worse I felt. I lost my appetite. I couldn't sleep. I was so jittery I couldn't carry on a normal, civil conversation with gas station attendants or the clerks who worked in the motels I stayed at. And when I got near Atlanta I froze completely. My foot didn't seem to want to push on the gas pedal. I thought I was losing my mind. I pulled over and sat and thought. Should I turn around and go back to Cambridge? Should I drive to Pittsburgh, and try to get a job working in the university, or teaching? Should I go to Europe—take my parents up on their offer? Why *was* I going to Atlanta? Who was *I* to presume to work in this strange part of America—having never spent a day of my life south of the Mason-Dixon Line? Then I gave up asking myself questions. I made a pact with myself: go to Atlanta, spend a few days there, see what you see, think about what you can do, if anything; and agree to turn around and go back North, quickly, if you decide that you're wasting everyone's time by staying.

I got there, and I've been South ever since, except for brief trips home, or visits to New York or Boston. The woman I was told to contact, Alice, became a wonderful friend of mine—probably the most important influence on my adult life. She's a black woman who is only five years older than I, but seems much too wise and thoughtful to be a member of my generation! She took one look at me, and knew the score—that I was a baby, a Yankee kid, rich as Croesus compared to most SNCC people, and in need of a gradual, *very* gradual introduction to the movement. If it weren't for her, I now realize, I would have drifted, and maybe ended up in a project someplace—where I'd have done as much harm as good. She spent hours talking with me, explaining to me what "life" was like in the South. She became my friend. She invited me over to her parents' home; she invited me to visit her relatives, and she had lots of them. She took me on one "field trip" after another, until I'd visited just about every SNCC project within six months of my arrival.

Meanwhile, I worked in the main Atlanta office, typing and answering phones and trying to run any errands there were. Day by day I began to realize what I'd done—changed my entire way of living. I was with people I'd never have otherwise met—people who believed in something bigger than themselves. All my life I'd been told to think of what *I* needed, and what *I* should do, and where *I* was going to go, and how *I* should do things. Suddenly I was with people, black and white, men and women, who were thinking of others not as lucky as themselves. After all, it was the *Student* Nonviolent Coordinating Committee; we all had more going for us than the Mississippi tenant farmers we worked with, or the poor black people in cities all over the South.

At last, Alice and I decided that I was ready to go "out in the field"—but not to do some "research study"! I'd become more relaxed in the way I got along with her family and friends—as she put it, less "awestruck" by black people. At first I fell in love with anyone who was black—a mixture of sentimentality, ignorance, nervousness, and, I'm afraid to say, condescension: the white queen who has come South on a romantic ego trip, and is anxious to find "objects" upon which she can bestow her regal benediction. I'm ashamed, as I think back to those days—the stupidity and naïveté, the gullibility and the smugness. But I'm not going to make myself, in retrospect, some monster. I had some decency in me: I was there; I was learning; I was doing work that had to be done; I was giving my energy to a damn good cause. In a few weeks I began to settle down; and in a few months I was able to help ''orient'' other white people from the North who had just come down South. And in 1962, believe me, we were getting dozens of volunteers from all over America—from foreign countries as well.

Who can ever forget Canton, Mississippi? Who of us in the Mississippi Summer Project of 1964 can ever forget those weeks? Even now, years later, I get all worked up thinking back—the dangers, the opportunities, the excitement, the fear, the sense of doing something that really mattered, that would really change the course of history—a little, at least. I loved the Delta as soon as I saw it—a hard thing to say, because it sounds as if I'm a foolish Yankee romantic who's cleverly adorning herself by waxing euphoric over a region she's lived in a few years; a region, by the way, full of misery and hunger and suffering and exploitation, if you're one of thousands of black people. My love for the Delta grew out of the love I came to experience there—the love I received from the families I stayed with, the love I learned to return to them, and of course the love between Paul and me. So much of my time was spent working with those people, walking the Delta soil with them, sitting under the Delta sky with them, listening to Delta sounds with them, that I'm never going to be objective about what I went through. I have dozens of intensely personal memories of Greenville and Greenwood, Clarksdale and Yazoo City—and above all, Canton.

I'd get up at five and be on the dusty roads of Canton a half an hour later. Black folk get up early in the rural South; they have to be ready for ''the man''—ready to do his agricultural chores or his domestic chores, or his warehouse or store or office chores. One black woman I knew said it all for me: ''I have to be a step ahead of 'the man'; I have to be an hour or two ahead of 'the man.' '' She'd be ready to go at sunup; she'd come home after sundown—a long stretch in a Delta summer for a maid. And *I* would bellyache sometimes, come three in the afternoon; and remember those nice afternoon teas at my grandmother's! But I learned to be happy with a Coke—and the company of wonderful people. Oh, I shouldn't generalize, I know. There were some selfish and mean blacks. No race, no class, has a monopoly on virtue. And I can't ever forget that I was white—and a woman. I was to black men in the Delta, especially at that time, a strange, untouchable figure. I was to black women a mystery.

But those women extended themselves to me so generously! They taught me to cook and sew. They showed me how to take care of children. They gave me the equivalent of a graduate school education in sociology and anthropology and political science—how a society functions, from the point of view of the people whose sweat keeps everything going, and whose position of jeopardy requires from them constant surveillance. Sometimes I'd wake up—in a tenant farmer's cabin, or in one of the rooms of a ''Freedom House''—and wonder how I ever got where I was: a long, long way from ''home.'' But I was never really sorry. After those first days of uncertainty, I felt grateful, always, to be where I was. And especially grateful after I met Paul.

I was having a rough time personally in Canton before Paul came. A couple of black men in SNCC had their eyes on me; more than that—they were constantly propositioning me, and making me feel guilty for saying no. Alice had warned me, from the start, to say no, no, no—no interracial sex. She was uptight, yes. But she was smart, too; remember, I'm talking about the Mississippi and Georgia of 1962 and 1963 and 1964. What I couldn't tell even her, what I had a hard time admitting to myself, what I still cringe at mentioning is this: I was a virgin then; but even more difficult to say—but it's the truth, and not only my truth!—I couldn't imagine myself having sex with a black man. I'd had plenty of sexual fantasies in high school, never mind college, and they all were of the same, basic kind: I'd meet a man, and he'd be tall and I might as well say it, blond and muscular. I'd be standing there, shyly; I'd be looking in a store window, pretending to pay attention to the exhibit; or I'd be waiting for a bus or to meet someone; and then he'd ask me out—and the next thing, I'd be in his arms. I lived off such nonsense for years; I never thought it was demeaning that I regularly pictured myself a passive, fragile, lost soul who was waiting, waiting— for a Nordic football player to sweep her into his lifelong grip! It never occurred to me, back then, to wonder what such endlessly repeated daydreams had to say about me, about my home life, my education, *my* kind of slavery! There I was in Mississippi, a white woman out to "rescue" black people—and yet for years I'd been having fantasies in which someone even lighter than I "rescued" me!

Paul had black hair, and was as thin as he could possibly be. I remember the first thing I noticed about him—with only his sweatshirt on: the boniness of this guy. It was a broiling Delta day, the temperature way over a hundred degrees and the humidity a tight blanket on all of us: no throwing it off, because no air conditioners, not for us in the homes where we were staying. Paul was quiet and retiring; on that count, too, he failed to be the man of my dreams! He had just come South, after a year of graduate work in history at the University of Chicago. He'd grown up in Cleveland; he'd gone to Case Western Reserve on a scholarship. His parents were first-generation Americans; both their parents had come here from Italy. Paul was, needless to say, the first person in his family ever to graduate from high school, never mind go to college. His father worked in a factory. His mother had five daughters, and then Paul. He was the favorite of both his parents—but because of that he had become upset by what he kept calling, all during his adolescence, the "unfairness of life." Instead of just enjoying himself, basking in the attention his parents poured on him all the time, he took to wondering (as we'd put it in Mississippi back then) "why that was the case." And he wondered why his sisters didn't even want to go to college. He even offered to work and help one of his older sisters finish high school, and go on further with her education. But she would have no part of such a plan.

When Paul finished college, he felt himself a stranger to his own family. He wanted to work with the poor in Cleveland, and his parents and sisters and their husbands thought he'd gone loony: all that education in order to become a do-gooder among the poor—meaning the blacks or the hillbillies of Cleveland! Paul couldn't take their criticisms; and luckily, a favorite professor of his pushed him toward graduate school. He'd majored in history, and he wanted to go on with his studies—especially American history. He wrote his undergraduate honors paper on populism, and went to the graduate school hoping to do more on the subject. And then came the same Freedom Rides and sit-ins that got all of us in SNCC going. Paul was torn between the inviting, scholarly life of the University of Chicago, and a desire to take part in the civil rights movement. When he saw several students he knew catch hell from a professor for mentioning that they might go South for a term, he became outraged. The two students were women, white women, and Paul was sensitive on that score, too: the professor had scorned their usefulness to the movement, because (he said) activist women down South, who were white, would only be an embarrassment to the cause. Paul urged them to stand up for their beliefs, but they folded. He ended up arguing so hard with them that he went himself!

I was a "veteran" of almost a year—a long time in the movement—when he showed up. I could see right away something different in him. He wasn't the "macho" man who came South to have another battle in a never-ending war to prove his strength. He wasn't the egoist—full of self-importance and bravado. I don't mean to say that most white volunteers from the North were arrogant and pushy; but some were—and some would show gentleness and tactfulness toward blacks, then turn on us white women exploitatively. It was Paul who began to see all that—the way we got along in SNCC as *men,* as *women.* I was, naturally, preoccupied with color; he had an eye for what sex meant, so far as our social behavior was concerned—and class, too. We'd be sitting around in those all-night "soul sessions," and he'd point out that so-and-so wasn't only black, or white, but a man, a woman—and did this kind of work or that kind of work. We'd be sitting around cursing the white people of Canton, and Paul would say: stop; take a look around you when you go to the post office in Canton; think about the different kinds of white people in the town. He'd point all sorts of things out to us—and soon I was noticing how southern *women,* black and white, both, were living. It was hard, listening to him. For a while I wanted to tune off. He made me angry. After all, we were there to fight the segregationists, and he was muddying the waters. And he made enemies for doing so—dangerous enemies: two black men, one of whom was a leader of SNCC; and a couple of white men who had been involved in the movement from its start.

One of the black men Paul took on had been pushing himself on me for months. I'd go to bed crying because I felt I ought to give in, but I just couldn't. He kept on telling me that I had "problems"—that I was still a "racist" at heart. I was devastated. I was also, at the time, a real fool. Because he was black, I thought, I had no right to question his assumptions. Talking about racism! He gave up on me eventually—because he found a more obliging white woman, whom he dominated completely. Now I can talk about what went on then calmly and with some psychological sophistication; but believe me, at the time I was confused, upset, anxious, desperately afraid—scared to stop, for one minute, and try to figure out what was really going on. And there were the white guys, too; they'd arrive, and the work they had wasn't enough to dampen their sexual interests. There was no reason for them *not* to be sexually turned on—that isn't the point. At the time, though, all of us SNCC women, black and white, were expected to be *there,* attentive and obliging to the heroes: the men.

I'm overstating the case a bit, but not all that much. I'm sure the men would see it, remember it, differently. That's what I've learned these past years—how differently even men and women who seem to share the same political goals end up looking at the world. The men who went after me in those early days of SNCC, black and white, were struggling to help the poor black people of the South, but were willing to try a few approaches toward women that certainly could be described as "patronizing," "exploitative," "manipulative," "condescending"—the words they used about plantation owners, sheriffs, other county officials. But there were days when many of us women didn't know, at least consciously, what was really happening—or, at least, speaking for myself, I had no idea of what made me so upset about some of the meetings I attended, when men kept talking, talking, and I kept saying yes, or keeping quiet, no matter what I thought, because I never felt it "right" (was never emotionally able) to speak up forcefully.

It was Paul who started educating me. He approached me intellectually, not sexually—a real shock to me at first! He wanted to be a friend. He wanted to talk. And later, I could see, he wanted to help me out, because he saw I was being hustled by a black man who came on strong, and a white man who was cute and clever and crooked when it came to sex—no matter how brave he was in the Delta. Paul would suggest that we go for a walk. At first I thought he was "after me"—not because I was antisexual, but because we were a small group, and there was a lot of tension coming at us from the outside, and it was natural for us to pull together "real tight," as we'd put it then, and often the men had their "ploys" to set the stage for a pass, and going for a walk was one of them. But Paul was a conversationalist, I began to see, not a talker in search of a willing listener, and a man after a woman. We would walk, all right. We would walk and walk and walk. Often we'd end up in the white section of Canton. Most of us had nothing to do with whites, except as adversaries. And the whites were rude to us when we showed up at the post office, or went shopping. They knew who we were, each of us. They had become for us a large, indiscriminate mass—a crowd of faces, full of resentment, prejudice, and narrowness of vision. But Paul wouldn't go along. He showed me that I'd been lumping everyone into two categories—the wonderful, decent, but vulnerable blacks, and the malicious, foul-mouthed whites. Through his eyes I began to see that prejudice is no one's exclusive property—that even in SNCC there was plenty of meanness to go around; the way we treated one another when we talked or made our plans or ate or took care of our living quarters.

For instance, Paul insisted on helping with the cooking and cleaning up after the meals. No other man would follow his lead. In fact, they began to snicker at him—the black men as well as the white men, and a few women, too, on both sides of the racial fence. Since he wasn't macho about sex, either, the snickering began to take a focus—he was too "finicky," and he was "like a priest," and he shouldn't be a "housekeeper." He managed to laugh at the remarks, but he was too sensitive, I knew, not to catch their implication. One evening, after we'd both cleaned up the kitchen, by ourselves, he suggested a walk. We'd scarcely got out of the house when he began to wonder, out loud, why people can be so petty—even people of high idealism, ready to dedicate themselves to a decent cause. I had no answer for him; but he did for himself—the "sinfulness" in each human being. I didn't like such talk; and I told him so. It crossed my mind that he *was* a priest after all! I was disgusted with myself for having such a thought. I guess I was so busy, then, being *better* than all the people I'd left behind up North, that it hurt me, threatened me, to be reminded that no gesture or commitment made a person all *that* special or superior. Paul must have felt that I was thinking such thoughts, or having such feelings, maybe without even knowing their exact nature, because he hastened to tell me that he wasn't denying the distinction between the "problems" of people and their *actions*. He was just trying to explain for himself and me the ironic moments we both were living through—smallness of character in people engaged in large and important deeds. And he was also trying to understand why people who were protesting racial exploitation weren't at least a little sensitive to the sexual biases that also cause a lot of pain for people.

I was in love with Paul long before I knew it. I was close to him, I admired him, I relied upon him, before I realized that I was attracted to him. It was in a sharecropper's cabin outside of Canton that I first felt myself flush at the sight of him. He was helping a black woman lift some wood, and I saw him take off his shirt because he was hot. I was embarrassed, but I didn't know why. Would you believe it: I thought to myself that Paul ought not do it—be so cavalier, strip down to his waist—in front of an elderly black woman. It was me, a young white woman, who really minded, though. I tried to look away. It's only his chest, I kept telling myself. My eyes would sneak back toward him—and finally, my thick, puritan head realized what was happening. I was jittery when we left the cabin, for no apparent reason. It was as if I'd met him for the first time. He noticed; he was always noticing everything. He asked me what the trouble was. I told him nothing was wrong. He said if I wanted to tell him, I could. I blurted out that maybe he'd made a mistake, being so "informal" with the lady. He said nothing for a minute or so—no explanation or apology or defense. Then he put his arm around my waist—as if he'd been reading my mind better than I ever could. I felt myself ready to cry. I fought to keep my eyes dry. I was afraid I'd start trembling, but I didn't. I searched frantically for something to say. Some hotshot white kid zoomed by on his motorcycle, and that got me going. I told Paul that the guy was probably full of bitterness, and maybe a young Klanner, by the way he roared his motor and kicked dust at us. Paul would have no part of my hunch. He said maybe the kid was fed up with his parents, like a lot of kids are—and if we got to know him, he might even be fed up with his parents' racial prejudices. I couldn't buy that! I was ready to talk, to argue. I was ready to pull away. I caught myself doing so—but Paul pulled me toward him tighter. I was confused. I remember thinking that if the sun wasn't out, and we weren't walking down a farm road in the Mississippi Delta, two "civil rights types," as they called us, then we might stop and kiss. Then we did; or he did, I guess I should say. That was the beginning of a new life for me.

Even in the worst hours of the Mississippi Summer Project, Paul was unhappy with the way we were all thinking—us against them. And he kept saying that southern white women had a lot to teach us—about prejudice and persecution. We all used to laugh at the "belles" we saw; Paul realized that they were not unlike blacks—ingratiating themselves, playing dumb, manipulating from a position of inferiority. He'd speak up, but he wasn't heard. When the Project was over, he decided that he'd better go back North. What did I want to do? Where did I want to live? I was speechless each time he brought up such subjects. I didn't know how to answer him. I wanted to be with him; that was all I knew. Well, not quite. I also knew that he would never let me be like that: the self-effacing woman, ready to abandon herself—her ideas, ideals, work, commitments of time and energy—to the will or convenience of a Mister. One day early in September of 1964, as we sat there in the Canton Freedom House, he asked me if I had any idea where I would be in a few months. I said no, I didn't. He said that he was asking because he'd like to be near me, and if I was staying South, he might try to transfer from the University of Chicago to Tulane or Emory or Chapel Hill, and if I was going North, he'd like to know where in the North for the same reason. I started talking before I even knew what I was saying; I said: "Paul, you can't speak like that, you can't! *You've* got to pave the way. *You've* got to supply direction. You can't throw it all on me. You've got to be a *man!* I'm waiting for you, for your signals. Where are they?" He didn't answer me. He looked away, and all I could see was half of his face—and way out there, the line of trees, and the late-afternoon sun, finally letting up on the land. I felt like running and not stopping until I hit the Canadian border. I hadn't realized until that second how tired I was, and how much I needed someone, needed him, Paul, to take the responsibility away from me, and say: let's go, it's okay to go, we've done enough.

It started out to be a sad, but also an exciting and happy day. We'd said our good-byes and we were "going home"—in the sense that for us the North was home. We had the names of a lot of black people—kin of our various Delta friends who'd also gone North, but under more desperate circumstances than we'd ever known. There had been a great big party for us, and we made sure that we left early, because it's painful to keep saying farewells, and because we knew that the actual departure would be very hard for us—despite the promises of a return, even though no one is sure if there will actually be one! I was driving; Paul was still sleepy. I saw the sheriff's car—the old enemy, out early to keep an eye on us. I got nervous; I always did when I saw that car. We were leaving, but the Project wasn't over, nor the harassment of the Project. I wanted to waken Paul when I noticed that the sheriff's car kept following us. I slowed down to fifteen miles an hour, about twenty below the speed limit. Too slow. I picked up to thirty. The sheriff stayed close for about two or three minutes, until we were on the highway. Then he turned off. I relaxed, pressed on the accelerator. I hadn't realized until that moment how scared I'd been all summer, and before that, for a year, for two years—but especially that terrible summer; three deaths, dozens and dozens of serious injuries, and threats every day. One last look in the window: no one in sight. I smiled, sang quietly, looked over: Paul was still dozing. And then, out of nowhere, that truck appeared, and came closer. I heard a pop, and looked out the window—as if it had thundered. I was looking for the rain. Then I heard another pop, and my stupid brain made the connection it should have made half a minute earlier.

The truck was almost inside our car! I pushed the accelerator down hard, to the floor. We jerked forward. Paul woke up. I screamed to him that "they" were after us, that they'd shot at us. He told me to keep going, keep going. I was sure we could pull away from them—a bunch of red-necks in a small pickup truck. And we did. The only trouble was that car, that Volkswagen. Suddenly it was on the highway, right before me. I hadn't even seen it come out of a side road. I tried to avoid hitting it. But we swerved, and I lost control of the car, and we went off the road on the other side—and that's all I remember; that's all I'll ever remember. When I woke up I was in the hospital, and when I asked the nurse about Paul, I could tell what happened by the look on her face. I started crying. I never *asked* anyone else what happened. I knew. I was told details later. I didn't want to hear them, though. When I met Paul's parents, and went to his grave, I was afraid they'd ask me for details. But they didn't want to know, either. His mother said it, the papers said it: he'd died in an "accident." But he was really killed in a war. He gave his life for a better country than we had then. We're still trying to make the country worthy of him.

It was strange, years later, when the women's movement got going. I'd managed, most of the time, to forget Paul. I'd long since met and gone out with and married my husband. I had a child, with another on the way. I'd become the "liberal" wife of a good, "liberal," southern economist. I'd stayed South, kept involved in the civil rights movement until it was "over." But the more I read the women writers who were bringing a new kind of civil rights movement to this country, and the more I heard some of them on television and on our campus, the more I thought of—a man, Paul! Meanwhile, a lot of my friends were coming to me, and telling me that I must join "women's liberation." Hadn't I fought hard in the South almost a decade earlier? Wasn't I one of the first white members of SNCC? Wasn't I still an "activist"? Didn't I know how to organize, how to launch a protest, how to take on a tough, vindictive enemy? And wouldn't I want to go to war again, take part in another important battle?

Yes, the answer has been yes. You bet. There's been only one problem; the harder I take on a lot of vain, arrogant men, and the more I challenge a lot of women who want to pretend that they are dumbbells, or moths hovering around some guy's big bright fire, the more I think of one man who really did take a woman, me, and help me grow and use my head and think straight, and think enough of myself to become—well, to become myself, and not someone's satellite or servant or slave. I met my husband when I was doing political organizing in Georgia, and also graduate work in economics. I stayed South because I loved Paul, and he died in the South. And I never forgot my talks with Paul—the push he gave me toward my own career. In a way, my career was his doing!

When I became active in the women's movement, I found myself trying to talk with a lot of men, who might (I reasoned) be useful and helpful to "us." Who was inspiring me then? Paul.

He would have been the first person (had he lived) to work on behalf of the women's movement. But he would have seen the "problem" as a joint one: of men, of women, of growing boys and growing girls. He *did* see the "problem" that way—years ago, when most of us women didn't even realize there was a "problem"!

Sometimes I look at my young son, Paul, and I think of the man he was named for, and I think of all he taught me, taught us, back then in another time, another struggle. I wonder what he'd be thinking and doing today, if that sheriff hadn't used his radio to signal those Ku Klux Klan people to go after us, in September of 1964. I guess Paul has become a god to me; when someone you've loved dies suddenly, so young, he becomes that—a shadow of grace over your life. There have been times that I've wished I had been the one to die, but I'm not one to be a martyr. I have to admit that I'm glad I'm alive. I only hope I live up to his ideals, occasionally. I'm trying to organize on behalf of women without becoming as "chauvinist" as the people we're battling it out with. Paul fought that way—watchful of the traps, the dangers, the personal hazards. I guess he was a victim of one kind of hazard; they got his body, the haters did. But they never got his mind. I hope I can be as immune to self-righteousness as he was. I hope my young Paul will know, one day, what a fine personal tradition his name commemorates. When someone calls me a "woman's libber," I think of the man who taught me years ago how to be gentle, and still uphold my convictions; how to be a fighting activist who smiles and reaches out—even to the people who are standing in the way, refusing stubbornly to give ground.

part four

CLIMBING THE MESA

FEET FIRST, she came out feet first. Her mother told her that more than once or twice: "When I would get into trouble, say something wrong, get hurt playing, I would be told this, exactly this: 'Maria, your head came last, not first, when you were born.' " The mother would then explain to Maria Sandoval that for some of her Pueblo forebears a breech delivery, as an Anglo doctor would think of it, had a definite significance: the head was a bit lazy, perhaps, or the legs and feet a bit impetuous. The moral for a child now seven or eight years old: be more careful with the lower body, be more reflective with the head.

Maria was headstrong, a trial to her parents. They were convinced that a "spirit" was responsible for the girl's behavior. Maria's mother remembers her this way: "I had seven children; Maria was in the middle, two boys and a girl older, two girls and a boy younger. But Maria was the only one who frightened me. I thought she was a sign, a warning. First it was her birth, the head last, not first. Then it was her body; it was always ready to go someplace! I had to run when she crawled. I had to run harder when she started walking. And she was a hungry child! She drained me. I never had enough for her. I am an old woman now, but I still remember how sad I felt: a baby who cries because I am dry! I was lucky to have the extra food to give her, lucky she would eat it. My mother had taught me to stay away from Anglo food—especially when the children are little. My mother had no money to buy Anglo food, anyway. But that was a long time ago! The Pueblos are different now!

"We thought Maria had an Anglo inside her when she was a girl. She noticed airplanes, and was always asking about them. She liked to see cars race by. She loved Anglo food—baby food, canned meat and vegetables. My father would look at her when she was a baby and say: 'She is an Anglo, sent here to keep us on our toes!' He wasn't angry. He liked the Anglos. He worked for one, on a ranch. He knew the Anglo writer—the one tourists have read and come and ask us about—always the same question: where is the ranch of Lawrence? We can see them getting ready to ask before they say a word. An Englishman who tried to find peace here in our part of the world! When Maria was a girl I wondered when *she* would find peace!''

Maria's grandfather, who had indeed known D. H. Lawrence, was a Pueblo Indian ranch hand, a man who knows how to take care of horses, gets to know rich Anglos. Maria's mother had married a more traditional Pueblo, a man who kept to the reservation, did subsistence farming, had much to do with the tribe's religious, ceremonial life. Maria's grandmother had died a young woman; Maria's mother feared strong winds, because she was told that one of them had taken away *her* mother. When Maria, at the age of five, responded so noticeably to the winds of northern New Mexico, the mother wondered if the baby's grandmother hadn't returned—restless, anxious to have another, and longer chance at life as a human being on a Pueblo reservation north of Santa Fe, New Mexico, in the second half of the twentieth century. But the grandfather of the girl overruled the mother: no Indian with his blood in her would be so attentive of New Mexico's Anglo technology. Hadn't he seen Maria run after the Anglo state police cars when they came near: a bad storm, and a road to be closed temporarily? Maria was an Anglo, all right—to a degree, at least, in her "spirit"!

When Maria was eight or nine, she bothered her parents, her maternal grandfather (both paternal grandparents had died before she was born) with questions—too many of them for a Pueblo girl of her age, maybe any age. She was especially attracted to the clouds as well as the wind. She wanted to know, insistently, where each cloud came from. She was not satisfied with the replies she received. She would go out and ask directly: "I can see myself, even today, standing there and asking the wind to reveal herself! I can remember asking the clouds to reveal themselves! I was sure that they were trying to tell me something. My father would say that I mustn't assume that *I* am the one being sent messages. But why not? I kept asking that question: why not? He never had an answer, because he knew that it *was* possible, that a spirit might have been trying to reach me, or that a spirit in me might have been talking with a spirit outside—across the land, up the mesa."

The mesa had been her spiritual home throughout childhood. She found it impossible—later on, when a grown woman—to imagine growing up far away from that particular mesa she had once known so very well. The pathways, the soil, the rocks and cacti, the desert flowers, the small wildlife, the birds, and most of all, the sheltering, watchful, energetic sky—all of that she heeded closely, conversed with, reflected upon. Her father pronounced her too self-centered, but she would not hear of his objections: "He wanted me to listen to *him!* He was the one who would stand between all of us and the sky, the mesa. When I told him that the weather would change, he wanted me to know that I was guessing, 'only guessing.' I would tell him that I felt a wind come up, and my skin got wet: rain. I have always known when rain would come. The sky may be clear, but I can feel the clouds approaching our reservation. My father says he is better at knowing when we will receive rain, but we have disagreed, and then I end up being right. He is not a mean man, though. He jokes with me. He says my mother's father was right about me—there *is* an

Anglo inside me: a man from the air force base near Albuquerque, where they try to trap the weather, so they can show where it is on their charts!''

Her father's brother had gone to work at that air force base—yet another Pueblo Indian who had found Albuquerque irresistible. As a girl, she found the uncle irresistible. He would tell her of his adventures, and he liked her stories—and her reputation. She was the most Anglo of his nieces and nephews, and he was a bit of an Anglo himself. He was also a storyteller, and she was enthralled by his accounts of the Anglo air force base, and not far away, the commercial aviation field. She remembers hoping against hope that somehow, her uncle would get up in an airplane. Then he would come tell her what he saw. Then she would be the luckiest person she knew. But such a moment was not to come—and she would, for a while, at the age of nine or ten, ask questions on that score, too: ''I was very silly. I would get an idea in my head, and it wouldn't leave me. I was sure that if my uncle had really wanted to go up in a plane, he would have been able to go. Each time I saw him, I asked, and each time he shook his head: no. But I wouldn't take his no for my answer! I would go up in the plane with my dreams; I'd picture myself flying, and looking down and looking up and feeling completely happy. I knew I was getting older, I knew I was no more a child, when I began to tell myself to stop having those dreams—or when I was no longer so happy when I *did* have them.

''I swore I'd spare my own children shame—the Indian bow to the white man's judgment! My father used to pride himself on being a faithful Pueblo. No Anglo had ruined his thinking! But he didn't know what had really happened to him, because he was always trying to make me be a good student at the BIA school. He laughed when I told him—only once!—that I'd flown a plane. He laughed at me for having such a 'silly idea' in my head. But that is what the Anglo teachers said, too—anytime we tried to be *Indians*. They kept telling me to change what I was saying, change what I was writing: I should become 'realistic.' The fifth-grade teacher who told me that all year was an Anglo named Mr. Brown—but he should have been named Mr. White!

"I asked him once what 'realistic' meant. He said 'truthful.' He said if you can't fly by raising your arms, then there's no point thinking you can. He and my father—a pair! All they both wanted me to do was tell them that I wasn't 'really' flying; I was just 'doing some imagining,' Mr. Brown's word that he wanted me to know better than any other! If only he had been doing some imagining when he listened to me tell about what I'd been doing!"

One day her uncle did take her to the air force base. She stared in mute amazement, and considerable horror. The blades of the planes frightened her. Their noise did, too. She didn't like the pilots: their clothes, their goggles, made her nervous. Now she pictured the airplanes up in the sky, but without herself in them. Now she felt pity and terror: the former for the clouds, the wind; the latter at the prospect of ever going up in such a machine. Her "imagining" became, at once, more combative, even apocalyptic, in its constructions. She found herself distressed rather than carried away pleasantly by what she found, inexplicably, in her daydreams: "Once I saw a plane up in the sky, and the pilot was an Anglo; he looked like one I saw that day with my uncle— heavy, brown hair, freckles, and a big smile for me. I tried to get him out of the plane. I tried to stop the noise by putting a blanket over the propeller. I tried to turn the plane into a glider. (Now I know that was what I was trying to do!) I thought to myself: if only I can get the Anglo out of the plane, it would become quiet, like an eagle or a hawk—coasting through the clouds. But the pilot wouldn't leave, so the clouds fled, and the sky turned from blue to gray to black, and the plane's noise was answered by thunder, and then lightning kept coming, coming—a knife into the plane, over and over again, until the noise stopped, the pilot fell out, the plane went straight down to the earth, and landed on the cement of the air force base. Do you know that today, years and years later, I will suddenly have that memory come to me— only the plane is headed right for this square in Santa Fe!"

She sells pottery she has made in the main square of Santa Fe. There is for her nothing "holy" about the "faith" the city is named for. Many Pueblos are Catholics, nominal or by conviction, but she is not one of them. She fought that in her father, too—his effort to feel a loyalty to his Pueblo heritage and at the same time be part of a longtime connection of a particular Indian people to Spain's exported national religion. When she hears the church bells of a lovely old Spanish-appearing town send their message of time and God's gracious presence to the surrounding pagan countryside (greedy tourists everywhere), she scoffs to herself, and remembers her father's desire that the children equate the ringing of such bells with a word from on high: "I would never listen! I would try to go to the river, and let the water speak to me. I would wonder whether a plane could manage to crash into a church, lose the engine, then become a bird that has been hurt, but suddenly is feeling all better, and so wants to celebrate with a long rise upward, then a gradual ride downward—toward the tallest aspen tree in sight. My father would see me, sometimes, not listening to him; he would tell me that there was a devil in my head, trying to take me over. He *was* a Catholic— more than he knew, I believe! He also liked the air force people—money to New Mexico! The Pueblo people have spent too much time being good in school. Their first teachers were the Catholics, and now there are the Anglo pilots!''

She may have ended up, as a woman, selling pottery to Anglos, but she never as a child showed an interest in learning how to make pottery, as did a number of girls of her age on the reservation. She was a constant source of exasperation to those girls, whom she taunted: why not leave the earth alone, and why not go to the mesa and look at the reservation, rather than decorate cups or plates? She was eleven, and mistaken for an Anglo sympathizer—when, of course, she was trying to be more Pueblo than her people knew how to be (she believed), and than she herself had figured out a way of being. She once declared her hands independently restless: "I was taken to an old woman, and she was to 'tame' my fingers—so I'd settle down and learn to make pottery. She told me what to do. I tried to follow her. I couldn't. She told me my fingers were running, always running. I told her yes, and I couldn't stop them. She told me *she* would! She made me sit down before her, and she told me to put my hands, palms down, on her knees; then, she covered them with her own hands, palms down, on mine. I sat there. After a few minutes she asked me if I was 'ready.' I didn't answer. Then she told me to work with her and make things. Once I took a bowl I made with her, and smashed it with a rock; I did that on the mesa. It was cloudy, but no thunder came, no lightning. I saw some blue in the sky. I think the clouds laughed at what they saw! I saw some hawks circling, circling. Nothing for them! But I was sure they liked what they saw!

"I knew then—only a girl!—that our pottery was going to the Anglos. My father would say that we are making the Anglos better people: when they buy what we have made, they learn to be like us! I saw my father's face when Anglo tourists came to our reservation. He tried to be nice to them, but he didn't tell us what he thought to himself. It was written on his face. I saw the writing, and told my mother what I saw; she said I look too hard, and I should learn to close my eyes more! I asked her to teach me! She said I was getting old enough to learn on my own. I was twelve then, I believe."

She can still recall vividly another moment with her mother; it also took place when Maria was twelve. She had awakened early one morning; it was still dark, but the day was beginning to make itself felt—the first, subtle light had made the slightest inroad on the dark. She was relieved; she had always, as far back as she could remember, feared the middle of the night. She lay there, listening: a coyote, birds beginning to waken and talk, a breeze coming upon her. She felt sick. She had a stomachache. She thought she was being reclaimed: "I was sure that I wouldn't be Maria when the sun came up. I was sure I'd be taken to the mesa, and I'd meet a spirit, who would be the one inside me, and we'd talk, and then I'd be there for a long time, and the spirit would be with me, and no more reservation life for a while! But I began to realize that it wasn't time; I was going to be around for a long time. I was bleeding, as my mother did! She had told me I would, and she was right. She had told me to be glad, and there I was getting ready to die and leave! Some of the older girls on the reservation told us we'd soon be bleeding, and they told us we could think of 'spirits' coming and going, or we could think of ourselves as becoming women: the flesh, as the Anglo priests in our Catholic Church put it! I wanted to go and tell a priest what happened to me. I was sure he'd be speechless. Priests don't like to be reminded of anything connected to sex. When I told my mother of my idea, she said I was a born troublemaker; and she reminded me again that I'd come out feet first!''

The mother had been comforting to Maria at the time of her menarche. Before that they had not had much to do with each other. The girl had argued with her father, sought the company of her uncle, listened intently to her grandfather—but, really, liked none of them at all. She had wondered whether she'd ever meet a man she'd like, then learn to trust. And she'd had no truck with the boys of her age. She was a loner, as her mother had noticed. Now, at twelve, the two of them could find themselves having a candid talk about the past—and not incidentally, getting a bit close for the first time: "My mother told me when I was born she knew I'd be the one to walk on my own, because my feet were already working before the rest of me came out. She told me that she kept looking at the feet when they held me up to her. The Anglo doctor told her she was 'wrong' to jump to her 'conclusion,' but she smiled to herself. I proved her right! I'd heard so much about my legs being born first that I would sometimes look at them as if they didn't belong to me, but were on their own! My mother told me, the time we had our first good talk, when my blood first showed, that we don't own ourselves, that the legs may be someone's spirit, that the blood coming may be someone's spirit calling to me.

"In school they teach you different ideas. I told my mother that the school nurse checked up on us, and always wanted to know about our 'periods.' A lot of the girls in my class had theirs before I got mine. I'll never forget the nurse telling me that Indians are dark, and we get our 'periods' before they do, the Anglos. I looked at her, and there she was: light hair and her eyes blue. I wanted to ask her how old she was when she got hers, but I said nothing. She told the teacher that I was a 'strange one,' because I didn't talk. I did talk, but not to her!

"I talked a long time with my mother that day. I told her what the nurse had said. For the first time in my life, the only time in my life, one of my parents talked honestly about the Anglos and the Pueblos, and what it's like to be a Pueblo among the Anglos, and what it's like to be a Pueblo woman. I sat there, hearing about the history of our people—how we fought the Spanish, but were not warriors, and only wanted peace, so that we could grow food and live quietly and take care of the land we lived on and the land nearby. My mother said some of the Pueblo men worry about the past: should they have fought harder? How hard should you fight, when another people show up, and they can wipe you out with their guns, because they live to fight and win and strip you clean, and you live to grow food and teach your children to say yes to the sun, yes to the sky, yes to the land, yes to all the world? My mother said that for a long time the Pueblos have gone back and forth between the Anglo cities and their own land, and it's been hard, but with each child there's a chance to be a *Pueblo,* not a reservation Indian who belongs to the Anglos— their children who start bleeding early, because they are dark!"

What does it mean to be a Pueblo? A Pueblo woman? Maria wanted to know, badly wanted to know. The mother was a bit put off by the ardent nature of the child's curiosity—as the child would never forget: "That was a hot afternoon: May, early summer. My mother told me I was making it hotter, with all my questions! I kept asking her about herself and her sister. She had one sister who left the reservation, and married an Anglo, and came back every year or so for a visit. My mother didn't want to talk about her sister. She didn't want to go on talking about the Anglos, either. She said that the best thing we can do is keep the Anglos out of our home—not mention them. When I asked her why her sister would ever want to marry an Anglo, she said she didn't know. But I asked again, and finally she told me what she thought—that her sister always liked to be different, and was always hiding, or taking long walks by herself, and later she met an Anglo who was fixing the road that goes from our reservation to the state highway, and they started going out, and that was how it happened.

"I wanted to know more! I guess I already knew more! I guess I wanted to hear my mother say what I knew—but she wouldn't. She never talked with me about sex. She was from another generation. Actually, I'm the only one in my family, of *my* generation, who will talk about sex. My sisters won't use the word! They say I've become an Anglo! They say I know too much about the Anglo world! But they have television sets, and they have eyes, and they have ears! Back then, when I was twelve, we had no television set, and my mother was really upset when I asked if her sister had a baby before she married the Anglo. She asked me where I got the idea. I told her I was her daughter, and I knew that babies don't just fall from the sky! Hadn't she told me all these years how *I* was born? That was when she took me and hugged me, and said I should be careful, because 'once a man gets to you, that's the start of a new life, and you're never the same!'

"My mother is a believing Catholic. I have never agreed with her on the subject of sex. I loved that talk with her—hearing from her own lips what she believed. But I knew that would be not only the first but the last real talk we'd have. She kept touching my arm and telling me not to 'worry' because the blood would only come for a day or two, and about as often as a full moon. I wasn't 'worried'; I was interested in what my life would be like, later on. My mother had the answer for me: a Pueblo man like my father would be my life! But my father was always telling me to behave myself, and stop running away to the mesa! I was not his favorite; the boys were! I almost asked my mother why she let my father be so unfair with his attention, but I couldn't get the words out of my mouth. I saw the answer in her eyes: don't ask me, because once I start asking myself a landslide will begin, and I won't be fast enough to get out of the way! As I sat there, glad to have a chance at least to be alone with my mother, I remembered the time I saw the rocks falling down off the mountains nearby, and the poor goats trying to escape. The birds were safe! I've wanted all my life to be a bird, the next time around—if there will be another chance!''

Her father wasn't quite sure about "another chance." Some Pueblos were prepared to imagine a cycle of birth and death and rebirth—a migration of souls, as it were. But the Pueblos are not the Hopis, he would remind his daughter—and when she asked him about the Hopis, he would fall into silence. When she asked him why the Pueblos had taken up so readily the Catholic faith, he would reply tersely: all over the world there are Catholics; it is not an exclusively Anglo religion. But she gradually began to lose interest in religion, in what her father or mother believed, in the Pueblos and the Anglos. When she was thirteen, she wanted to leave school, get a job—any job. She kept dreaming of Albuquerque—not of the Anglos there, and not a fast life there, but a store or an office where she could work, make money, and be *alone:* "I think it fair to say that I *hated* everyone in my family at that time, even my mother—especially my mother! She was always telling me to be 'good,' to stay at home, and stop going on my walks. But if I didn't go away and talk with myself, I'd have shouted all day at home. In school I was no good. I didn't like the teachers. They were the worst kind of Anglos—always ready to pat us on the heads and say we are 'nice,' and we should 'try harder.' Try harder to please them! As far back as I can remember—my first years in school—I stared at the teachers until they would notice, and ask me what was wrong. Once I was told I had eye trouble! Another time the teacher really meant business; she called the nurse in, and told her to test me, to see if I *had* to stare! I told the nurse I was doing as we were supposed to do—pay attention!

"When I turned fourteen I refused to go back to school. I knew I'd be told to find a job, so I went and got one before I told my parents I wasn't going to school. I took the bus to Albuquerque, and I found my aunt. My mother kept telling us that she didn't know where her sister lived—only that it was someplace in

Albuquerque. But I knew her name, her husband's name, Fred Haley. What more did I need? I looked up the name in the phone book, and called from the bus terminal, and sure enough, it was my aunt on the phone. She said to come over. I forgot to ask her how to get there. But I asked and found out at the terminal. An Anglo man heard me asking, and wanted to drive me, but I said no thanks. It was the first time I'd had to stop and think about myself like that: sex. I knew he had it in mind! Suddenly standing there, waiting for a bus, I wished I was back on the reservation. But I talked to myself. I told myself that birds have to fly all over, or they'll go hungry; that the sky isn't always clear blue; that the aspens lose the gold of September and October, and are naked for months, before they get a new green dress. I remember the sky that day—it was without a single cloud. I wanted to be on the mesa, watching the Indians below, not standing there with Anglos all over the place, not very nice to each other. When the bus came, I got on and sat down and closed my eyes. The bus driver said he'd call the street, and I didn't want to see anything until I heard him tell me to get off!''

She was welcomed by her aunt, who had a Maria of her own, aged five, at home; there were three older children, at school. The older Maria was tongue-tied, now that she had arrived at her destination. She seemed so intractably silent that her aunt asked if anything was wrong. No. Did she plan to stay in Albuquerque? Yes. But that was all the visitor could do, answer with a yes, a no. Soon the aunt was staring at her and she was staring back— and beginning to feel faint. Through her head a vision flashed: the schoolteachers, and her eye battles with them. Was she doing the same thing here, in her maternal aunt's home? She began to fill up with tears. She didn't know why. She could only offer yet another "no," when asked whether anything was wrong. But the aunt knew that something was indeed wrong. She told the little Maria to go get some cake and milk for her namesake. The aunt also stopped asking questions. She turned off a television set, whose quiz program had intruded upon the tense air. She went up to the girl and without saying a word guided her gently, a hand on the elbow, toward a seat.

Maria ate hungrily. She's always had a craving for sweets. While she worked her way through the middle of the first piece of chocolate cake, she saw her cousin whispering something to her mother. Soon a second piece of cake was there, waiting. Maria went after it, but stopped her hosts from implementing their plan to offer her yet another slice. Conversation got going, thereby: "I said it was too early to be eating so much cake. My aunt said I sounded like one of her Anglo relatives. I asked her why. She said they worry about desserts—but eat more of them than we do. I told her I could eat cake all day. She asked me if I do. I said no, because my mother doesn't let me. She asked me if I'd really want the cake, if my mother said she didn't care how many pieces I ate. I smiled, and she smiled, and my tears went away! We began to talk about Albuquerque, and her life in the city, and the reservation, and my life up there. I asked her if she missed living with her people. She said yes, but only sometimes. She was sure, then, that she'd never want to go back—only for a visit. I told her I didn't want to leave for good, but if I was older, and could get away for a while, I'd grab the chance."

The aunt offered her niece sanctuary, an opportunity to find her bearings in the city. In exchange for room and board Maria could help with the house and the cooking. Maria had to go home and report on the offer. She also had to decide if that was what she really wanted. In fact, she knew, as soon as the offer was made, that she was tempted, but inclined to say no. When she got home, she found herself unable even to bring up the subject of her proposed departure from the reservation. After repeated vows to initiate a conversation, she did what she'd always loved to do—walk, walk alone, walk for miles, early in the morning, until she was out there, climbing the mesa, looking behind occasionally to gain confirmation of her rising altitude, and also looking up skyward repeatedly: "I've never talked to myself so much. I was talking about my life: what I should do. I wanted to leave the reservation, but when I saw my aunt, I realized that she wanted to get out of her home in Albuquerque. She didn't want to go back to the Pueblo people, but she wasn't so happy there in that house they'd just bought, even though it was a lot nicer than our house. I knew I didn't want to take care of my cousin. I was sure my aunt wanted me to do that. I began to dislike her! She looked like my mother! I decided that I was no good. I'd gone to church enough to know all the bad names to call myself!''

She felt better for such a self-confrontation. She sat on her favorite rock, and watched a few clouds go lazily about their respective ways. If only she could become some part of nature—an aspen tree, a cloud, if not one of the hawks she had, for so long, admired! She felt a wind come up, saw some tumbleweeds being chased farther and farther away from the mesa. She was like them—unable to make up her mind, a lightweight spiritually, at the mercy of various external forces. If only she liked school better! If only, she added emphatically to herself, school *were* better! If only she could simply accept her fate—a Pueblo young woman who would, soon enough, be ready to become a Pueblo wife, a Pueblo mother. She needed no one to tell her what was ''wrong'' with herself; she knew only too well: ''I was being pulled by my feet, just as my mother said. My feet wanted to go to Albuquerque, but when they got there, they wanted to go home, and when they got home, they wanted to go to the mesa. The only place where they were able to rest was on the mesa; but in my head I knew I couldn't stay there for the rest of my life. When I came down from the mesa that time, I knew I had to say something to somebody—*do* something. But I didn't know what I wanted to do—because I was a 'misfit.' We learned that word in school, and it was one word I didn't forget. I even took the word home to my family. I told my parents I'd learned a word: misfit. They hadn't heard of it. I told them it meant somebody who wasn't sure what she wanted, so she didn't fit in anywhere—she was off by herself. My mother laughed, and said that the Anglos must have invented a word just for me! I laughed myself!''

That had been a year earlier; now, she wasn't laughing. Now she was calling herself that Anglo ''name''—behaving critically toward herself, and all the while getting angry at what had come to pass: ''I've never in my life felt more confused. I thought of going to see the priest. I figured he'd call me everything bad, and then I'd at least stop doing the same to myself. Then I thought of going to the school, and talking to the principal. He used to tell us he was one-quarter Indian, though we always considered him one-hundred-and-fifty-percent Anglo! I couldn't talk with my mother and my father; they think of us as part of a chain that started back in time and will continue far into the future: hundreds of years, either way! They think you should take the world as it is! When I was fourteen, and a 'misfit,' I wanted to leave the world behind completely, or change it a lot, or find a new world—though I didn't know where that world was, and neither Albuquerque nor our reservation was the place I was dreaming of going to.

"After doing nothing for a while, I decided to give up and return to school. My mother was pleased. My father told me I was coming to my senses. They sounded like the Anglo teachers. I went back for one day, and heard more congratulations for my decision, and knew when I got home that I'd never again set foot in a BIA school. The lecture they gave me almost made me scream: in this world, without a diploma you're no good to anyone. *No good to anyone!* Who were those teachers to say that—*to anyone?*"

She boiled over. She raged within herself, said nothing to her family and friends. She approached the church one day, but turned her back on it: more pieties that would fuel her resentments, her loneliness, her quite fussy sense of herself. On a Sunday, while the others were in church, she again went to the mesa—a personal pilgrimage she would never forget: "I'd been there many times, but this was a different trip. I had to decide what I would do that next day, the next week—for the rest of my life. I was talking to myself on the way. I was trying to find an answer. All of a sudden I saw two men, Anglos. What were they doing there? One had a camera; one had spyglasses. The man with the camera was taking pictures; the other man was looking up at the sky. What was he looking at up there? I saw—a hawk. I wanted to fly up to the hawk and tell it to get away, before they take out a gun and try to shoot.

"But they didn't have guns. They weren't Anglo hunters. They saw me, and came toward me. They were full of excuses and apologies. They didn't mean to be on our 'property.' They didn't realize where they were until they saw me. They were trying to take some pictures for a magazine. They lived in Santa Fe. They were born in New Mexico. They had great respect for us—for Indian people. The man with the camera had lived with the Navahos. He knew all about their history, and all about the Pueblo history. At first I thought to myself: Anglo teachers, like the ones at the BIA school, all full of talk—and themselves. But they were trying so hard to be *nice* to me. I wanted to tell them that *I* didn't own the mesa; and even the Pueblo people don't own the mesa. It's just there, and they don't have to tell me everything about themselves; they can just go ahead and take their pictures. Then they asked me if I came to the mesa a lot, and I smiled, and I laughed out loud, and I said I practically *lived* there. That's how we started becoming friends. That's how my life changed."

She showed the two men the terrain she knew so well. They walked across the mesa, down a gradual descent, up a steep one. They walked up a hill, through groves of aspens, over a lush meadow not far from the Rio Grande. So many scenes on that reservation—from a semi-arid desert to a lush expanse of vegetation nourished by a river, at that point, full and strong. Touched by the continuing interest the men had shown in the sky, *her* sky, Maria found herself pointing to it at one or another moment, as an especially commanding, awesome view came up. The men were even more taken than she ordinarily was. She was surprised at the emotions she felt: rivalry, possessiveness. Who were they to linger so long, be so obviously appreciative? But she also was becoming appreciative; they were a breed of men she'd never in her relatively short life encountered. And she regarded herself as, in fact, a rather old person—all too thoroughly aware of the world's hypocrisies and corruptions, Indian as well as Anglo. Here were two men, however, who appeared different, and a strong challenge to her premature worldliness, if not cynicism: "I was only fourteen, but I was thinking like a seventy-five-year-old Pueblo woman I know thinks. I had given up on a lot of people, as she has, but I believed that the mesa would survive, the sky would, and they were my faith! The two men weren't acting like Anglos, and weren't acting like the Indians I knew. The two men were like small children, trying to discover the world. They made me remember what I'd been like when I was half my age—seven, instead of fourteen.

"I took them all over; I took them everywhere I knew to take them. I ended up going places I didn't know. They were interested in the river, and I had always liked to look at the river from far away. It's not so noisy. When I was a little girl my mother took me to the edge of the Rio Grande, and I started crying. I wouldn't stop until she took me away. She had two rivers on her hands! I was afraid we'd be grabbed up. I couldn't swim. And there I was, ten years later, and I still couldn't swim! The men saw the look of fear on my face. The man with the camera in his hand kept telling me to call him Jack—and not to worry about the river. I said that the river can flood our land, and he thought I was afraid that would start taking place when we got to the edge. I told him I wasn't worried; I just liked to see the river down below, not right beside me.

"They told me of the rivers they'd seen in other places, and I was listening to them, and forgetting about the Rio Grande. The next thing I knew, I was standing right near the river, and hearing it, and enjoying it, and enjoying myself. I'd lost my fear! I'll never forget the sun on the water, and my face staring at me from the water, and the foam. I fell in love with the river, and I've gone back to it many times, and I owe that to those friends. They were the first people I'd met whose spirits really belonged to the mesa, and the river. I used to want to drive others away, even my own people. I used to imagine myself with a gun; I'd shoot any-one who came near. But now I had two others who would help defend the mesa and the land that stretches beyond it and away toward the river."

She did get to call him Jack, and she called the other man Rod.

She was intrigued with Rod from the start: where did he get the name, and why was he always looking at the world with binoculars? For that matter, why was Jack aiming, always aiming, that camera—then click, and click, and click? She was a great one for *picturing* things. She had often wondered whether others, too, carried around visual images so constantly, and used them similarly, as a means of shutting off other sights. In Albuquerque she had pictured for herself the mesa. Inside the BIA schools, she had often closed her eyes and seen the sky. At home on the reservation, in her bed or at the kitchen table, she would conjure up the hills covered with the golden leaves of autumn, or a single cactus—her favorite kind: a cotton tufted one. But what were these men up to? They were "doing a story," but they were not greedy Anglos, or phony "Indian-lovers," two kinds of white people she'd heard about and caught a glimpse or two of. Nor were they like the Pueblos she knew—farmers, keepers of livestock, workers in various Anglo businesses near the reservation, or alas, idle. These men were self-employed, energetic watchers—and a young woman who had kept her own eyes on the world so intently for so long could not help but be intrigued with two fellow creatures who were stalking her native soil with not only their own eyes, but additional ones.

When they asked her to come see them in Santa Fe; come see, too, what they had done—the photographs developed and printed up and enlarged—she was not about to be shy or say no, while intending a firm yes. She asked for their address, was given a card. She asked what would be a good day; they said anytime. She asked for a good time; they said mornings. A week later, still apparently aimless, confused, lost spiritually, she boarded a bus for Santa Fe. She had always hated bus rides—the pavement, the desolation beside the roads, the incursions along the way of Anglo faces and beer and soft drinks and automobiles in the form of billboards, and also, the honky-tonk Indian invitations: beads and more beads; foolish trinkets for children; postcards with idiotic scenes; fake pottery, some of it, she knew, made by Anglo hands in factories, and bought by huckster Indians, willing to acknowledge ownership of anything a gullible tourist was willing to buy. This time the bus ride was different. Her eyes were mostly closed. She saw nothing.

She was remembering the time she had with Jack and Rod. She was wondering whether she'd be spending a few minutes, an hour, a whole day with them. She was asking herself if she'd dare ask Rod about his name's origins. She was thinking that she might invite them back for another visit to her particular preserve. She was hoping they would have an invitation or two for her: to go with them again—to another "spot" they intended to "cover." And she had one additional "thought," fanciful and quite improbable, but not to be dismissed from her consciousness: might they possibly need, from the likes of her, some help? She knew nothing of photography. She was no experienced "guide." She was not a naturalist, or an Indian "informant," skilled at helping Anglos, for one reason or another curious about Indian "ways," obtain some answers to the many questions which seemed constantly to enter their ambitious, eager, hungrily grasping minds. But she knew she had an affinity for them, intangible but real; and even if they didn't know that, or weren't able to offer her the outstretched hand she so much craved and needed, she was already stronger on their account.

Why? She asked herself why and didn't know the answer. They were, she did realize, two kindred souls. She had wrested something inexplicably from their presence—enough to feel excited by hope: "I wasn't calm. I was nervous. I'd never wanted to be with people so much! I was afraid of my own wish to see those two men again! When I got off the bus I had a grinding stomach. I was sure I'd vomit. I was sure I'd had a dream, and those men didn't exist! But in a few minutes I knew they did: I saw the address, and Jack's name, and Rod's name. I pushed the bell, and I expected to hear thunder! I even looked up at the sky, but there weren't any clouds! Then Jack was there, and in a few minutes we were talking, and they were showing me their photographs. I'd never seen anything like them—pictures of everything I'd been seeing for years. I was silent for so long, I stared for so long, they wondered if I'd ever speak. Finally, I knew I had to say something, but I couldn't talk about their pictures. I just thanked them. They told me they were honored I'd liked what they did. I told them I was glad to be with them when they did it. Then they made me coffee, and we sat down, and at last I got up the courage to ask the questions on my mind—though to this day I can't remember the words.''

She had wanted to know what kind of name "Rod" was. She had wanted to know how old Jack was, how old Rod was. She had wanted to know where they came from, how long they'd been doing what they were doing, and how much longer they intended to pursue these special interests. She saw clearly the difference between them and some other Anglos. She was not a complete stranger to Anglo conservationists, environmentalists, naturalists, youthful social or political dissenters, religious cultists or anthropological investigators—the kind of white people Pueblo parents had for many years held up to children as expectable parts of the New Mexico human environment. These two were working people, she concluded—two young men trying to make a living by doing what they liked best: photography. She noted the modesty of their work—no flashy "shots," no effort to turn an already dramatic territory into a melodrama of color, shadows, heights, and depths. If anything, the pictures downplayed the beauty Maria had always recognized and appreciated. An utter novice at something called "photography," she was able to convey her sentiments explicitly, enthusiastically: "I told them they didn't leave the white man's garbage on our land. I told them they weren't the *Conquistadores*. I told them that the wind and the sun and the sky and the river and the trees and the mesa and the hills had given them their love, and they had accepted what had been offered. I didn't understand as I said that, how I dared speak those words! When I finished, I was silent again.''

They were not silent. They told her they wanted to see more of her. Did she come to Santa Fe often? What were her plans? Was she at school? Out of school? How old was she? Had she ever held a job? Did she want one? And then the last question, the one she'd caught herself anticipating in her wildest dreams: would she like to help them out? They had a darkroom. They had a lot of work in that room. They required help, but were as fussy about who would be with them, near them, as she was about who came to her beloved mesa, the hills beyond it.

She told them yes. She told them she would do whatever they needed done. When they brought up the subject of money, she was reticent to the point of mumbled phrases. What she tried to say was that she didn't want any money at all. She wanted to learn from them. She loved, already, their adobe house, the warmth inside it—despite lean furnishings: a single Navaho rug; a couple of cots; a couple of simple unpainted tables, with accompanying wooden chairs; an old leather chair that went up and down; and books, more books than she'd seen even in the library of the BIA school, more books (she realized quickly) than she'd ever seen before in her entire life; and most of all the photographs, some on the walls, some on a brown card table with metal legs, and some delightfully scattered over the floor. She felt as if she were in the presence of an intense mystery: "The priest told my mother once that he thought I believed in magic. I was never sure what he meant by 'magic.' They taught us about Cinderella and 'magic' in school, but I thought that was a stupid story. Cinderella should have walked out on that stepmother long before she met the Prince. And what was so good about him, besides his blond, Anglo face? They never told us that! But that morning I knew what 'magic' was!"

And the mornings that followed. She became their friend, their "assistant." She rode the bus from the reservation to Santa Fe every weekday, came early, and left late. She learned how to use a camera. She learned how to work in their "laboratory." She learned how to display photographs—how to combine things visually. She became so taken with the process of photography—the results, as well—that she lost interest in the visual reality that had, for so long, been a psychological mainstay of hers: the mesa. Besides, she often came home after the sun had set, except in the warmer months; and she came home tired. On weekends she had books she'd borrowed from Jack or Rod—collections of photographs by various practitioners of the art. She would spend many minutes with a particular photograph; she would absorb it thoroughly, then turn away and stare, or close her eyes and stare inward. In either case, she was "looking" at what she'd just seen. After a while, she knew in her mind every detail of a given picture, to the point that her friends, and bosses, and increasingly, her mentors, were telling her that she had an extraordinary memory—"total visual recall." She knew that if such was the case, she was not in possession of a gift—something that fell into her lap, willy-nilly. She had to work hard with each photograph—sometimes hours of dedicated eyeing of details. But there came a moment when she could feel utterly the sovereign of what she'd regarded so loyally, persistently. And the more she used her mind that way, the more she found herself seizing upon certain arrangements of the outside world as a photographer does: *there,* it is *that* I wish to record for others to view.

She was soon enough given a camera to use; and she used it with great enthusiasm, with intelligence, with proper discrimination. She became, within a year and before her sixteenth birthday, a colleague of Jack's, of Rod's. She went with them on their trips to various parts of northern New Mexico, and often suggested ways of going about a certain documentary effort. They came to rely upon her enormously—her prodigious enterprise, her analytic approach, done entirely without pretense or pomposity, her natural, friendly manner. She was, as they kept on telling themselves and her, "intuitive." She knew when she first heard the word that she didn't like it: "I tried to tell them that I had to work hard before I could understand what to do—how to use a camera, how to understand what they were doing when they arranged their photographs in the order they did. But they wouldn't listen to me. I was a 'born photographer,' they kept telling me—and I was 'intuitive.' I told them just to call me a 'mixed-up Pueblo.' I liked that expression they used—about themselves: 'mixed-up.' They meant that they weren't the usual Anglos; and I knew I wasn't doing what my parents thought I should be doing, and I wasn't even doing what I would ever have thought I'd end up doing."

When she had her sixteenth birthday, no special attention was paid at home or among her friends, but Jack and Rod gave her an "office party"; the three of them sipped wine, went out to supper, sipped more wine, cut a cake afterward, baked by Rod, who was the cook of the trio. He was also, at twenty-two, the more accessible of the two men, and the younger. Jack was then twenty-four, and had been married several years earlier and quickly separated. His wife, also an aspiring photographer, had become severely depressed, had required hospitalization, and in the midst of it, killed herself. Maria had appreciated the sadness in Jack long before she knew the facts of his life. She had also appreciated the reflective decency in him—the constant sifting of things he engaged in, the search for meaning.

He was, she once told herself, an old Pueblo at heart—very much like a woman on the reservation who was reputed to be over one hundred years old, and who gave advice sparsely but tellingly. She was often seen taking brisk walks—astonishing in their length for her age—and they were solitary by choice. But occasionally she held court: "We went to her once, my mother and I. My mother wanted to talk about her sister, about moving to Albuquerque. My mother wanted to change our life—be near her sister. She was sick, and asked us for help. My father said no; he said: 'Let her come back home.' My mother didn't know what to do. The old lady listened, and told my mother that she should only go to Albuquerque if she wanted to go there herself. She asked my mother if she did. My mother didn't answer for a long time, then she said yes, she did. The old woman said we should stay where we were. She understood my mother's life.

"I was glad then; I wouldn't have known what to do in Albuquerque! But I had never before understood my mother as well as I did after that meeting in the old woman's house. I knew from that day on how much my mother sacrificed to keep peace in our home, and keep our family together. My father would never go ask for anyone's advice—unless he knew the person would agree with what he wanted to do in the first place. My father has always told us that the Pueblos would not be here today if they hadn't been tough, and kept on a path, and never left it. The old Pueblo woman wasn't like that; she saw what had to be done, but she could bend. My father has an Anglo heart. It took me a long time to realize that. My mother has become his Anglo slave. Jack and Rod were the first Anglos I'd got to know well. They reminded me of that old Pueblo woman!''

She not only learned how to take pictures as an apprentice to Jack and Rod; from the latter she learned how to cook—Spanish and French cuisine, along with a number of ordinary Anglo staples, such as cakes and pies. Her mother was not a very good cook. She threw together cans, relied upon the frying pan—and sweets to take up any slack. Maria was surprised to meet a man who obviously enjoyed cooking, who did such a good job at it. She was also astonished at how delicious food could be. When Rod asked her if he could teach her how to prepare some of his favorite dishes, she readily assented. They cooked up a storm, and Jack had all he could do to be an adequate consumer and judge. The kitchen intimacy caught hold of the two; soon, Maria was wondering if she were in love: "I couldn't get through a morning or an afternoon without thinking of Rod. I wanted to be near him all the time. If I didn't see him for a day or two—and I didn't on most weekends—I was sick in my stomach. I couldn't eat—partially because I missed him and his food, and partially because my mother's cooking tasted so bad now that I knew something better. I was thinking of him when I woke up, and I was thinking of him when I went to sleep. On the weekends I'd go to the mesa, but even then he was on my mind. I'd walk and walk and think to myself that it wasn't like the old days when I'd go up there and forget about *everyone*. *He* was up there, so far as I was concerned.

"After a while I went to the old woman, and told her I was only sixteen, and I'd fallen in love with an Anglo man, and he was twenty-two. She didn't say anything. I tried to tell her more. I told her his name, and told her how I met him, and told her what I did in Santa Fe. Then she stopped me and said I was 'making too much' of my friend. I wanted to turn my back on her and walk out. I looked at her face, covered with lines, and saw her squinting, and leaning forward, because she couldn't hear, and I thought to myself: what does she know about me, and my life? I stopped talking, and we just sat there. Then I told her I was sorry, I had to go. I thought she'd fallen asleep. Her head was falling forward. I was afraid she'd fall down. But she surprised me; she got up and came over to me, and put both her hands on my shoulders. She stood there. I didn't know whether I should get up or stay seated. I looked into her eyes—and suddenly she smiled. She said a few words to me: 'You are strong, and you will get through this. You are a Pueblo woman, and you will learn what is best to do. Our people have always known what is best to do. We are still here, after everything!'

"I didn't like her message, though I was beginning to like her. She was really trying hard to be nice; but she had been giving 'smart' advice for so long, she thought every word of hers was the right one, and the person listening was supposed to get down and pray to her. I realized that she was trying as hard as she could to make me feel good, and somehow she succeeded. I thought to myself that it would be great to live as long as she did, and sit there giving advice to people. I thought to myself that by the time I got to be half her age, I'd no longer be thinking of Rod all day and half the night!"

But later that day and into that night, Rod was back in her thoughts. She began to notice, a week or two afterward, that it wasn't just her problem: Rod was indeed paying her a lot of attention. Finally, he began to talk openly with her about his affection for her. He "liked" her. He "enjoyed" spending time with her. He wished she lived nearby, so they could "go out" in the evening. She listened and smiled, but she found it hard to tell him how much she reciprocated his regard: "I was afraid that I'd never be able to tell him how much I liked him, how often I thought of him. I wasn't shy. I wasn't ashamed of the way I felt. I didn't know how to find words to say what I wanted to say— that I was a Pueblo and he was an Anglo, and I was younger than him, and I didn't have the education he had; but that I had a better time with him than with anyone else I'd ever met, and so all I could do was wish I was with him more and more and more!''

Her silence confused him. It continued—until he stopped showing her attention, began to pull away. One afternoon, as they worked at developing photographs, she declared herself sick. She had to go home. She thought she was getting a bad cold. She began to ready herself for a walk to the bus station, when he told her he wanted to drive her home. She said no, she didn't need a ride; he said yes, he would take her in his car back to the reservation. She reluctantly agreed. On the way home she was silent. So was he. She stared out the window, felt herself getting the chills. She asked him to let her off a mile or so from her home; she wanted to walk, and thought she'd feel better for doing so. But he wouldn't oblige. She became, thereupon, quite angry. She told him that she must get out immediately. He pushed harder on the gas pedal instead of letting up. She fell apart emotionally. She started sobbing. She started screaming: he must leave her alone, let go of her, drop her off right away. She was going to quit her job. She never wanted to leave the reservation again, not for the rest of her life.

She talked as if she had five minutes to say everything in her heart. Then she fell into silence. Meanwhile, he had driven by her house, on toward the mesa. She had not noticed for a while; she was talking continually, looking nowhere, seeing nothing. But when she stopped speaking, she began to use her eyes: "I suddenly realized where I was. I felt as if I'd gone to sleep, and had been dreaming in it, talking in it. I'd told him everything on my mind by the time we got to the mesa. I felt like I used to feel when I was six or seven—glad to be there, and ready to start climbing. He stopped the car. I got out. I ran ahead, because I wanted to get to my favorite spot. When I got there I stood and looked, and saw him coming up toward me. I was quiet. When he saw that I wasn't upset anymore, he started talking, himself, and he did a lot. I learned from him that I'd been so busy thinking of how *I* felt, that I'd never stopped and thought of him!''

She found it hard to give an account, years later, of what her friend Rod had said to her. But, in essence, he told her that he loved her. He told her, also, that because she was a rather young Indian woman, he had feared even trying to get involved with her. The Pueblos, of course, have been no strangers to the Anglos, and vice versa; he knew that. But he also knew that Maria was a proud, sensitive, aloof person; moreover, she had been of so much help to him, to his friend. He feared that any gesture on his part toward her would deeply offend her. Years before there was a "women's movement," he worried about Anglo domination of New Mexico's Indians, among others; about the difficulties and vulnerabilities of the poor—whether Spanish-speaking, Indian, or for that matter, Anglo; and not least, about the way men get along with women. Of that last concern she has distinct memories—his words, given to her, and later recalled: "When he talked about men and women, I knew why I liked him so much! He told me that he grew up in Texas. His father ordered his mother around as if she were his slave. He loved his father; they worked together on a ranch. But he loved his mother, too—and he saw how hurt she'd become. She would cry, but never tell him why she was crying. He vowed one day, to himself, that he would not be the same kind of man his father was—even though he had his name: Rod, for Roderick. He told me his ancestors came from Scotland.

"I told him my ancestors haven't been so perfect, either—the way Pueblo men treat Pueblo women. I was only sixteen when we had that talk, but I knew as much about Pueblo men and women then as I do now! I'd been hearing my father command my mother for years! An Anglo general, ordering the Indian around! When I'd hear about the cowboys and the way they fought with the Indians and tried to take everything away from them, I'd think of the women on our reservation: the men run everything, and the women do what they're told to do. Rod was very nice after he'd heard me tell about the Pueblos; he said we'd learned it all from the Anglos: how to win a war, and rule people—our own, our women! To this day, the word he used, 'war,' has struck in my mind. I remember, a week or two later, watching my mother and father, and realizing that an Anglo man, Rod, had given me the biggest clue about my own people! Now when I hear Indians say that you can't trust any white man, I say no; I trusted one, and he was the best teacher I've ever known."

They became lovers. She would not use such a word. She said—once and tersely—that she had become "very close" to Rod. She said—another time and tersely—that she had gone to the hospital at the age of eighteen with a miscarriage. But she was not about to spell out the psychological details of one of the major personal episodes of her life—for reasons she was willing to bring up, in her thirties, with two other Anglos: "I read in the paper these foolish letters of men and women who are unhappy, or disappointed in love. Everyone is told, today, to pour out words, to say *all*. Pueblos have become Anglos; a lot of my people read those newspapers, and I know a Pueblo woman who wrote a letter, and it was printed, and it told of her love for an Anglo. How terrible! How wrong! If I knew her I would take her to the mesa, my old home, and shake her until she could think better. I would shake her the way I used to shake aspen trees late in the fall, when only a few, dead leaves were left hanging, and I wanted there to be a clean start for the spring to follow! I would shake her until she got rid of her stupid idea that strangers should know of her complaints.

"As for the 'answer' she got, I cannot speak of it without wanting to throw my food up! The Pueblo was told that 'interracial marriages' can mean trouble, so you have to be careful. Who is going to pay me to write such garbage? If I wrote like that—I'd pray to God, pray to the sky and the stars and the moon and the sun, that a strong spear of lightning would be sent down and made to go right to my head. Maybe then I'd become smarter, afterwards. Maybe then I'd stop being a fool. Maybe that Anglo who writes those letters to people who have written her letters should be put on top of one of our hills, and left there—to speak with mountain goats for a year. She might come to her senses.''

Maria apologizes for a certain bitterness of tone. It is not right, she says, to criticize others, then join their ranks. If newspaper columnists can be presumptuous, so can a Pueblo critic of theirs: ''I think there are some people who won't respect other people. And there are some people who won't even respect themselves. Rod was a fine, fine person, because he encouraged me to stay silent when I wanted to be silent. These days, everyone wants to talk about all their worries and all their wishes for the future! I hear our Pueblo boys and girls, on the way to school, or playing on the reservation—and they are so *open* with each other! I want to run away, so I won't be ashamed. I am ashamed for *them!* It is all right to tell another about your life, but to expect in a letter from a stranger advice about what to do—that is holding out for a miracle that won't come. I suppose the person who gets the advice uses it to make a decision. But maybe it helps—to receive a distant message. Maybe I am wrong. Maybe when people give strangers all their thoughts—give themselves to strangers—it can make a big difference. Who am I to know!''

Her miscarriage marked the end of her close friendship with Rod. She talks about it, two decades later, only by indirection. She does want to refer to it, though; she has good memories of a fine, young man—and they are to be shared, if discreetly: ''I wanted the baby. We had decided not to marry, but I wanted the baby. He did, too. But when I started bleeding, I was glad. I hadn't realized until then how frightened I was. What would my family think? What would the others on the reservation think? And what would I *do?* I had no money, and he had no money. I was not going to let him devote himself to me and the child. When we decided not to marry, we decided to take different paths. I joked with him; we'd meet at the end, up the mesa. He would get tears in his eyes. He was, as some Indians would say, 'a strange Anglo'—and they would mean an Anglo who is kind, and not out to stamp on the floor with his heavy boots, and hold his hands on his rifle, or his pistol, and show everyone how loud he can talk.

"He took me to the hospital; on the way I told him the blood was a sign. It was meant for us to say good-bye. He said no, I was making a sign out of an accident. I said an accident can be a sign. We realized we were seeing different worlds. I said that to him several times, and he agreed. When I left the hospital, he was there. I felt better. He was crying hard. I asked him, please, stop. I told him we had to look ahead, not backwards. He was sure I'd lost a son. When he told me that, I got angry. I said it was a girl, and I knew, because it was *mine*. That was our first fight. We had to fight, I guess. We had to separate. Whites and Indians have fought for hundreds of years, and they still do today—in their thoughts and their hearts. We were becoming an Indian and a white man, an Anglo. He wanted his son; I wanted my daughter. Maybe we were fighting the way a man and a woman do! Maybe I shouldn't blame it on the Pueblos and the Anglos—but on Rod the man and Maria the woman. The world isn't only made of cowboys and Indians, Pueblos and Anglos. That day, leaving the hospital, was the first time I realized that I was a woman, not just a Pueblo, and not only a Pueblo woman—but a woman who is Pueblo, but different from a lot of Pueblos. I guess women are different from each other, too—women who are Anglo, or who speak Spanish, or who are Indian. But women are different from men—I was beginning to understand that: no matter if they're Pueblo or Anglo."

Would she care to specify those differences? Of course not! Would she care to say more about what went wrong between her and Rod? Not really. Not directly, at least. It has been years and years since that time—and always, she insists, she lives under its shadow. Ironically, that love (rather than a hate-saturated experience) led to a certain tough-minded awareness: "It may sound crazy, but it was the blood of a baby who wasn't meant to live that turned me into a woman, and Rod into a man! We both had lost a child, but he had lost his, and I had lost mine! I had always, before, thought of him as a good *mother* to me! He liked to cook for me, feed me his 'dishes.' He liked to choose clothes for me. He worried about my teeth; they needed to be brushed! But I saw him, that day we left the hospital, as a father, cheated of a son. And I saw myself as a mother, hungry for a daughter."

He wanted to continue to see her, but Maria said no. She loved him, loved Santa Fe, loved Jack, loved the working life with the two men friends, but she wanted to leave all that, go back to the reservation, go back to the mesa. She was "depressed," Anglo psychiatrists might say—a reaction to a loss, a "traumatic experience." But she had other thoughts about what had happened, and how she wanted to come to terms with herself: "I had to stop in my tracks. There is a Pueblo story—about one of our hunters who kept trying to find his way back home, but he couldn't. He went in one direction, and then another, and then another. He followed every path he could find. He was still lost. Finally, as he was running up and down the paths, the sky filled with clouds, and it began to rain, and there was thunder. The hunter stopped running. He found a place of shelter, and sat down. He thought to himself. He closed his eyes, and tried to remember all he could—how he got where he was. Finally, he saw in his mind a path; he'd forgotten about it. He realized what had happened, and after the rain stopped, and the thunder, he walked slowly and found the path. He got home.

"It's best to know when to sit on the mesa and look at the reservation, and the Anglo land beyond—and the sky above both. Sometimes it's best to talk to yourself and only yourself. I went to the mesa and I watched a lot of clouds pass over me. And I listened to the wind, until I thought I heard something I could understand: I was not the person to live with Rod, be his wife. I wasn't meant to be an Anglo's Indian—held up and admired by good men, Jack and Rod, and their friends. I was me—Maria; not a 'victim,' as they kept telling me, an Indian who had 'suffered' from Anglo 'injustice.' I was a woman who knew 'injustice' in her own home! I wanted to leave home, but not the mesa! I wanted to live in Santa Fe, but not the way I'd been living there before. I wanted Rod to marry the woman he was destined to marry—not me!"

Maria found it hard imagining a return to the reservation, a return to the life she once had lived—as a young girl, as a child at school, as an adolescent in hope, always, of some adventure. She had left the reservation mentally, spiritually—even though she had not moved out of her parents' home. She had not told them that she had gone into the hospital; she had pretended to go to Denver to see a cousin. And her mind began to think of Denver, as (at the age of seventeen) she began to contemplate her future life. She talked to herself a lot, argued with herself constantly, weighed alternatives—an urban, working world, or days and nights on the reservation, helping with the brothers and sisters, and hoping soon for a marriage, a career of motherhood. She wanted neither possibility to become a reality. She wanted something, but she wasn't sure what it was.

Soon she found herself accepting the inevitable—helping out her mother at home. She knew that it would take initiative to seek a job in a city—and the odds of obtaining work in the least satisfactory were slim. She had been spoiled, she realized, by the Santa Fe experience she had stumbled upon. Two persons like Jack and Rod weren't going to show up again on one of her reflective walks near the mesa. Anyway, she'd rejected that alternative as well: the undoubted attraction of being a white liberal's showcase Indian. And she'd been hurt—not really by Rod, but by her own continuing attachment, she had realized, to her people and their fate.

At eighteen she seemed strangely at peace with herself. She had become proprietary about her younger brothers and sisters. She had become, seemingly, indispensable to her mother—who had begun to ail badly from rheumatoid arthritis. And even if Maria found her father's self-important, pietistic, ungenerous personality a constant source of irritation, she had learned to appreciate a better side to him—the stoic confidence he had in the future of the Pueblo people, come what may. She began to wonder whether she would ever marry. She wasn't upset by the prospect of living a single life, but she was troubled by her growing doubt that she would ever be attracted to a Pueblo Indian. Was she destined to be drawn only to white men? Did she, for some reason, shun her own tribe's men? Or had it been a matter of luck, so far—the accident that brought her together with Jack and Rod? Would the "clouds" break eventually—so that she might meet some attractive man: the sun of her life?

She had used that imagery often, but began, at nineteen, to dislike such a way of thinking. On the other hand, she worried that she was turning on her own people—a way they have not only of speaking, but regarding the world: "I didn't want to think of my 'future,' because every time I did, I thought of men—the Pueblo men who wanted to start going out with me, the two Anglo men I'd known, and the Anglo men I'd seen on the reservation. I began to wish there weren't any men around! I didn't hate men. I just didn't like the way I was living from day to day—waiting for a man as if I was a plant, and had to have him: the sun; or waiting as if I had to have him: the rain. I didn't like the way I was brought up to think of men—the ones who gave life to women, as the sun does to the earth. But I didn't want to be against my people—and I knew the Anglos spoke worse words about their women!

"It was no use talking to my mother or to any other Pueblo women I knew; they had surrendered to their men. On my nineteenth birthday I told my mother I was sure I'd never marry; I didn't like any of the men I knew. She became very upset. She said I thought too much about what *I* thought, and who *I* liked. She told me that I should think of the children a man would give me. Otherwise, I'd be 'a desert,' a 'cactus plant,' all by myself. I turned away from her. I was upset. I wanted to walk away and never see her again. I almost did that. I looked at the door. I looked out toward the mesa. I asked myself why I ever came back to this—to listening to my mother speak her words. She told me she hadn't liked my father when she agreed to marry him. She was thinking of us—of *me!* I was supposed to thank her! And I guess I did. I knew that without her I'd not be alive. She got me thinking about my children; she got me thinking like her! I didn't leave. I went back to the dishes. All I could think of was some girl who would be born to me—*my* Maria. I was very upset.

Should I 'kill' that girl by being 'cold' to the men who wanted me? Those were my mother's words: I was 'killing' my future children by not going out with men, marrying one, having the children I would then have. I was selfish when I was 'cold' to those men.''

The young Pueblo woman became haunted by a vision of children as yet unborn. They were, she would later comment, all girls; and she knew, even at the time, that the girls were a collective version of herself. Her life was the result of another woman's avowed sacrifice. Ought she not continue such a tradition? Who was she to do otherwise? Why was she thinking so differently, so much of herself? The accusations had become her own. Once she took to asking such questions she was, in fact, changing the direction of her thinking—embarking upon her mother's road. She would see men, now, as enabling agents of a sort—sperm to eggs. But she remembered her miscarriage. Had that not indeed been a sign—a reminder to her that she might not be destined to have children anyway?

Her mother had a ready answer for such a question—and Maria knew it, without hearing it: ''My mother had told us for years that she had several miscarriages. I'd almost been one of them, myself. What could I do, go tell her that I'd already had one? I tried to find a few minutes for myself. I went to the mesa, and talked; I talked both her side and mine. But she was persuading me—the bad pain in her legs and hands, and still she worked so hard for her children. I was getting in the habit of doing the same; most of the time I wasn't thinking of anything but what I had to do for one of my younger sisters, or for my mother. She had more and more trouble moving around the house. She was in bed a lot. She was getting sicker. And my father was giving me his orders every day—what to do in the house, and what he wanted for supper, and what he didn't like about the house, and how he expected us (me, it was!) to make the changes. I would look at that mesa and wonder if I'd ever get to go there. Days went by, and I was glad to have a chance to go outside in the evening, around ten o'clock, to look at the stars before going to bed.''

For months, for two years, the stars became her mesa. She didn't go visit her old stalking grounds even when she easily might have. She looked up at the evening sky, wondered what secrets it held—wondered, often, if somewhere in that incomprehensibly vast universe there was not someone very much like her, staring into space, perhaps at the star that is our Earth, in the hope of finding a much needed echo. But she knew better than to give herself without qualification to the black void. She had loved the mesa for its life—the small animals, the plants, the grasses, the trees, the water of the mighty river nearby, and of course, the sight of the reservation and its people down below. She knew that space was an alien world, quite likely lifeless. She'd been told that by her schoolteachers. But she'd heard some Pueblo speculations to the same effect: "My mother's aunt used to say that this is where people are—and up in the sky there may be 'spirits,' but no reservations like ours. My oldest brother asked her how she knew. She said 'it has been handed down.' Then he told her that she was right, because he'd been told the same thing in the BIA school! Our aunt smiled, and said that my brother had been given a gift—something 'handed down' by the white man. I waited for my brother to tell her that the white man doesn't 'hand down' anything; he *knows* everything. But my brother didn't open his mouth.

"I think the old woman had got to him! I think she made him realize that the white man has his ideas, and he 'hands down' what he believes; and we have our ideas, and we do the same. Since then the white man has gotten himself up to the moon, but what did he prove—that an old Pueblo woman, our aunt, was right! I'm glad I didn't spend all my life staring at the small lights of the night. They are meant to remind us that we are alive; they are lights in the dark for the eyes of men and women and children. One day I decided to stop leaving my life—of going to the mesa, or to the moon's sky. I decided to let myself live—to let myself have a life on the reservation; to let myself fall in love with a man."

An interesting construction of speech—and she is by no means unaware of what she is saying, or in need of anyone's help in pointing out the implications of her way of putting things. She decided that she had to join the world around her; the alternative was to die—and join the stars, not the mesa: "The soil moves with the wind, knowing there will be a new home. The trees bend, and so does the grass. Who was I to stand still and stiff? I decided to stop counting my birthdays, and stop looking at the stars; I decided to forget the mesa for a while—and listen to the music of the radios. Before the hi-fi sets, there were radios on our reservation! The boys loved them, and so did the girls—and so did the boys and girls when they were together!

"Then Frank came, and because of him I became a true member of our people's family. He had a job with the Federal Government, working with the forestry service—the same job he has now. I was really impressed: a Pueblo man who made a good living, and loved the mesa. I began to think of him, and when I did I got hives! I thought I was sick. I thought I might be getting my mother's illness. But I noticed that it was Frank who caused the hives! I went with my mother to the doctor, and he told me what they were—hives. He said it was my nerves. I already knew! When Frank asked me if I wanted to go for a ride with him in his government truck, I knew I wasn't the same Maria anymore. He wasn't sweeping me off my feet, though. He was like me, and I'm not ashamed to say it: I liked him because he made me think I wasn't a strange one; there was someone else who didn't mind spending a day alone in the woods, near the river, up the mesa—and to do that was his job!"

They were soon married. It was later to be described by her as an "even marriage." She loved helping him in his work—cutting down trees, planting other trees, keeping track of the water level, the vegetation on the reservation. He never pressed her on children; if anything, he wondered whether he really wanted any. She was stunned when she heard him speak his mind on the subject: "We'd been married two years, and I was happy. I didn't care if I never left the reservation again. I hadn't understood how much there was to know about our reservation. All I wanted was to keep working with Frank. Then he told me that he didn't want me to leave him; he couldn't go back to being on his own. He didn't think he even wanted children—'not even one.' I thought he was kidding me, at first. But he wasn't. His face told me so. But he didn't want to have a long talk with me. He seemed upset. I cheered him up, but then I got upset. I was better, though, at hiding my feelings than he was.''

At that time there were no oral contraceptives. Nor were they of a ''background'' that would bring them in close touch with a gynecologist, who could fit a diaphragm. Frank suggested that he use ''rubbers,'' but Maria would have no part of them. Neither she nor her husband knew exactly when a woman becomes pregnant—the pattern of the ovulatory cycle, not to mention its idiosyncratic variations for particular women. For a year they thought fate had heard them; and they were happy. Maria became known to other foresters as a hard-working, knowing helper. She began to wonder why she couldn't become, officially, a forester in her own right. But there weren't any women foresters then—even Anglos. Frank fought the issue out with his Anglo bosses, almost lost his job doing so. Then Maria ''lost'' her period, and she knew what was coming. They had both become saddened by the failure of their efforts to obtain official recognition for Maria as a co-worker. She welcomed the change of vocation: ''I was happy. I knew Frank wasn't. I knew he loved the life we'd lived—the two of us out in that truck he loved; the two of us walking up a path, ready to do something to prevent a fire, or hold the earth down in a place where it might be restless. But I told him that he'd love his child, when it was born; and I kept going out with him—until, one day, I knew I was going to have my baby. He took me to the government hospital, and it took a long time—but our son was born.''

It took too long; and the care she received was not particularly attentive or experienced. For long stretches she was left alone, unheeded in her increasing agony. Her son would be retarded—brain injury that might well have been avoided under other circumstances. The retardation was not severe, but demanded patience—a mother who could free herself of her disappointment and sense of personal injury, and attend to the *child*. She became such a mother. She became an extraordinarily sensitive and effective parent.

She prayed for another child. She wanted to have many children. She had been told no by the foresters; she would say yes to herself, to the whole world, through her children. Her husband was of another mind, however. He was twice bitter at the Anglos—their treatment of her at work, of her in the hospital. They argued about children, argued about sex, argued about where and how to live. They began their marriage at the edge of the reservation; with their baby, they moved near Maria's parents, but she wanted a larger home—and Frank wanted to stay put. More rooms meant to him more children. He had, anyway, wanted a girl. He had never had a close friend of his own sex, had always thought of himself as the parent of a daughter—if a parent at all.

Eventually Frank began to relent: one more child. Eventually she was born. Their son was named after his father; their daughter after her grandmother, Dolores. And eventually they moved to Santa Fe; Frank got an office job, a good one. He missed the work out in the "field," but he enjoyed planning "operations" throughout New Mexico. Maria resumed her friendship with Jack, who had stayed in Santa Fe and had become a good photographer indeed. Rod had gone East. Maria also began to take an interest in Pueblo Indian crafts. She abandoned her hopes for more children; turned to pottery and weaving as her two children became old enough to go to school: "I was torn, at times, between living near the mesa, and living here in Santa Fe. It can be *too* pretty, this town; and there are a lot of phony people here, people who put on airs—and rich, rich people who want to buy everything they can get their greedy hands on. But there are a lot of nice people here—and when I walk to a certain spot, I can see hills, and then higher hills, and then the sky. I can see a valley; I can see land folding into land, hill upon hill. When the sun goes down over those hills my children clap their hands, and say that tomorrow will be another day, and aren't we lucky to be here! They've learned from me what to clap for!

"Now that the children are going to school, I think of the mesa. If I was at home, I'd be there a lot. We go home on the weekend, but only for a short visit. I worry that my children don't live on the reservation, but they are more interested in their people, in the Pueblos, than I was when I was their age. My children ask all the time about their Pueblo ancestors, and they are happy when we take them back to the reservation. The Government is trying to do a better job. I'm not sure whether it's working, but money comes from Washington for jobs—to give us Indians a chance to build ourselves up. Some Pueblos have started learning our language; many of us know only English. And more Pueblos are learning the old crafts of our people—pottery and rugs and other crafts. It is a way to be in touch with our ancestors, and it is a way to make money. I suppose we're doing it for the money. But we live in a world where money is important, whether you like it or not. I know; I have to go buy food.

"Sometimes I wonder what it would be like, living near the mesa, trying to find food, grow food, hunt, and fish. I never lived on the mesa, though; I lived as the Anglos live, only poorer than many of them. When I sat on the mesa and looked toward the sky, across the valley, and up the hills, I thought I could feel my ancestors. The wind, the rain, the thunder talked to me—the voices of my ancestors. The sun spoke to me, the heat of Pueblos long gone from the reservation! Now in Santa Fe we wonder how our ancestors once lived—without mortgages and bank loans and signs that say you are entering a reservation.

" 'Are we really Pueblos?' My children ask that question. They see me selling Pueblo 'handicrafts,' and they ask me why. I tell them we *are* Pueblo, and I sell what I make because I am proud I made it with my own hands, and because I want others to see and know what we as a people can do—try to make good, honest, lovely things; *and* because we need the money. Are we not also Americans? We buy food. We wear clothes made in factories. We use furniture made in factories. We drive a car. And I own a camera; with it I take pictures of our Pueblo land and our people, and my children look at those pictures. I tell them all the time they are many things; we all are: people on this earth, men or women or children, Anglos or Spanish-speaking or Indians.

"The children want to know why, why. I tell them that is what they are, too—young ones who ask why! Then they ask me if I ever ask why. Yes, I tell them, more than I let on! A day doesn't go by that I fail to ask one or two whys. Usually I will be selling a rug, or some jewelry, or the pottery we make in the cooperative, and a white man comes by, and he grabs and touches and pokes and throws something down as if he doesn't care, and hasn't noticed how much work has gone into something, and how easily it can hurt. Then I start with my questions to myself: why are there people like that, and when will our world be free of them—the cowboys and rustlers and trigger-happy soldiers and gold-hungry explorers, who made life so unhappy for my people for so long? I have no answer. The Pueblos have lived for a long time without answers. We try to be good to the land. We try to remember our ancestors. We try to live in peace with others. And we try to live in peace with ourselves. As the Anglos of Santa Fe would put it: that is a tall order!"

Sometimes those "Anglos of Santa Fe" get to her; she hears a remark or two from them, and she feels the blood in her face, the words at the tip of her tongue. Once she heard herself characterized—an Anglo mother to an Anglo child: "There, over there, is a Pueblo, a Pueblo woman." Maria was ready to go over and say to the child: "And there, over there, is an Anglo woman." But a few hours later she had cooled down, and was grateful to her: "If she had been nearby, I would have gone right up to her, and said yes, you have put your finger on me, and I'm glad. I would tell her that I'm glad because I am what she said I am, and I'm glad because it's clear to her, to the whole world, that I am what she said I am: a Pueblo woman. I wonder what kind of woman she really was. What kind of Anglo? There are so many kinds! I know what I am: a woman who is a Pueblo. My photographer friends used to say: 'looks can deceive.' I hope I didn't deceive that Anglo lady and her child. There are many kinds of Pueblo women, too, I guess!"

part five
DREAMING

PATIENCE—ALL through her childhood Eileen heard it extolled: a great, a prized virtue. Her father had known a lot of patience in his youth; he experienced the joblessness of the Great Depression. Now he lives in an adjacent town, comes once a week to visit. When others visit, Eileen insists that he speak for himself. On one occasion he says this: "My daughter can't forget the Depression, even though she was born at the tail end of it, in 1940. I'll tell you the reason: on my deathbed I'll be thinking of those awful years. Every American workingman who is young enough not to have lived through that time should be told what it was like. I told Eileen what it was like, as soon as she was old enough to understand. And her sister, I told Jean, too. And my son, I told him; I told Eddie so many times, he said once that he felt as if he'd been in those long lines, waiting for a handout of food. The big boys, who owned the country, didn't give a damn what happened to the poor people. Millions were out of work. The country was paralyzed. All people wanted was work—no handouts, just work. But we got nothing—only hunger and cold-water flats and lines for soup.

"I would have joined a revolution then. I was desperate. My parents came over here from Ireland, and look what they found. My mother got pneumonia and died in 1934. But it was her heart, not her lungs; her heart was broken. I left school after that, and tried to find work, any work available. I was a teen-ager. I wanted to collect garbage, sweep floors, run errands—but no one wanted me. My father was sick, too. He had tuberculosis. He refused to stay in a hospital, because he wanted to be with us. My uncle tried to take us all in, but he had no job, either.

"He was an electrician, but a lot of good it did him, the apprenticeship he had with a master electrician. I used to see my father and my uncle cry, like babies. When grown men are reduced to that, you don't forget it. I was in tears myself, after all the nos I got. Then I met Eileen's mother, and we fell in love. She was lucky, very lucky; she'd landed a job at a Woolworth Five and Ten because the manager liked her looks. He made passes at her, and she refused. She was sure she'd be fired. But *he* got the ax—because he also flirted with a few customers and one of them reported him. I'm ashamed to say it: I got married on my wife's nerve, and we lived on her money until 1939, when the war began, and President Roosevelt began to rearm the country, and everything picked up—the economy and, let me tell you, my spirits. I got a job in a General Electric factory, and I stayed there until I retired."

Eileen remembers her father leaving the house for work, early in the morning. Years later, decades later, she could capture for herself or her guests a moment, often repeated—in fact, daily lived out—of her childhood: "I was always an early riser. My mother would tell us that I was God's reminder to her and my dad that the day was soon to start! When I was one or two, apparently, I would start crying at five thirty or six o'clock, and they'd know that it was time to get up. When I was old enough to go to school, I just woke up—always, it seemed, a few minutes ahead of the sun. I'd lie there in my bed and wonder when I should get out of bed and go to the bathroom. I'd ask my parents if they minded, when I got up; they said no, I was entitled to 'meet the day' any time I wanted. That was my father's way of saying it—'meet the day.' He was an early riser, too; of course, he had to be one. He left the house at a quarter to seven every morning. When I was young, we had no car. He'd take the bus to the factory. Later, we got a car, but he would still leave early. He liked to stop at a diner and get a cup of coffee in his stomach, and those donuts. My dear Lord, how our dad loved donuts! My mother used to tell us that the biggest failure of their marriage was her inability to make donuts. She tried for a while, but she couldn't do the job. My father would look at the donuts she made, and he knew in advance what to expect. He'd try to be brave and pretend; he'd say 'good, good' while he gobbled up one or two of the pile—but she knew, my mother did, what was truly going through his head.

"I remember the last time she tried. He came home, and there was the stack. She'd covered them with a lot of powdered sugar. He must have hoped that he would have luck, this time. He grabbed two, and pushed them into his mouth. Then he said they were 'great.' But even I knew he wasn't being sincere. My mother started crying. She said she was going to get a job, so she could buy Dad his daily quota of donuts. She was only kidding, but I remember the joke—I guess because it's the first time I ever heard my mother talk about the possibility of working. I recall asking her where she'd work. She told me in Woolworth's, in the Five and Ten, as she had when she was first married. Or, maybe, in the drugstore: Evans Drugstore, where she could hand out free ice-cream sodas to me and my sister and my brother! She told us she was only kidding—because we must have all looked as if we were worried!

"More than anything else, work for me meant leaving the house early, the way my father did. So I must have wondered what would happen if they *both* left the three of us young kids before seven o'clock. But I now realize that my mother never could have held a job down for very long. She was too religious; I mean, she was always interrupting herself at home to pray. She would have done so at work—and got fired! I never could understand why she prayed so much—until I began to see that it was her way of calming herself down, and not losing her temper (the way I do!) around the house. I wish I could pray the way she did! I wish I could believe in God the way she did!

"She'd pray for my father as he'd leave the house. More than anything else, I remember that: he would be putting on his coat, and getting his lunchbox under his arm, and saying good-bye to us, and she'd be saying a prayer for his health and his safety. We'd be standing there, waiting to be kissed good-bye. We hadn't had breakfast yet, but we could smell the coffee he'd made, and sometimes the toast or eggs. He'd often give us a little sermon before he left—about how we should pay attention to our mother and to our teachers, and we shouldn't fight with each other,.and we were two sisters and a brother, and we should be close together, and if we weren't, then that would be very sad for us later on. Or he'd remind us of a chore we had to do. Or he'd tell us that he'd see us soon, just ten hours or so later! He was so cheerful—and I used to wonder why. I knew he worked extremely hard. I knew he came home dead tired and needed a long shower to get the dirt off him. He used to tell us never to follow in his footsteps. He used to tell us to try to get ahead, and 'do better in life.' Mainly, he'd tell my brother Eddie that; but he also wanted my sister Jean and me to have an easier time than he'd had. I don't want to give the wrong impression; he wasn't unhappy, and he wasn't the complaining type at all. He loved having a job to go to. He never let us forget what it had been like when he had no job—how 'lousy,' how 'rotten' he'd felt. He'd leave the house happy to be going somewhere. And he left the house happy for my mother's prayers, and for the sight of us, standing and smiling at him and waving good-bye. I think those early-morning times had a strong influence on my life, but don't ask me what kind!"

She was always qualifying her obviously astute, introspective reflections with a disclaimer, or a renunciation: far be it for her to have answers, or even to pretend to know what it is all about— life. But she asks, rather commonly asks, that question, a "leftover," she calls it, of her mother's religious way of putting things: "All my life I've had a habit of looking out the window, and asking myself whys—one after the other. Why am I me, and not someone else? Why did God put us here? Why did my sister Jean get polio? Why was my daughter born retarded? My mother used to tell us that there are no answers this side of Heaven to the really big questions in life; only God knows why everything is the way it is. But she told us to pray for His guidance, and I guess I do that a lot. Sometimes I just think, though. My mother worked those beads of hers overtime. I'm more like my father. I ask questions about life, but I don't ask them of Him, the good Lord. The way I see it, He's got a lot more important people to listen to than me.

"Who am I, after all? I'm just a housewife, an American woman with a husband and three kids, so why should Jesus Christ Almighty stop in His shoes and listen to my whys, and my bellyaching? But even if He's not listening, I have to get away and be by myself and let my head settle down. I used to hear my mother say that; she'd tell us when we were little that she could take us most of the time, no matter how much we fought and no matter how much trouble we got into; but she needed a few minutes every day to be all by herself. So, she'd demand that we sit in separate chairs and look at books or listen to the radio, and she'd go into her room, and she'd do her praying—have her talk with Jesus, I guess it was. My father believed in his religion, too; but he said he had all he could do to get by, from day to day, and he didn't have time to pray.

"I remember the routines of our life—when I was a kid, growing up and not even knowing that I was doing that. (Children don't know what's happening to them until it's happened, and then presto, they're no longer children!) I remember my father whistling, then saying he didn't know what he was whistling about, then saying he *did* know—we had our next meal coming, and a roof over our heads, and clothes to wear. I remember my mother telling us not to become 'too worldly.' It took a long time for me to figure out what she meant. I'd ask her what she meant, and she'd say that when we fought over toys, or complained that someone was getting a bigger helping of food, then we were being 'worldly.' But she'd save and save, and then she'd buy us nice presents! And she admitted to me once, when we'd gone downtown, that she would like to have a fur coat.

"I must have been ten, then; I was becoming a little bolder with my thoughts, and my words. I said: 'Mum, don't let yourself get too worldly.' She looked at me real hard, and I was afraid for a second or two; but she smiled, and said I was right. I felt like a schoolteacher must feel. But then I kept having a dream afterwards—that my mother was walking into the house with a fur coat, and that I was beside her, and I had one on, too, and that my father saw us and said he was proud of both of us. The dream wasn't completely happy, though. My father's face would suddenly change, and he'd tell us both that now we were in debt, 'bad debt' (he was always telling us about being in 'bad debt,' even if it was five dollars he owed the druggist or variety store) and he'd have to work and work to get us 'clear.' That's when I'd wake up, and I'd feel terrible—as if I'd gone and done something real bad. I never dared tell my mother about that dream. It was as if we'd both conspired to be evil, to commit a sin. I had the dream maybe ten times—until I decided to confess to the priest that I was guilty of the sin of greed. He said yes, I probably was, but I'd be forgiven, and not to worry. He had a nice, friendly voice, and it worked a miracle on my mind: I stopped having the dream. I forgot about a fur coat. I've never had one; I've never wanted one. To tell the truth, if I won a million dollars in the lottery tomorrow, the last thing I'd want would be a fur coat. It must be because of my childhood memory—like the psychologists say!"

When she was a year older, eleven, she had quite different dreams—nightmares, actually—based upon a real and terribly upsetting family experience. Her younger sister Jean got polio—before the Salk vaccine was available. She had to go into a respirator. She nearly died. She was left with a partial paralysis on her left side, affecting both the arm and the leg. She required, of

course, prolonged hospitalization, and constant outpatient re-
habilitative efforts for months after that. For Eileen such an event
would prove unforgettable and decisive. Indeed, years later she
would say, without any qualification, that her sister Jean's illness, more than any other single occurrence, had shaped her life:
"I am the person I am because my sister's struggle with polio
made all of us different. We had to stop and think about life. We
had to ask ourselves what we believed in. Were we going to
stand by Jean, and fight for her—so that she'd be able to live a
halfway normal life? Where would we find the time and energy to
do so—and still live our own lives? And the money—how would
all those bills be paid? And over and over again, my mother's
question: why did this happen to us? I think she drove the priests
crazy asking it, even though she knew they had no satisfactory
answer. One priest, Father Tim Connell, finally asked her to
come see him. He told her she must stop asking that question; he
told her she was behaving in a 'disedifying way'! She came home
and told us that she would no longer bother any of us with her
questions. She let us know what Father Connell had said. I remember thanking the Father in my mind.

"My mother had become so wrapped up in Jean, in Jean's illness, and in her religion—her questions to God!—that I felt like
an orphan at that time. My poor father had a second job, to help
pay the bills that were coming at us, one after the other, so we
never saw him except for a few hours on Sunday, and he'd be
sleeping, the poor man—'resting his weary bones,' he'd tell us.
My mother was living in two worlds: the hospital and the church.
At home she'd be a ghost of herself. Jean was gone. Eddie was a
sad lad of five or six, always crying. They drove me wild, his
tears. I wanted to hit him—or hold him tight. I remember running
out of the house. Lucky for me I had a good friend; her name was
Kathleen. It was her house that took me in. It was her mother
who got me through the worst of that time—a small, thin lady,
very kind: Mrs. Clifford. She was a nurse.''

The comfort of another home. The outlook of another kind of
woman. The good health of a friend. But that health was not

taken for granted, for reasons Eileen needed no one to explain: "I was always wondering, those days, whether I'd get polio, too. And the closer I got to Kathleen, the more worried I got about her, too. Would she get sick, as well? Nonsense, I know now. But I was a kid, then—a girl whose family was in tough shape. Not that Kathleen came from rich people. Her father drank a lot. He was an automobile mechanic. He was rough. He'd swear all the time. I remember Kathleen blushing when she'd hear him say some awful word. She was very light-skinned, and she'd suddenly turn red. She'd leave the room; she'd go lock herself in the bathroom until she was back to her regular color! Her mother was the strongest woman I've ever met. She seemed able to put up with anything. She looked weak, delicate; but she was made of iron. She ran her home as if it was a ship. Everything had to be just right. She was like a clock—everything on schedule. Four afternoons a week she left for the hospital—the three-to-eleven shift. I still remember her—the white uniform, white shoes. Not a spot anywhere. Lots of starch; I remember the crinkly sound as she walked. And her nurse's hat—very glamorous to any kid; and a touch of magic to me, because it was the nurses who'd worked so hard to keep my sister alive, and to get her going on the road to recovery.

"I can remember the exact moment I decided that I wanted to become a nurse myself, when I grew up. I was visiting my sister Jean; Kathleen and I came to see her. She wasn't feeling too good that day. She was moody with us. She said she'd been wondering what her life would be like—partially crippled. I was afraid she'd start crying, and never stop. I used to think, at the time, that life was really rotten and unfair, and that if I'd been in my sister's shoes, I'd have just given up completely. Then a nurse came in the room, one of two or three nurses Jean had become attached to. It was miraculous. The nurse didn't coddle my sister. In fact, I thought the nurse was being a little tough. She told Jean to eat. She told Jean to straighten out the table beside her bed. She told Jean she should dress herself, rather than stay in pajamas all day. And Jean ended up smiling and going along. Later, I realized that when you're in a low state of mind, sympathy isn't always so good for you, because the danger is you'll wallow in pity and self-pity. I felt better myself, watching the nurse check up on my sister, and straighten everything out in the room.

"I began watching the nurses more carefully that day, and I remember thinking that there's no better profession for a woman than being a nurse—and if I could, I'd be one when I grew up. I told Kathleen that on our way home, and she told her mother, and they both said I'd make a good nurse, and I was really proud to hear them say so. When I got home, though, it was a different story. I think my parents were so worn out, because of Jean's illness—so tired of sickness and hospitals—that they were beginning to feel trapped. When I mentioned being a nurse, it was as if another door was being closed on them! My father said it was 'depressing work.' When I started to disagree, he fell back on money—his old standby. He said you had to pay big tuition bills in nursing school, and you lose money for a few years because you're not working in a regular-paying job. And where would they ever get an extra ten dollars, never mind hundreds of dollars to pay my bills? My mother joined in, too; she said that the Lord had given us a 'big problem' to face—Jean's illness—but that we shouldn't 'overdo it.' I wasn't even sure of what she meant. I'm not sure she was. She was fighting back tears when she said that to me; and in a few seconds was off holding her beads. I dropped the subject."

But only for a while; in high school, even with Jean much better and out of the hospital, Eileen held fast to her ambition: nursing. She favored science courses. She especially liked biology. Unlike many of her girl friends, she took a strong interest in dissection of frogs. For doing so, she began to be known as a bit "peculiar." At the time girls were not supposed to have such inclinations—at least so thought a number of her classmates, young men and women both. Few students in her class were headed for college, anyway. When, one day, she told the three co-workers sharing a table with her in the biology lab that she would like to be a doctor, even though she knew she probably wouldn't have a chance to become one, she was greeted with surprise, cynicism, and not a little contempt by the one young woman and two young men: "I thought the girl would be on my side, but she was the worst of the three. She only took biology because she was terrible in languages and had flunked social studies. She was trying a 'new course.' But she wasn't doing well in that course, either. She was very good at typing; she wanted to be a secretary—and she kept razzing me: who did I think *I* was—not wanting to do what 'everyone else' was quite pleased to be thinking of doing! That line got the two guys going. One said something I'll never forget, I guess because he hit the jackpot: you have to be rich to become a doctor, and none of us were in that league. I couldn't argue with that—not when my father had told me that for me to be a *nurse* was more than he could ever afford. I just mumbled that I was only dreaming.

"Next, the other guy told me off: he wanted to be President of the United States! I told him I'd vote for him! He said that when he got elected, he'd pay my way through medical school. That silly, stupid girl then started lifting her eyebrows and cooing: was he proposing to me? I asked her if *she* wanted to be the wife of a future president—maybe! No, she said—she wasn't like me; she wasn't one to put on airs! I wanted to tell her that it wouldn't help her, even if she did put them on; she was a jerk then, and would always be one. But the longer we kept talking about medicine and nursing, the more uncomfortable I felt. I wanted to drop the subject cold. Thank God, the bell rang and we had to break up and go to the next class. But I wouldn't forget that table talk—ever."

Long after her sister was home and well on the way to a reasonably active, useful life (she went to a special school, did quite well there, eventually ended up marrying a man who also had fought his way to a successful recovery from polio), Eileen found herself walking near a hospital, not the one Jean stayed at, in order to look, "just look." She knew that the nurses' shift changed around four o'clock, and so she made up excuses for herself to happen by then. Scenes lingered in her mind afterward: nurses rushing into the hospital, or leaving it for home, often in pairs, sometimes in larger numbers—a flock of white uniforms hurrying along; nurses playing tennis in an adjacent hospital-owned court; a doctor and a nurse walking out of the hospital together. The stuff of soap operas. So some of us all too easily might conclude—forgetting the banalities, the obvious clichés of thought and feeling, the predictable directions of our own particular lives. For Eileen the hospital was a place of purpose, action, achievement; the nurses she saw were admirable, accomplished human beings, living enviably exciting lives—of a kind she wished for herself.

If she had, by high school graduation, given up her dream, she was not without a certain stubborn resourcefulness. She scoured the want ads for hospital jobs, found none. She adjusted her hopes to "reality": why not become a secretary in a hospital. She'd been taking "typing and transcription" courses as well as biology, and she could at least, she concluded, work near nurses, if not become one. But to be a medical secretary required additional schooling, she learned. And her parents had for some time taken her continuing interest in nursing to be a dangerous sign of sorts—an invitation to fate: once again the family would be entangled with the lame, the sick, the halt. They had had quite enough of doctors, nurses, wards, intravenous setups, shrill and demanding pages, ambulances whining their way through traffic to an emergency ward. They had been, for years, trying to free themselves, emotionally and financially, from an overwhelming assault. Why must their daughter Eileen keep trying to remind them of a world they badly wished to forget?

The mother talked of the "sin of pride"; in some way and for some reason Eileen had decided to leap over the normal "course" of her life—entertain large, immodest visions of what ought be in store for herself. The father saw himself confronted with an increasingly independent young woman who had lost, it seemed, a proper respect for the realities of *class:* how dare someone, virtually penniless, her extremely hard-working parents in serious debt, aspire to a *profession?* Hadn't Eileen's mother taken a job in a nearby bakery, selling pastry for eight hours, and glad to be doing it—because the hospital bills arrived unrelentingly, and they (like millions of others at the time) had no health insurance plan of any kind? Didn't young Eddie talk of following his father to factory work, or learning a trade: welding, he hoped? As for Jean, her boyfriend's father knew a politician, and she had been promised a clerk's job in a city hall, as befitted someone still with the "residues" of polio. And there Eileen was, still with "stars in her eyes."

The expression was not one spoken behind the young woman's back: "It got bad at supper. My mother was more tired than she admitted to herself, never mind us. She'd be up at the crack of dawn, so that she could go to an early mass before starting work. She was on her feet all day. I knew, then, that she hated the work, but I would never have dared say so. She was always pretending—the *nice* people she waited on, the *good* pastry she sold. She never brought any home, and I could understand why: she had her fill of it at work, the sight and smell of the stuff; and besides, she'd never bought any there before she'd started work, because to her they were as "heavy as lead," the donuts my father once or twice had got there. The harder she worked, and the more she put on a happy face, the more intense her praying became, and the more irritable she became with me when the subject of my 'life' came up, as it did, the nearer graduation day came. What would I do—meaning, what kind of job would I get? And if I dared mention anything remotely connected to nursing— medical secretarial work, lab work—I heard about the 'stars' I was seeing in my eyes. I began to resent them, all of them at home. I wanted to leave, but I didn't know where to go, and I was only sixteen or seventeen. Besides, I felt terrible for having such feelings. So, I'd go to church—but sometimes confession didn't help, either."

One priest reprimanded her, several times—which she did not believe she deserved, in fact was convinced she did not. As a result, she stopped going to confession—at a time (the 1950's) when she could expect from other Catholics far less sympathy for such a decision than would now be the case. She even contemplated refusing to attend church—but to do so would signify an open break with her family, especially her mother. She could, of course, lie—pretend to go on Sundays, but not do so. She had often gone to a late mass, whereas her parents always rose early on Sundays, too, and headed for church. Indeed, one sign that she was virtually grown-up had been the churchgoing habits she had developed; attendance on her own was taken for granted as a "right" by others in the family. In church, at the time, her mind turned to fantasies of escape—miracles she had no expectation that God would deliver her way: a handsome doctor to drive off with her; a sudden windfall of money, left her by a relative no one knew existed; a letter from a nursing school offering a full scholarship, and then some in extra cash, to appease her father, who continued to think not only of what a "career" for his daughter would cost (an impossible sum), but what would be, thereby, forsaken in the weekly income that a job provides.

A week before Eileen's graduation a "sign" did come. She saw an advertisement in the paper for "help wanted": a person to work in a hospital—the laundry department. She had never before connected in her mind the words "hospital" and "laundry," but now she realized her error—realized the source of all those sparkling white doctors' uniforms and nurses' uniforms, and the wonderfully starchy and clean sheets that were always being changed when Jean was sick in that hospital bed. Telling no one, Eileen went to apply for the job, was interviewed, was questioned hard about her motivation—did she realize that the work was tough, sweaty, sometimes quite unpleasant?—and was, finally, promised the job. She was strangely euphoric, in view of the work ahead of her: "They must have thought I was crazy, those people in that personnel office. I guess I *did* have 'stars' in my eyes! I was going to work in a hospital, at last—one way or another! But to them, I must have been a strange one—actually *anxious* to take such a 'dirty job.' I remember them cautioning me that way: 'It's not always easy work, and sometimes it's a

dirty job to do.' I smiled and said yes, I understood! I was thinking to myself, at the time, that being a nurse wasn't so easy,
either!''

The laundry was located in the basement of the hospital. Eileen
had to report to work at seven thirty, and leave at four; a half
hour for lunch. In a large, windowless room the machines did
their job—clothes soaped and washed, clothes dried. But before
that could happen, someone had to collect a busy hospital's
supply of dirty bedsheets, dirty pillowcases, dirty gowns, dirty
uniforms. They came down a chute, each day's harvest—from
one ward after another, load after load. It was Eileen's job to be
on the receiving end. Each early morning she walked into a small
room, its walls of unpainted cement, its floor covered with piles
of material for the huge washing machine in the laundry, across
the hall. Much of the linen was foul-smelling. The room, needless to say, reminded Eileen of a toilet. She was wont to breathe
through her mouth at first, until she had picked up several loads
and pushed them in the cart to their destination. She felt better
when she had dumped her load in the waiting hot water and soap
of a boilerlike washing machine. After she closed the door, saw
the red light go on, a signal that the linen was being worked on,
she turned and walked away, breathing once again through her
nose.

At first she tried hard to be stoic, lest she be caught grumbling
or downhearted by the manager, or some of the women who had
other jobs—moving the wet laundry to the drying machines, sort-
ing out the finished loads, arranging piles of sheets, pillowcases,
gowns, uniforms, for various wards or outpatient services. But
there were moments of strain and doubt: ''I was all right a lot of
the time; but every once in a while there was a terrible mess to
sort out and load—as stinking a collection of laundry as anyone
could ever imagine! I'd walk into that room, and it would be
early, very early in the morning, and I'd have had no breakfast,
because I knew what was ahead, and I'd not be breathing through
my nose, but even so I'd get sick, bad sick—my stomach. I'd
feel like vomiting. I'd feel like fainting. I'd feel like quitting! I'd

just stand there, paralyzed. I'd ask myself what in the hell I was doing there—and for no big salary, either. I was getting a low salary, much less than I'd have made if I'd been working as a secretary, or even a clerk in a store. But it was a tight market then, especially for women. And I had this crazy idea that I'd be happier in a hospital than anywhere else.''

At times, she was. During her coffee breaks, ten minutes in the morning and ten minutes in the afternoon, and during her lunch period of a half hour, and during occasional "slow periods," when the machines were operating at full capacity, and the major backlog of "dirty stuff" had been cleared away and handed over to a row of carts, she could wander off safely and look and listen and dream—and return strangely exhilarated to her smelly if not brutish basement reality: "I'd go up to the coffee shop and sit there and sip my morning cup of tea, and have the first food of the day, a donut. I'd watch the people come and go. I'd try to make out what they were talking about. I'd enjoy myself, imagining myself one of them, a nurse or a lab technician, or a medical student. Every once in a while there would be a woman among those medical students—the luckiest of the lucky. I didn't envy her as much as I imagined myself being her! Well, I probably did envy her; but, you know, if you were born as poor as I was, and your parents were as humble in their outlook as mine were, you don't set yourself all those big goals, and so you don't feel too disappointed or jealous when you see someone up there, on top of the world! That's my psychology—my explanation of why I admired those women, and didn't begrudge them their success.

"I was a busybody. I'll have to admit that. I was always trying to overhear people, or figure out who they were and where they came from. And I kept my eye on the hospital romances—the doctors and the nurses, the medical students and the nurses, and the boyfriends of the nurses who came to the hospital to meet them for lunch or coffee, to pick them up at the end of the day. Sometimes I got lost in what I was seeing or hearing; I'd come back to work a few minutes late. But by then I'd proven myself. I was a hard worker. After a few weeks the boss told me to take an hour off for lunch, because by the middle of the day, there wasn't much for me to do, anyway. With that bonus of time, I could go exploring—over to the nurses' dormitory. I could watch them coming in and out, and have my dreams! But one day one of the older women who worked in the laundry saw me hanging around near the dormitory, and she guessed why. Later, during a coffee break, she took me aside and gave me what she called a 'heart-to-heart.' She told me I was an 'attractive colleen,' and I was wasting the best years of my life in that 'dungeon,' lugging around soiled linen, and sweating off pounds I couldn't afford to lose, and taking all those salt pills. She said I should escape, fast. I told her I needed a job, and besides, I liked working in a hospital. She told me I should try to become a nurse's aide, if I couldn't become a nurse. She knew my mind! I was surprised at the time, but now I realize it must have been so obvious, how I felt, when she saw me during that lunch hour near the nurses' home.''

After several months of conscientious, exhausting labor in the laundry department, Eileen did begin to think of an alternative kind of work. But she feared that she could not, as an employee, inquire about the nurse's aide training program. And she didn't want to be a nurse's aide; she wanted to be a nurse. The summer had worn her down, though: outside heat on top of inside heat. She began to slow down at work, to stop wandering around the hospital as if it were a magical place, and instead, to stand near the pile of dirty clothes and linen with a feeling of melancholy and, increasingly, bitterness. She became prone, at home, to self-pity. And she had virtually no social life, because she was so tired after she left the hospital. On weekends she wanted to stay in bed late, and on the weekday evenings she wanted to go to bed early. She attributed such obvious lassitude to "salt depletion," a syndrome she heard much about in the laundry. But how much salt could make up for a person's moody resentment at her fate in life? She knew enough to ask herself that question. Finally, after four months of "sticking it out," she decided to quit. She was about to hand in her notice when another kind of fate beckoned her: a chance meeting in the coffee shop with a medical student.

Years later she had no trouble recalling the first conversation they had: "It was crowded, and he had to sit at someone's table, and I was looking at the morning paper, and suddenly I looked up, and there he was. I smiled a little, but I was too shy to say hello. He was a friendly sort from the start. *He* said hello. He saw me reading the sports page, and he began talking about baseball. Then he introduced himself: David Stein. I told him my name, and I felt myself blushing! He asked me if I worked in the hospital. I said yes. Suddenly I didn't want to tell him where I worked. I kept quiet, mostly. He talked. He told me he worked in the hospital, too; he was a medical student. He was in his third year. It was the hardest of the four you had to go through, if you wanted to graduate. He was rushed, I could see. He gulped his coffee down. He had to go. But just as he was leaving he asked me if I wanted to meet him later and 'grab a bite of lunch.' I nodded. I was too shy even to say yes! Those were the 1950's! But all I could think about was him, for the next two and a half hours. I even started singing, and the others in the laundry room noticed. When I saw them smiling at me, I began to worry: they'd see me with him in the hospital cafeteria! I was all worked up! It's easy now to laugh at myself. At the time I had no sense of humor!

"When I met him, I was silent because I was excited, rather than out of shyness. I tried to smile and be friendly, though. Luckily, he was a great talker. All I had to do was listen to him! He was full of medical student stories, and for me it was like going to a good movie; I got lost in his world. When we'd finished our lunch—I remember, we both had grilled cheese sandwiches and milk—he asked me if we could have lunch the next day. I said yes; and from that moment I waited for the next twenty-four hours to pass. I even had a dream about him! Of all the crazy things (I thought at the time), I dreamed that he and I were walking, and we bumped into a priest, and he said he was lost, and could we help him, and I said yes, and pointed toward a road, and there was the church, in the distance. I woke up nervous and upset. Later, months later, when I had that dream again, I'd be much clearer on what my mind was thinking!''

They met for lunch day after day, but that was all. His pressing medical school burden made him reluctant to plan his social life far in advance. She found herself depending upon those lunches; they became her sun and moon. She would comment, long afterward (and in the midst of quite another life) that she never, except then, had been so time conscious. For her the noon hour was a reverse of Cinderella's midnight. Eventually they started "going out." He liked jazz. She knew little about it. He taught her what he knew. He told her of books to read. He bought them for her. He introduced her to the world of art; took her to a museum she only vaguely knew existed. It didn't take her long to fall in love with him; but she kept wondering why he liked *her*.

And it was the 1950's, and she was of Catholic upbringing, and he was a studious young man who hadn't had the most active love life: "I suppose that these days we'd be considered a strange couple! For a long time, a couple of months, David never touched me. When he did start kissing me, it was a very quick kiss he gave me! I'd never really gone out with anyone more than a few times. And my parents were very upset about my going out with David, because he was Jewish. I had to be home early, and they kept telling me I was headed for trouble. My mother started praying for my soul! When I kept going out with him, she started praying for *his* soul! My father kept telling me I was risking a 'bad fall.' He said it wasn't only the religious problem that worried him; it was his background and mine—the difference. David was going to be a doctor. Where was I headed? When my father talked to me that way, he really got to me—more than he expected. I started crying. I felt terrible. I felt stupid. I felt as if I'd been leading David on. I hadn't hid anything from him, but I hadn't reminded him of who I was—a woman who worked in a laundry. The daughter of a man who worked in a factory, and a woman who worked in a bakery. I decided to tell David what my father said.''

She was stunned by what happened when she did manage to get up the courage for that talk. Her boyfriend reminded her that he, too, was of not especially rich stock: the son of a storekeeper. He reminded her that he'd been lucky—the recipient of an uncle's largesse, which enabled a medical school education. He also reminded her that he was a man, that it was easier for men to "work their way up," and that because he was Jewish, he was (maybe) a bit more desperate. She lived in a city overwhelmingly Catholic; her parents had been hit hard by their daughter's severe illness; and in the Church they found solace, but not the driving encouragement for "success" that an often scorned minority has to inspire in its young, for the sake of survival. And anyway, why didn't she try to go to nursing school? Wouldn't she, at least, let him make inquiries? Didn't she realize that he liked her a lot—precisely because she didn't put on airs, and because she was "nice," and because they had "fun" together, and because she was "pretty"?

He made his inquiries. He obtained the application forms. He helped her fill them out. He talked with an attending physician at the hospital—a doctor he'd gotten to know well in the course of a rotation through the surgical service. Eileen was accepted. She was given a partial scholarship. David insisted on loaning her some money. She refused it. She was told by the school that she could borrow money, pay it back at low interest over the years. She began her nursing education a year after she'd graduated from high school. Her parents thought they'd "lost" her. They wondered what would happen next: an engagement to a Jewish man, who was well on his way to becoming a doctor? Nor could the priest help. Eileen had for a year or two attended church irregularly—something her parents could not rationally blame on David, though they did connect the lapse to his arrival in their lives.

At the same time they couldn't help liking him. For a year, their daughter's first year in nursing school, he became a fairly constant weekend visitor—the young man who was taking out their daughter. And they couldn't deny the obvious glamour of the two—her uniform and his, her career and his, her future life and his. In the father's words, their daughter was headed "across the railroad tracks, way across," a blessing but also an occasion for a little sadness and, not least, a touch of envy: "It's hard, even now, to talk about what happened. My parents were nice enough on the surface to David, but he (and after a while, the both of us) made them nervous. I was the first one in my family, on either side, to graduate from high school. But I was even going beyond *that*. I began to realize that I was upsetting my parents more than my sister's polio did. They could take that easier!

"When I'd come home with a new book, or a program from a concert, I could feel the tension in the air. My father would take a look; my mother would take a look; my sister and my brother would take a look—the big brain, who was going up, up, up on the social scale. It was ridiculous, but it was true. And, remember, in the 1950's the Church was different about marrying 'out of the faith'; and people were tighter about 'intermarriage.' Even among Catholics, for an Irish person to marry an Italian was an *event*. And then there were those 'railroad tracks' my father kept mentioning. I'm surprised David and I stuck together as long as we did! Of course, his family was three hundred miles away. If they'd been in the same city, like mine were, we might never have lasted a week together!"

They lasted a year and a half. They became close friends. They became close physically, though she would later take pains to point out, with the detachment and wry amusement that comes with age, and with the attitudes of a later decade, her ultimate hesitation, and her boyfriend's as well: "We used to do everything but . . ." That was the way, she would observe years afterward, almost sociologically, "many couples felt they had to get along." What caused them to split, finally, were those very matters her father and mother had kept alluding to, if not mentioning. Her family. His family. His career, too. He took a very prestigious residency in a different city—and she had another year of nursing school to go. When she found out he'd be moving, she knew their "days were numbered." She told him so, but he refused to agree. She wasn't heartbroken when she began to realize that he was making increasingly feeble efforts to stay in touch with her from the distance of his new home: a hospital in a city 250 miles away—and about fifty miles from his boyhood home, his parents' residence. She loved nursing from the very beginning, and continued to do so until she graduated, when she was given a prize as the student who showed the most "conscientious spirit" in work done with patients.

Another decade's language, if not clichés, would enable her to sum up an important moment in her life: "I guess they'd say I was going through a 'stage' then, a 'crisis'; the psychologists I read in the paper would have told me that, if they were around them. But in those days they weren't as many of them as there are now. It took me three years of nursing school to begin to settle down and see life through a regular window—not the rose-tinted one I'd been carrying around with me. I had had a lot of dreams; I was going to be a nurse and I'd be married to a doctor, and we'd be happy ever after. I'd never really thought very hard about David's way of thinking and mine.

"Every once in a while he'd do something or say something that stopped me cold; and I'm sure I had that effect on him. He was a beautifully organized person, and very 'deep.' I was always building castles in Spain: my mother's habit of praying to the Bleeding Heart of Jesus, and then assuming her prayers would come true! Toward the end of nursing school, as I spent so much time with dying patients, I fell back on my religion. David could never understand that—not because he was an atheist or a 'bad' person. He just didn't believe in organized religion. He suspected them all—Judaism as well as the Protestant and Catholic Churches. He was an agnostic, very self-sufficient. He was a loner, really. I needed friends; I wanted us to spent time with others—double-date with my nursing friends and the men they were seeing.

"I suppose, looking back, I was rising up in the social scale: to be a nurse. But there is so far you can go! In my class there were women who came from much better circumstances than me. They could have gone to college; at least they had the money and 'background' to go. But they really wanted to be nurses—maybe were better at *doing something,* rather than studying all the time and taking of lot of tests based on books rather than practical matters: the care of the patient. They were the ones who ended up marrying doctors—well, some of them did. I shouldn't be too general; I should be specific. But we did sort out, all of us—and the years have taught me how important a person's background is in shaping her life! When I graduated from nursing school it was the biggest, most important moment of my life; but I was more subdued than I would have thought a few years earlier. I was still getting over the slow breakup with David. We decided that he shouldn't come to the graduation exercises, but I was very sad, not having him there. Had it not been for him . . ."

She got a good job in a busy city hospital. She had her choice of jobs, as did her classmates. Most of them chose "better" jobs: in private hospitals, or teaching hospitals carefully restricted with respect to admissions by the requirements of medical education. But Eileen was her father's daughter. His memories were admonitions of sorts to her—then, as a freshly graduated nurse, and in the years that followed, as well.

These days, so much power is granted certain childhood experiences: "oedipal," "toilet training," "separation" or "individuation," or experiences more broadly, and alas, no less banally, described as the "child-rearing process.' But children are also influenced by what their parents say, think, and believe *substantively.* A certain kind of parent, half-crazy, say, psychotically manipulative, is justifiably regarded by psychiatrists as an important influence in what turns out to be the catatonic schizophrenic life of a child. Emotional disorders live on and on—handed down by mothers and fathers to children, "world without end." Yet psychopathological traumas are not the only inheritance. For Eileen, at twenty-two, or for that matter, forty-two, there were indeed important childhood influences to contend with, and they included what mother and father had told her and her sister and her brother many times, *ideological* messages she would always have to reckon with: "My mother read to us, all the time, from Christ's Sermon on the Mount. She read to us from St. Thomas a Kempis: *The Imitation of Christ*. She read to us from the saints—Francis of Assisi and Catherine of Siena. She taught us to think not only of ourselves, but others—and, most of all, God: what does He want of us. She's 'too religious,' some would say; and I used to think so myself. But I never doubted her sincerity, and I now realize that more than anything else I learned an attitude from my mother: don't just do what suits *you;* think of what is right, by divine law; think of God's will, as much as your own; think of His life, the example He gave us.

"Of course, my father was also a big force in our lives. He'd never let us forget the depression of the 1930's. He'd give us speeches sometimes; he'd tell us how the poor got treated by the big companies. There weren't labor unions then, not the kind we have now. A few cheated their way to millions on the stock exchange, and the rest of us had to hold our breaths as the economy went up and down like a rollercoaster. The ordinary person had no protection: no Social Security, no unemployment compensation, no minimum wage—the good old days! Some of these politicians would like to go back to those days; my father told us never to trust a politician, or a big business type of person. Maybe Dad was unfair; but you can't forget those old sermons your parents gave you!

"When I went over to the City Hospital, I felt I was Dad's true daughter! I could help with the poor people, the sick ones among the poor; and I could give back what the good Lord had given to me—so I was my mother's daughter, too! They both had worried that I was 'overreaching' myself when I went into nursing. Stay in your own place, where God has put you! But they were proud of me, once I started in; and they were always grateful to David for 'inspiring' me—as my mother would put it! And so am I, now—when I think back to the past. I do sometimes, I think of old times, when I'm by myself. I'll always be a nurse; even when I got married and started having children and 'forgot' about nursing, I was still a nurse. I wouldn't be the person I am if I hadn't got that R.N. for myself; I know that.''

It was through a friend of hers, a nurse she went to school with, that Eileen met her husband Tim. He had gone to high school a few years ahead of her, and on to a business college. Like her, he came from a working-class, Irish Catholic background, was the first in his family to go beyond high school. He had always had a flair for mathematics, and he put it to good use; he became an accountant, then an officer in a small company, with the responsibility of keeping its financial affairs in order. Eileen at forty could look back a bit nostalgically at her initial involvement with Tim, and later, the first years of their married life. But she remembers, occasionally, the tougher times they both had to face ''back then,'' a phrase she likes to use more and more as she gets older: ''It was simple back then; that's what we say, but we should know better! Prices were low, all right. But who had a good job? And what kind of salary did you get? I sweated and sweated to pay off loans for my education. And when I met this guy Tim Halloran, he was as strapped as I was. He used to say that all he wanted was a good job, some security to it, and a decent wage. His father had worked for years in a warehouse until he got into a bad accident. In those days, there was no Social Security or Workmen's Compensation to protect you. They'd fire you; and you'd put yourself at the mercy of the city—go on relief, and try to get half-decent medical care at the city hospital. It was called becoming a 'charity case'!

''Tim remembers his parents giving him lectures like the kind I got from my parents. His mother had to find a job; she got one in Fanny Farmer's, selling candy. She got very little for long hours, but as we used to say back then, in the good old days, beggars can't be choosers! Tim remembers thinking to himself when he went to bed: I'll work like a dog, I'll slave my way through school, so long as I don't end up poor and broken like my father. A teacher told him he had a 'gift' with numbers, so Tim grabbed on to that as if God Himself had sent a message. He memorized his numbers, and he did extra work in math, and he tried his best to plan ahead, by asking the advice of teachers. They told him it was useless to aim big when you haven't a cent to your name. Even if he'd gotten a scholarship to a fancy college, it wouldn't have taken care of all the expenses he'd run up. And for him, every single quarter, never mind dollar, mattered a lot. As he used to joke: his mother didn't work in the candy store for no reason!''

When Eileen started going out with Tim, he was struggling through business school on a part-time basis; he had to work to pay the tuition bills—and to help out at home. After a while Eileen wanted to help him, financially—but he said no: pride. She asked him how he would feel if the situation were reversed. He hesitated not at all; he would insist on helping her. In retrospect, that was the first discussion, if not argument, she had that centered on the connection between sex and one's various rights, responsibilities, and obligations: "I got rather upset. That was almost twenty years ago, and we had no 'liberation' then. But I told Tim that if a woman has a good job, she ought to help her boyfriend; and if it's the reverse, fine. I told him I was glad to pay for myself. I'd be glad to pay for him at a restaurant, too. He'd have no part of it. He wanted to take me out. He didn't want me to take him out—and that was that. I got angry. I told him he had a double standard; besides, he was being foolish, and we were both suffering needlessly. I wasn't rich, but at last I had a halfway decent job, and the least I could do was share what I had with someone I liked a lot. But he got more and more tense, and I let the matter drop.

"In all these years I'm not sure he's really changed! He probably would phrase things a bit differently now. After all, he has me to contend with—still! And his three daughters! And his son, as a matter of fact. Children are different today. They have different ideas. They believe in 'equality' more than we did. They live different lives than the kind Tim and I lived. His parents are gone. Mine are very old. I don't talk to my own children in the same way my parents did to us. This is a comfortable home we have. We're not doing so bad. The kids have a lot more hope than Tim and I did when we decided to get married. Even though we were both 'on the rise,' I guess you'd say, we were scared that suddenly there'd be a crash, and we would both be out on the street, like our parents had been, without a cent to their names, and as my father used to put it, 'with fear staring us in the face every morning and every evening.' I tell my children what it was like back then, but the words don't ring true to them. When Tim and I remember our first years together, we wonder how we did it—get to where we're at. Not that we're in danger of becoming all that well off!''

They became engaged after a year of ''going out''; but they waited two more years to marry, because Tim was still at school part-time, had absolutely no money to spare, and continued to insist that until he was ''on his own'' he would not consider marriage. Eileen saved money regularly during those months, no huge amount, but enough (she knew) to buy some furnishings for their first home—which turned out to be a small city apartment. They lived there longer than they had hoped. Tim's father died—a stroke. Tim had the responsibility of his mother and several younger sisters to share with his one grown-up brother, no wealthy man himself: a carpenter. For several years after they were married, Eileen and Tim struggled to meet their respective family obligations as well as their felt obligation to themselves. Believing Catholics, they did not seek to practice birth control. Yet, they wanted no children ''at first.'' As the duration of that phrase grew longer and longer in their minds, the two of them began to experience substantial difficulties of both a psychological and moral nature: ''Tim never wanted to talk about sex. He was brought up to ignore it. So was I. My mother and father never even kissed in front of us children. His parents were a little more open, but Tim never dared ask his parents about sex. To be honest, I learned about the subject only when I met David; and in biology class during nursing school. To be honest again—well, I was the one who explained a lot about sex to Tim. Oh, I don't mean that he didn't know the basic facts! But he really didn't understand how a child is conceived, and what happens inside a woman, and where.

"Remember, we're talking about the 1950's; both schools and the Catholic Church were different then, and so were families like his and mine. The only reason Tim and I *ever* had a talk about sex, the first time, was because he kept on saying that he 'hoped' we didn't have any children for a while, and we were 'lucky' because so far I wasn't pregnant. At that time there was no pill, of course; and at that time the Church was much stronger against birth control than it seems to be now. Today the Church is taking its stand against abortion, and it's my opinion that a lot of our priests—at least the ones I know in this town—close their eyes and ears or even wink when the subject of birth control comes up. I told Tim, back then, that if he wanted our 'luck' to hold out, we'd have to do something about it. He turned as red as the setting sun on a midsummer day. Finally, he said he didn't want to talk about 'the subject.' I knew not to push anything on him. I said all right. Then I asked him if he wanted me to try to figure out when I was most likely to become pregnant, and stay away from him during that time. He said 'good,' and we never spoke a word more on that score! He grabbed that newspaper of his as if he was in a canoe, and it had tipped over, and he needed a life preserver real fast."

She was a nurse, she kept reminding herself then—as she would on other occasions in the coming years. She was a nurse, and as a nurse, as a woman who was also a nurse, as a woman who had studied biology and knew the workings of the reproductive system—that is, her own body—and as a Catholic woman, married to a Catholic man, she had a particular course to follow. She used the thermometer. She ascertained the nature of her ovulatory cycle. She stayed away from her husband during that period. And for a while she did not become pregnant. But one month she "miscalculated"; or, in retrospect, as she thought about it, forgot to abstain from sex an extra day or two on both sides of the day she ovulated.

She had been taught in nursing school that the sperm are hardy, tenacious; she remembered that apparently stray piece of knowledge when she noted the absence of her hitherto quite regular period: "It's funny how you can learn a 'fact,' then forget it completely—and suddenly it's on your mind all the time! I realized, even before I was *sure* I was pregnant, that a month or so earlier I'd forgotten that fact about the sperm. Well, today Tim and I can laugh about all that, but at the time I hardly knew what to say to him. I was afraid he'd be upset with me, for failing him! Such a stupid way of thinking! There I was, the one who was pregnant, thinking I'd done something wrong, and would be criticized by my husband, the one who had everything in the world to do with getting me pregnant! Back then we were so poor, though; and back then we were very shy about sex. You get older, you have children, the Church changes, the world changes—the attitudes of people—and pretty soon you're a different person yourself. Oh, not completely different; Tim and I aren't what you'd call a 'swinging couple,' full of a lot of today's sex talk and ready to try anything! We're just a plain old suburban couple, I guess. But we've been influenced, over the years, by what has happened around us.''

Their first child was a girl, Louisa, born three and a half years after they were married. Their second child was a boy, Tim, Jr., born a year later. Their third child was a girl, Patricia, born two years after the son. Then came another girl, within a year and a half, named Maureen, born with difficulty, and eventually a slightly retarded child. And then Eileen and Tim became concerned, if not alarmed: "I was becoming overwhelmed; I told Tim so. I had four children within five years. Were we going to have eight in ten years? Twelve in fifteen years? I wouldn't say I got depressed after Maureen was born, but I found myself staring out of the window—dragging my feet, because I was thinking too much. Once I did break down and cry. I remember thinking to myself that I was glad that Tim wasn't there to see me, the tears coming down like a rainstorm. But an hour later, changing the diapers and listening to those children cry—oh, the crying undid me back then!—I suddenly got angry, real angry: why *wasn't* Tim there? Why wasn't he, at least, there more often than he was? The answer he'd have given I knew without asking him. He had to work, work overtime, in order to keep the job he had, and keep up his chances for a promotion—so that the money could keep coming in, and we'd be able to have a roof over us, and food, and the kids could have those damn diapers to wear!

"I confessed later that week to the priest; I told him what I felt—mostly. I told him the kids were getting me down, and I was taking to blaming my husband, when it wasn't his fault that life can get hard for a mother with babies to bring up. The priest only made me feel worse; he said I was right to say what I did, that it wasn't my husband's fault! I got almost sick to my stomach when I left that church. I was mad as could be; I went and got myself a coffee ice cream soda, and I felt a little better. But I can still hear the words going through my head while I had my soda: 'It's okay for those priests to give us their sermons; let them try bringing up the big families they think are so wonderful—on the average person's paycheck.' Of course, you never say those things to the people you think them about!"

On her own she decided to begin practicing birth control. She went to a gynecologist and got fitted for a diaphragm. Only then did she tell her husband what would be happening. She expected an argument, or at best a long discussion. She was wrong. He seemed to want no part of any conversation on "the subject." However, she was annoyed rather than relieved by that development. Why wasn't he more explicitly worried or, at least, concerned enough to want to discuss what was, after all, their common future as parents? Why did he leave the whole matter up to her? What would have happened had she in fact done nothing? More pregnancies, no doubt. Or "rhythm" practiced, yet somehow in a less-than-perfect way—hence the repeated pregnancies? Obviously, she felt overwhelmed by the increasing number of children she had to bring up. But she was also unhappy with herself because of what she concluded was a failure of hers: a consistent lack of success at the only kind of "birth control" the Church gave its sanction to.

When she took her own kind of initiative, though, to break out of that cycle, she was met with her husband's seeming indifference. Or possibly, his continued prudishness. Or, she speculated, his preoccupation with the demands of his career, his life as a breadwinner. She found herself both resentful toward him and quite understanding of him—a mixture sure to survive the fog of forgetfulness that descends on less complicated emotional configurations: "If I'd been *only* angry, I would have had an explosion, probably, and we would then have sat down and talked the whole issue out. If I'd been looking at the problem from his point of view, *and* the Church's, *and* my mother's (who *couldn't* have any more children after my brother was born!), I'd have said nothing, *and* done nothing. But I was going back and forth in my feelings toward Tim, and I guess that's the reason I still remember how I felt back then—because it went on for so very long, the trouble between us, as we tried to figure out what kind of family we'd have and, I now realize, what kind of people we were going to be.

"When I first told Tim what I'd done, he literally was silent, not a single word. He got red. I assumed he was embarrassed, and didn't want to talk. But he was cool to me that evening, and I began to think: he's mad. Then *I* got mad: what was *he* mad about—who was *he* to get mad? But I didn't say anything to him. We were going around and around, keeping a good face for the sake of the children—a whole week. Then we made up—in bed! And I realized that Tim had not really wanted to take advantage of the diaphragm I'd gotten. He waited until he thought it was 'safe' by the rhythm method! He was willing to be frustrated until then. The diaphragm, in a strange way, helped the rhythm method to work better! But we couldn't go on forever without talking about the whole business; and we did, eventually.

"Tim finally told me he was 'upset'; I'd gone and done something without 'consulting' him. And I was violating our Church's teachings. And he didn't really want to 'get involved' with a 'gadget.' He felt it 'made sex something artificial.' I asked him if he even knew what a diaphragm was, if he'd ever seen one. Boy, did he explode! It was the worst fight we'd ever had! Today, a lot of Catholics, like others, use the pill. Then we didn't have the pill, and I *was* doing something most Catholic women wouldn't have considered doing. He told me I thought I was a 'big deal' because I was a nurse! He went on and on about my 'airs,' just because I'd gone to nursing school. I told him he thought *he* was a big deal—because he was a man! I gave it right back to him: who has to carry the children for nine months, and take the medical risks, and stay with them every minute, every hour—while he comes home and expects them to be in bed, asleep, or looking all dolled up, so they can smile at him and coo a little, and get kissed by him—the big treat of the day?

"I never thought I had such bile in me. I felt terrible afterwards. But I also kept thinking I'd been right. And I never confessed to the priest; I couldn't bring myself to mention what I'd done—got myself that diaphragm. I carried the secret inside me—and I had bad dreams, real bad ones: someone choking me. I'd wake up in a cold sweat. I couldn't talk to Tim about it. I was brought up by a very religious mother! You can't just walk away from your childhood, the psychologists say! After a while, several months, Tim and I learned to live with the diaphragm. But it took longer for me to learn to live with the Church's attitude toward birth control. When the pill came along, I had lots of company, lots of Catholic women to share my experience with, if I'd needed to talk with them. But by then I didn't; I'd found some peace with myself. The nightmares had stopped."

She had, at the worst moments, thought of seeing a psychiatrist, because those nightmares were followed by serious insomnia—tossing and turning until morning made sleep no longer possible, because of the demands of young, hungry, diaper-wet children. As her husband began feeling comfortable with the diaphragm, and applauding "their" decision to keep the family at what he would call a "reasonable" size, she found herself not only able to sleep without the kind of frightening, disruptive dreams she had previously experienced, but also to contemplate a future for herself: "I knew I wanted to go back to nursing. I knew that the day would come that my last child was in school, and I had a lot of time on my hands. Once we seemed able to get together on birth control, Tim and I, my mind became more relaxed, and sometimes, while changing a diaper or spooning in the Gerber's, I'd think of the hospital wards I'd worked on, and my old uniforms, there in the closet, hanging in a corner, all starched up and ready to go! Oh, that was hard work, too. I'd remind myself how much I had to do as a nurse, starting at seven in the morning. I'd remind myself of the bedpans, and the change of linen, the 'diapers' I had to put on the elderly, incontinent patients we'd have!

"It's strange, how one thing seems attractive when you're in the middle of something else. I was so thrilled to be pregnant; I was glad to leave the wards. But when the kids were young and a lot of hard work, I forgot all the burdens a nurse has to carry. I pictured nursing a wonderful breeze. It helped even to *think* of a change of scenery. It's spoiled of me to talk like that, my mother would say; but she didn't have some of the choices I have, and so she had to defend *her* life—just as a lot of women today stand up for what they believe is right. I may not agree with my mother; but I won't forget how tough it was for my parents, and how hard they tried to do the best they could. It's too easy to turn your back on the past, and be pleased with yourself and your own life, and forget what others, before you, had to face."

She did go back to nursing when her youngest daughter had entered the first grade of a special school. By then there was beginning to be a shortage of nurses—the result of greatly expanded hospital facilities, an inadequate number of enrolled nursing students, and a declining interest in the profession, the last a matter Eileen noticed with great interest and increasing alarm. As the civil rights movement emerged, gave way to the antiwar movement; as the women's liberation movement came on the American social scene; as Eileen's children moved along through the primary and secondary school grades; as Eileen's husband began to earn a larger and yet larger salary (eroded all the time, however, by inflation), the question of a nurse's work became for one woman a means of approaching a nation's moral climate: "I went back to nursing because I wanted a change, I guess. We also could use the money. We weren't desperate, but we've always been an average family, and when prices go up, and your family needs more and more food and clothes, something has to happen: you borrow, you work harder, or you make do with less. There I was at home, with the kids in school, and I thought to myself: why sit around and look at the television and read the paper three times over, and nibble at butter-crunch, my fatal weakness! (I put on five pounds, while I looked at various nursing jobs, but hesitated to make a firm decision!)

"I tried full-time nursing at first, but I had to give that up after a week. It almost drove the whole family crazy. I don't agree with those people who say: go to work as soon as your youngest is in school—or before, by using day care. Let me tell you: that week I went to the hospital early, and it meant I was leaving the kids to themselves! Sure, Tim helped, but he had to go to work, too. My mother had to come stay with us, so she could be there when we needed her, early in the morning. If I'd worked the three-to-eleven shift, she'd have had to be there in the evening, to make supper. Tim couldn't arrange his hours to suit our needs; he'd have been fired on the spot!

"Today, some women would say he should have quit, helped out at the house, and tried to get a more 'flexible' job. Do they know the reality of the job market, for a person like my husband? He's not a doctor or a lawyer or a man who owns his own business or 'consults.' He's a workingman, a lucky one, with just enough extra education (after high school) to give him a little edge over a lot of other workingmen, but not all that much of an edge! He's 'completely replaceable,' like he says. There are a dozen men looking for his position—more than that number!

"And the kids: do you just walk out on them? Do you throw them at strangers? Even their grandmother, I soon realized, was a stranger to them. They wanted *me* around when they got up and had to start facing a new day! Well, people say that in time the kids would 'adjust.' I'm sure that's true. Hell, kids will 'adjust' to anything! I've seen some of the day-care centers today's kids have learned to 'adjust' to! My sister-in-law *has* to work; her husband is paralyzed from the waist down, an auto accident.

They've been fighting the lousy, crooked insurance company for two years! She is heartbroken when she leaves those children off, every morning. She knows what will happen. But she bites her lip, and she tries to be cheerful. She'll tell you that it's all right, it's all right—the kids are learning how to 'socialize,' and how to be independent. But twice she's pulled me aside, and tears have come to her eyes, and she'll start talking—and then she has to sleep. She's right to stop, I guess. Like my father used to say: there's no point crying about what can't be helped; you have to do the best you can.

"Of course, these days, no one talks like that. Everyone wants to do better—to get the best of all possible deals for themselves. I see the change in my own profession. For a while I worked part-time, and I was off in a geriatric ward, and I loved it. I've always liked working with elderly people; and after I had children, I was even better at geriatric nursing, it's become called. Soon I began to see, when I could spend a little more time at work, how really valuable a person I was to the hospital—because the younger nurses didn't want to do the kind of work I was doing, and enjoyed doing. A lot of women who might have once gone into nursing have been having second thoughts about the profession—saying no, it's not for them. Why? I've talked with nurses; I've talked with students—and with young women graduating from high school and thinking of what's ahead for themselves. I keep hearing that it's 'menial,' the work we do—*I* do. I keep hearing that there are 'better' jobs—meaning work with more 'dignity.' I've heard nursing called an 'old-fashioned' job. I've heard women say they want no part of bedpans, changing beds. I've heard talk of doing 'shitwork' for the doctors!

"It's hard to keep your cool when people say such things to you. They're not being insulting to *me;* I realize that. Actually, in my opinion, they're being insulting to themselves! They're talking about 'liberation,' but then, who do they think will do the work that has to be done, if the sick are to get better: *other* women? Or other men? But I hear young men talk the same way: I don't want to do this, and I don't want to do that. Everyone wants to sit behind a desk, and have 'dignity'—and shout orders to the next guy, who doesn't need the same 'dignity'! I'm sounding like an old preacher; maybe I'm losing touch with the young—and that would be a disaster, now that my own children are teen-agers! But there's something wrong when people think of hard work as demeaning. There's something wrong when women say they won't go into a profession like nursing because for years it was the work women were allowed to do by men.

"To me, it's been a privilege to take care of patients all these years. I don't think of my work as being a woman's job; it's *my* job—me trying to do something worthwhile for other human beings. Isn't that why the good Lord put us on this earth, to prove ourselves before Him? I *am* becoming preachy, I know. But I've loved my work, and I wish more people—men and women both!—would go into nursing, and let the past be buried. I'm not against women becoming doctors, or anything else, but when a high schooler who lives near us tells me that she doesn't want to became a nurse, when she can become a doctor, now that women are 'liberated' and don't *have* to be nurses anymore, then I feel my blood pressure going up to over two hundred, and I want to scream, I really do."

She doesn't, though. She stops and reflects, and often enough, reverses the direction of her thinking. Yes, she has her ideas, her ideals; but a new generation, that of her three daughters, her one son, has a right to come to terms with *its* world. When she has spent a full day at home, alone, she is apt to be most introspective, most willing to examine various issues from a number of different angles. She loves those days home; as a matter of fact, when her children had moved along into the middle school grades—sixth, seventh, eighth—she decided to cut back, work less than half-time. She wasn't even sure why at first. A "mood" came over her, and she obliged it.

But soon she understood what the emotional side of her was saying to the more intellectual side: "I was wondering myself why I began wanting more days off. Was I getting tired of work? Was something wrong with me—physically? Maybe it was in my head? Were we doing better financially, so I was just slackening off because I knew I could? Should *I* go back to school, and get some administrative job? No, I was in fine shape, and I loved my work, and we can always use extra money these days—a family like ours, not on the top and not on the bottom, just trying to make ends meet. I began to realize that my children need me now as much, maybe more than they used to. It's different; before I had to wash and clean them, feed them, keep them from hurting themselves. You still have to keep an eye on your children as they grow older—get their meals, check up on their clothes (they grow out of them so fast!), and make sure they take showers. But more important, you have to help them with their schoolwork, talk with them, listen to them, teach them, and learn from them. That's a job, too. I don't want my kids out on the street with God knows whom, or sad and lonely at home, because there's no one there—just when they need their mother and their father to be with them, help them figure out what's going on, and figure out where they're wanting to head in life. Tim tries to give his whole weekend to what we call 'family projects.' He's taken time off, come home early, when he's thought that one of the kids or all of them needed him, or when I've said: 'Tim, we've both got to do this'—whatever it is!

"When I was working over half-time, I began to feel rushed when I got home, and impatient with the kids, and drained. How much energy does anyone have? If you're honest with yourself, you'll realize that you have to *pretend* that you're living the best of both worlds, being a good mother, and being a good, full-time nurse. But the children are picking up the tab, if you ask me—or the patients are! When I have a full day off, I'm much better with my children; I read with them at night, and before that I have a good time talking with them about school. I don't mean to tell others what to do. There's too much of that going on in this country now: people pointing their fingers at other people; people telling other people what's absolutely right and what's absolutely wrong. But for me, the main thing in life is my family.

"I hear women say to each other: what about *yourself?* They go on and on about *their* lives! I feel my pulse get faster! I want to interrupt; I want to say that for me, my family *is* myself, *is* my life. I don't know how to distinguish between what I want for what they would call 'myself,' and what I want for my husband, my daughters, my son. We're all part of this family—the Halloran family! My mother used to tell us about the 'Mystical Body of Christ'; I couldn't for a long while understand what she meant. She'd try to explain—that Christ was 'in all of us.' I wasn't sure how, or where! But once she explained to us that when we sat down as a family and prayed to Him, or when we kneeled as a family and took Communion, we were joining His Mystical Body—then I suddenly got it! It was us, together, joining Something Bigger—Him. And before we did that, we also joined Something Bigger—our family. Why should I go running away from that, in order to say I'm not 'old-fashioned,' or I'm a 'new woman'?

"I've been working most of my life; it's no big deal for me. I know the thrill of a paycheck made out in my name. I have my profession. And good God, I know the pleasure of throwing in a hundred dollars, and then another hundred, to reduce the flood of bills that keeps coming toward us. We'll drown in those bills, I sometimes think! But for me, the struggle recently has been to stay at home *more,* not leave home. Maybe it's because I do have a tough job. Maybe if I could go to a nice office and sit back and give orders and go on long lunches, I'd feel different. Maybe if I'd gone to college, my mind would have a lot more questions, and I'd be more ambitious for my own career. I can see it through the eyes of others, sometimes. But do the others think of us—how someone in your ordinary American family, how a woman like me, living in the suburbs, thinks about life?"

She changes from such a rhetorical and, arguably, self-serving question to a more meditative vein of discussion. The word "suburbs" has caught her mind's notice. That is it, in a way—the critical element in her life: the place where she and her husband live, and bring up their children. In the particular suburb where she has lived these recent years, her destiny is being worked out:

"I'll be at home, and I sit and have my morning coffee, and think to myself: this life has been good to me! I mean, I'll walk into my children's rooms, one after the other. The rooms are empty, but the spirit of each child is there! I can see the child in my eyes—and in her possessions, or his. I heard on television someone calling us in America 'materialistic.' Maybe so. But the things my kids have are books and toys, and their hobbies: stamps and a bird and coins. No huge, lavish gifts come into their lives! One of my daughters loves plants; she cares for them beautifully. Her room is a garden. I go into it, and I feel so touched— by her, by God in her, as my mother puts it. The whole house gives me that feeling a lot of the time; we have a sign in our kitchen: *God Bless Our Home,* and I do believe He has heard our request, and honored it—'shed His grace' on us, as the saying goes.

"Maybe I'm getting more like my mother in my old age; maybe I'm becoming mystical, but I think of our house as part of us—a place where each one of us becomes a member of a family and, I hope and pray, a part of God's family. If others say it's 'dull' in 'suburbia'; if others say we're all alike out here, and we are the blind following the blind, and we don't have any individuals left—then let them have their high-and-mighty opinions. I know from my own life, my own experience, how different each family in this circle is, and how much fun we have here—and how much thinking and wondering and hoping and praying go on. It's too easy for outsiders to give us a bad name. You can take any place and find rotten apples, or make fun of what you see—the people and their habits. I don't want to move, ever; or until the kids are grown up and leave. Even then, I'll want to stay—hold on to the memories of our family's life. Why should I say good-bye to those memories? Our dreams, they've been nourished here in this house."

Her dreams: she often talks about them. Not the dreams of night, which she rarely recalls; and not the daydreams that come and go as she goes about her business at home or in the community hospital serving the suburb where she and her family live.

She has dreams that are quite explicitly conscious and carefully fashioned. She works at them, too. She is, she repeatedly makes clear, "a worker." Why shouldn't her mental life reveal that characteristic? She will be sitting at the kitchen table. She will be sipping black coffee. She will be eyeing the cream: to use or not to use? How many calories can she afford? How many has she recently spent, or saved? She anticipates her critics—and performs the labor of dreaming: "I know, I'm another spoiled American. I read in the paper that over half the people on this planet are hungry. And here I am, trying to lose those ten pounds. I do—and then they come back on me. I'd share what we have with others. I don't want others to go hungry. But God put us here, not in Africa or Asia. We're lucky, I know. Our ancestors knew hunger in Ireland. Even today, the Irish suffer: Belfast and Derry. I wish the whole world would know peace.

"I don't just think of my family; I try to think of others, around the world. I dream that my kids will be grown up, and they'll be living good lives, and they'll marry good men, a good woman. I dream about my grandchildren—that they won't go hungry, and they'll have jobs, and they'll be able to look themselves in the mirror and say that they're doing the best they can to live up to God's commandments. But you can't just hope and pray and dream for your own blood. We're part of a country—a wonderful one, that's been good to so many of its people. And we're part of the world: if there's a war, these days, we'll all know about it, you bet your life. And we *will* be betting our lives—because the next war could wipe us all out. I know that. Tim does. My neighbors do. It's wrong, when you hear that we're 'in a shell' out here in the suburbs. A man said that on one of the talk shows, and I wanted to sit down and write him a letter and tell him what is on my mind!"

She didn't, however. She is no letter-writer—not to talk shows, newspapers, politicians. She has never been asked by any pollster what she thinks about any subject. The longer she gives forth, the more complicated her opinions become—she well knows, hence her frequent assertion that she sees "too many points of view." But that inclination—a reflection of a nature at once even-tempered, sensitive, and essentially nonpolemical—is countered by a decided capacity, as she has put it, to "hear voices." The psychiatrist need not, at this point, take serious notice. Eileen may have her "problems"—may, like all of us, have a few "illusions," a worry or two that is a bit excessive; but the "voices" she hears are real fragments of her family's past, and mental responses of a kind to America's continuing social and economic reality.

Once, in a spirited, though unselfconscious, defense of her neighborhood, its values and customs and rituals, she made reference to those "voices," and added one to them—hers: I'll be cooking, and I'll smell the roast beef, and it will get something going in my mind. I'll remember my mother, cooking a ham, and saying that she'd been saving dimes and quarters for that ham, and she wanted us to eat it up, but she hated to see it go fast, because she didn't know when we'd be getting another one. Why should a woman of forty, living in a nice home in a nice town, think of that? I guess it's a reminder. When I go to the shopping center I'll hear my mother then, her voice; and my father's voice, too. I'll hear them talking in the small, dark kitchen we had, in that apartment house. They were talking, so often, about money—whether they had the rent, and what to buy in the grocery store: 'The best you can get for the cheapest price,' my father would always say.

"Today, I walk from store to store, handing over those credit cards! I never even carry much cash. I get what I want and need—within reason! It's a different world—though as a parent I think I still wish for my children what my parents wished for me, to be a 'good, God-fearing person,' my mother would say; to be 'happy in life,' my father would say. I guess, sometimes, they are contradictory messages! As the priest told us one Sunday, God wasn't always 'happy'; in the end, He was very unhappy, on the Cross! When my children are with me shopping in the mall, I tell them to listen to me; I tell them that life isn't only getting, it's giving, too. Then, they ask me who they should give to!

They'll see a Heart Fund box, or the Salvation Army lady, and want to give!

"It's phony generosity, maybe! It's being charitable in the midst of a place built upon greed! Everyone is buying, buying. But we have a good time there, browsing and meeting people. You can look around and see what a great country this is—all it offers you. Sure, they're always trying to sell you things, and much of what they have to sell isn't completely necessary. But people have common sense, a lot of us. We may waste some money, now that we make more—unlike my parents, who never wasted anything!—but we don't go throwing all that much money around like drunken fools. How can we? We're tied to weekly wages. That's what it means to be a worker: you're not rich; you don't have a lot of stocks and bonds and real estate—the 'investments' they write about on the financial page. Tim and I never read that page. No one I know does. That's for others. The shopping mall is where we 'invest' our money—on clothes, on food, on a lawn mower or a snow remover. Then we'll have a bite to eat in the cafeteria, and if there's time and a good movie, we go and sit down and munch our popcorn and watch!

"While my kids pay attention to today's stars, my mind will wander off, and I'll remember Bette Davis or Rita Hayworth or Joan Crawford, the old actresses my mother used to love seeing. She'd be feeling low—not knowing how we'd get through that depression, and she'd get out a quarter she'd saved, and take herself to the movie, and cry her eyes out because of Bette Davis's troubles. My father would silence us if we complained that she was leaving us; he'd tell us that our mother is with us all the time, and enough is enough, and we should be glad that she's going, and someday we'll know how she feels, and we'll want to go to see a movie, just as she does. I still remember him saying that. When the subject of 'women's liberation' comes up, I often think of those words of my father!"

She does more than simply recall them; she uses their import to talk with her daughters and her son about the past, the present, the future. She tries to make sense of the world that was, is; and she tries to see ahead. She reminds her children that they are heirs to the hard work of their grandparents, their mother and father. But she also, modestly and shrewdly, makes clear her conviction that it has been larger forces which have shaped their rather satisfactory, if not completely assured, present situation: "My father used to tell us that you can kill yourself working, and get nowhere if the country's economy is no good; and my mother always talked about God, and how He had a hand in your life. I've tried to remind our children that you mustn't take yourself too seriously. I had a friend in nursing school who always said that to herself. She was a beautiful woman; but she worried that it was going to her head. She was wise! I worry sometimes that 'the good life' they say we have here in suburbia is going to my head, my husband's head, our children's heads. I try to remind myself of where we've come from. I try to save a little, in case suddenly there's a lot of trouble in the country. What more can you do!

"When I drive off, going to work, I'll catch a glance at the house, and say I'm lucky, and so are the kids. I tell them that when I come home; and I also tell them I'm lucky to have a good job. I think of my mother, watching those Bette Davis movies, and penny-pinching in the five-and-dime store, and I realize how much nursing has meant to me. If I hadn't become a nurse, I wouldn't have met Tim. Because I'm a nurse I can earn a good wage, and help make our life here easier. And now, I can give my own life more meaning than it would have if I weren't a nurse. I must be a mixed-up person: some mornings I leave the house, and I almost want to stay, and just sit there and enjoy what Tim and I have built up for ourselves. Other mornings, on my day off, I get restless, and I miss the hospital routine. I actually hear those bedpans rattling and I see myself throwing the dirty sheets down the chute—and even (on a real strange day!) catching them, like I used to, when I was a kid. A kid! I was a young woman, trying to get myself a leg on life, as my mother and father used to say we should do. And now I'm a 'suburbanite,' a woman trying to hold on to a good life, trying to keep steady in the place where I've settled myself!''

part six
EPILOGUE

No part of our work together these past years has brought us more pleasure than the communication we have maintained with the five women whose stories make up this book. We have stayed in touch through letters, through Christmas cards, and through occasional visits. Once in a while, a special event has prompted a phone call. Snapshots sent through the mail have helped our memories evolve. Even as gray has appeared in our own hair, it has graced the hair of several of these women, too, in the decade since this second volume of *Women of Crisis* first appeared. In her 1988 Christmas message to us, Eileen called attention to the changing color of her hair, to the passage of time: "Each year brings more white hairs. I kind of enjoy them by now! I wouldn't want anyone to think I was having too easy a time!"

We all have "easy time" some years and not-so-good spells in other years. Laura Willis, whose life we present in "Bossing," for all her social and economic success, has had to struggle with her husband George's long-term illness (a chronic leukemia). For a few years, her daughter Joanie's lack of interest in school became a source of great concern to a mother of working-class origins who often worried that somehow, sometime, she'd "end up poor, and that would be that." But then, in 1986, George went into a surprisingly sustained remission, one still in effect at this writing; and when she entered high school, Joanie suddenly became a conscientious and capable student.

"I've had lots to worry about," Laura wrote to us early in 1988. "I'd wake up for years in the middle of the night and everything—I mean, *everything*—would go racing through my poor, tired head. It's funny, I've gotten through life by pushing a lot of stuff out of the way, way out of the way; but when the stuff mounts up, an alarm must go off, someplace in my mind, telling me I can't brush everything under the rug. That's when I start waking up at one or two in the morning—it's always then—and there are these thoughts in my head, and they won't go away, they just won't. First I turn over, and try to go right back to sleep. That works, sometimes. But a lot of nights, it doesn't. So I lie there and think. I look at George, and he's snoring away! I think to myself that he's the one who should be awake, given the trouble he's fighting. But no, he sleeps like a log. I think it's because he'll take a couple of highballs after supper, watching the TV, and that's his ticket to a good night's sleep. Not even those highballs will work with me, though—not if there's enough worrying me in the back of my mind. I told my hairdresser: there comes a time when the back of your mind becomes the front of your mind, and with me, it's one o'clock in the morning—my moment of truth!

"I worry about everything! [We had asked.] I worry about George, I worry about Joanie, I worry about my work, I worry about my health, I even worry about people I see on the street, total strangers. There's a homeless man who is always stationed near our building in the mornings, and he's begging. I see people give him a little change, or lots of change, or they say no, they don't have any change, or they ignore him, totally ignore him, and the other night, I woke up thinking of him! I wondered how he survives—where he sleeps, and how he takes care of himself.

Does he ever brush his teeth? What about his gums? I'm having the worst trouble with *my* gums, and I go see the dentist twice a year, even more. He must never see a dentist! Now, I ask you, why should my mind have such thoughts? I asked a minister we know, and he said it's my soul talking to my mind in the middle of the night. I liked that—the way he said it. The next morning I took out a couple of dollar bills, and I had them ready when I came near the building, and there he was, and his friend was there, and I gave him the money, and I could see that he was surprised. He looked right at me; his eyes and mine really met. He bowed his head, and he said, 'Thank you, lady.' I smiled and with my lips said, 'You're welcome.' I don't know why I didn't use my voice. Later on, I was sitting and sipping coffee at my desk, and I wondered why I didn't say 'You're welcome' right out loud.

"Later in the day I figured out why, maybe: I felt ashamed for him and for myself. The homeless are a judgment on us, a friend of mine said once. I was angry at her when I heard her say that. I thought to myself, If you work hard, you won't be homeless. But some people can't work hard—they're sick, or they're in personal trouble—that's what my *daughter* said. She's not grown up yet, and she talks like that.''

Her daughter's troubles at school worried Laura deeply. She began to realize why Joanie was an indifferent student for so long: "She is bored. In one of my middle-of-the-night insomniac soul sessions I finally got the message—that Joanie is a really kind-hearted kid who can't stand teachers who are brusque and rude. Joanie watches closely and hears everything, and she thinks about what she sees and hears. She has told me what her teacher does, and when I seem to be insensitive, she pushes me: 'Mom, that teacher goes easy with me, because you're a more important mother than some kids' are. I think she has in her mind whose parents are making which amounts of money, and her words follow the income.' I was shocked when I heard that. 'No,' I said, almost by reflex. Joanie answered me with one word: 'Yes.' That was the best way [for her] to do it! If she'd argued with me, I might have argued back. But she just said what she knew to be true, with one word, and I knew in my heart she was right. So I said 'Yes,' too, and we just sat there in silence. A few nights later, in the middle of the night, I remembered that moment. I had to reach for a Kleenex. I was crying there, in bed. I wasn't really upset. I was proud of my daughter. She told me the other day that she loves the car we bought for her, and she loves the life we have here, but when she's older, she'll go in the Peace Corps! I was all set to ask her why and to start trying to change her mind, but I stopped myself. I did what she does, and said, 'Yes.' She looked at me to see if I really meant it. I'm not sure what answer she got, because I'm not sure what I really thought: it was both pride and worry, my usual mixture of emotions!''

Soon enough, after those comments, Joanie was off to college, a strong-minded, independent person with an energetic social conscience. This conscience prompted her to tutor children in the ghetto, causing her mother more of those middle-of-the-night alarms. The time came when Laura really believed her daughter *would* go into the Peace Corps. Just before this new paperback edition of our book went to press, Joanie has begun considering such a step: she has written away for information about how to do so.

In a memorable note, Laura Willis described the evolution of her relationship to her daughter: ''Once I was pretty tough with her, a real boss at home, never mind work. Now, I look up to her. At first I thought I was failing in my responsibilities as a mother— to stand up and be the parent, not a friend or someone who goes along with her daughter because it's easier to do that. But I gave all this a lot of thought, and I think my daughter is a good, good person—a good soul might be the best way to describe her. And so I let *her* guide *me* some of the time—not all of the time, but some of the time.''

Maisie, much of whose life was spent ''managing,'' has also moved toward humble acceptance of another's wisdom in recent years. Not that she wasn't always impressed with her husband Donald's decency and goodness of heart. Still, she was a bit of a "manager" with him too—a practical, older person, she provided for him and on numerous occasions mediated between his gentle idealism and innocence on the one hand, and the skeptics, cynics, and outright confidence men out there in the world on the other. When Donald graduated from college, he was prepared to dedicate himself to a civil rights organization, to a charitable cause, to any group intent on helping those in need. But Maisie had her eye on the checkbook, on their debts, and on the bills she knew would be coming in week after week. They took a long walk together one Sunday and had the argument of their life. In a letter to one of us, Maisie made her point, though a bit apologetically, for she had by then deferred morally to her husband: "I'll be reading the papers, and I'll think of the checkbook. Don has never written a check in his life, or not since we've been married! That's the difference. I wish I could have his ideals. It's true—I'm materialistic."

Despite these differences, over the years, the two have built a strong marriage. Donald was a youth worker for a while, then went back to school and became a social worker. He was tireless in his devotion to the hurt and impoverished children he constantly met in the line of duty. He also became, at times, terribly depressed: "I hate that word *burn-out*; it's a cop-out word. But dammit, there are days when I'm ready to throw in the towel totally. I'll be going to work [by subway and bus], and I'll see a skyscraper in the distance from a hill, and I'll imagine all the comfortable offices and the nice restaurants—and the people there who aren't all messed up. Sure, maybe they are, in their own way, like you said—but at least they're going along in life, and they're not so wasted as these folks here are, *so wasted!* I try, and it's like in that 'myth' I read about—Camus, I think: you roll the big stone, the boulder, up the hill, pushing, pushing, sweating like you're in a hot shower, muscles creaking away, and you think you might be getting somewhere, this time, yes, getting there, but then, the damned thing starts coming down on you, and you'd better get the hell out of the way, *fast*. I don't know if that's what Camus described—it's been years [since he read the essay "The Myth of Sisyphus"], but it's sure what happens to me; and when that happens, I'm just destroyed. I feel so lousy and stupid. I'm ready to call some stock brokerage company and ask them if they have room for me to make calls, to get people to buy whatever Wall Street is selling.

"There's nothing wrong with selling stocks. I'm getting snotty. Maybe people on Wall Street get depressed the way I do. I have no right to feel sorry for myself. All day I see awful things, so I should thank my lucky stars. I do, too—especially when I stop and realize what Maisie has done for me. If it hadn't been for her, I'd never have done this kind of work, and lasted. There are days when someone will thank me for what I've done, and I'll tell them, don't thank me, thank my wife. They think I'm being 'nice' or 'modest'; but I'm being truthful, that's all."

Their marriage has been all that he says it is: a bond that enables each of them to express for the other—for the two as a couple— certain qualities of mind and heart. Maisie's goodness, she herself often said, got lived out as her husband did his work. With her competence as a "manager" at home as well as at work, indeed, at times he could even imagine himself as the stockbroker he sometimes summoned in his blue spells of fantasy. Maisie lived out that side of life for him: he said to us, "You folks shouldn't just stick with the women you're meeting! Let a few of us [husbands] put in a word or two about them. Maisie gives me lots of inspiration, but I egg her on a little, too, you know. I've noticed that she likes me to be forgetful about money; that way, she can work the harder at running our house—the bills. But she wants to hear every word of what I tell her at supper about my work, and I have my little ways of keeping track of our checkbook and the savings we have. It's a marriage, I guess—a good one!"

A similar overall harmony, strong enough to contain differences, has characterized Sue's marriage. Her "fighting" spirit has in no way become attenuated this past decade. She has become, in her own description, a "hardworking Southern liberal"—in the late 1980's, a somewhat lonely vocation. She works for a small weekly newspaper that takes on controversial matters shunned by the daily press. She can be counted on as a critic of federal cutbacks that affect the poor. She is a signer of petitions, a willing marcher in one or another political cause. Often her husband is, to use her words, "quite shocked." We ask why, knowing that he basically supports the same causes. "My husband isn't conservative in his political views: he's a liberal, too, a Southern liberal. But he *is* conservative in his personal life, in the way he behaves with people—and that's where, I guess, I fail. I wish I could be as quiet and tactful as he is—well, a lot of the time, I don't want to be like that, and I wouldn't if I could, to be honest! I'm what I am—I mean, *who* I am. To some Southerners, I'll always be the brash, outspoken Yankee outsider, no matter what the subject is: the brand of cereal you buy for your breakfast! There are still differences between people up North and people down here. There are lots of similarities, of course: suburbia is suburbia in certain ways."

Sue brings up all the "variables"—class and ethnic background and race and region and religion. In the intermittent conversations we've had with her, she keeps going back to her own childhood, to the constraints and anxieties she experienced growing up—her father's mean-tempered manner, fueled by the consumption of alcohol, and her mother's strange, even "loony" ways of behaving. She had always been one for voluble psychological introspection, much of which we quoted at length when we presented her to the reader a decade ago. Each time we have met her since then, or heard from her—long, self-analytical letters—we realized how hard she has had to work to rein in what she once called her "egotism"—an unnecessarily harsh word perhaps, but one she has insisted upon using: "I've been talking with a psychiatrist lately [in 1986]. I don't like to talk with him about myself for an hour at a time—especially when the major problem I have is that I think about myself too much! You two write about 'ironies.' There's one! But I had to do something. My husband is a very patient and polite person, and yet lately he's had his fill of my egotism. He's never called it that, no, but I can tell when he'd rather be hearing something else besides my voice dwelling on my thoughts or my deeds. It's only recently that I've figured out that it wasn't my dad's drinking that 'did me in' when I was a kid; it was my mother's personality—she was really big on herself! She had a way of twisting everything so that it came out being about her. Even her friends called her 'kooky'—behind her back. They'd feel sorry for her. They'd say she was lonely, and she'd had a tough time growing up. But a lot of people have had a lot of trouble, and they don't act as 'nutty' as she did. I think I wanted to explode at her, but didn't because I was afraid she'd totally 'lose it' if I did. My doctor said 'nutty' people can use their 'nuttiness' to intimidate others, especially their kids. They can even hand it down [to their children]. I've tried not to be like her; boy, have I tried. I don't stare into space all the time or talk with her goofy voice, or manipulate people emotionally, the way she would—until Dad had three choices: tell her to go to hell, which he couldn't do, unfortunately; get depressed, which he did; or drink, which he also did. Then everyone called him a drunk, and they felt sorry for my mother, and she loved that.

"You see, I'm talking and talking about me and my childhood. I'm sorry! I should spend my time trying to help the poor. That's what Paul would be doing if he were alive. Whenever I'd start talking about myself back then, he'd change the subject to the blacks, to their problems. My husband is too tolerant of me, I sometimes think."

Sue was not, when she wrote this, very "tolerant" of herself, but a year later (1987) she slowed up a bit with respect to her psychological self-criticism. She was back to political activity: she would "try hard" not to "bore" us with "personal details," she said, and told us of various social questions she was examining, various "local matters" that pressed on her mind. Once, wistfully, she spoke of her son, Paul: "He reminds me of his namesake. He's a good person. I hope he doesn't become disappointed by life." Sue herself has experienced moments of such disappointment, but in the main she'll always be the fighter she thought of herself as being, the brash Yankee activist down South.

In our minds, we sometimes compare Sue with Maria, another

headstrong woman. They are separated by miles of land and belong, of course, to very different cultural traditions. They are also temperamentally different, as mothers and wives, even though each was, for a while, fairly impulsive and determined. By the late 1980's, however, Maria was quiet and watchful of others, while Sue was talkative and intent on coming to terms with herself. Maria, after a fashion, was slowly returning to the "mesa" of her childhood. Not literally, but in her mind: "I sit and watch them [Anglos] and sometimes I wander in my spirit—my spirit wanders, I should say! I'm back on the mesa, feeling the wind, watching the tumbleweed roll along, or a bird trying to use the [wind] currents to get someplace, and almost falling, but not [falling], and rising suddenly: its will does the job! I try to tell my children about will; you must be clear about what you want to do, and then, you must do it. My children have their own ideas. I guess they don't have to hear me talk to them about 'will.' I remember Rod talking about 'willpower.' I must be turning into an Anglo, after all! Pueblos, we—we sometimes go with the wind too much."

Not her children, though. They grew up in Santa Fe, and in many ways found their mother hard to fathom psychologically, culturally. They had a number of urban Indian, as well as Anglo, friends. As teenagers they looked forward to a life in Albuquerque, perhaps, or even in California. Maria applauded such "will" on their part, but lamented what had happened to all of them as a family: "I may have started all this [acculturation]. I was the one who loved our land, our reservation; I was the one who wanted to spend all my life on the mesa—once. I was the one who left, though. I haven't the heart to tell my kids about my [earlier] life. I thought I'd forget it. But I don't. I see those Anglo artists and photographers, and I'm interested in them—too much. My kids have seen my eyes, the look on my face. They want to know the same thing—all about 'them.' "

Maria saw this curiosity of hers as something to be fought. For her children, however, things would always be different: "They are further away from our people than I have ever been. They know we are Pueblo Indians, but they have their hearts set for the city. They won't stay there just a year or two: I think they'll live in some city all their lives. Fine! Before I die, I hope I can return to our reservation. I'd like to die on a sunny day, but a windy day. I'd like to hear the wind talking to the land!''

In middle age, Maria had once again become the dreamer she had been as a child. Eileen, our "dreamer" in this book, never lost her own, determined dreams. Hers are not the unfettered dreams of a Pueblo woman but the stuff of urban, ethnic history— to keep on the "rise," generation after generation. In the years since this book first appeared, Eileen and Tim have devoted themselves mind, heart, and soul to that ascent—working hard, saving money, setting goals and standards for their children and for themselves. In her 1987 Christmas letter, Eileen told us how well her family was doing, how earnestly they were all working. "We're doing fine," she wrote, and spelled out in some detail how each of the children was "moving along." One of her daughters was an excellent student at a first-rate college; another had become a nurse; another was "into computers"; the son was hoping to go to college; and she and Tim were doing their best to keep the family afloat. "I love being back at nursing. I love the work, and I love the chance to make fairly good wages, at last. We were given a good raise last spring!''

For Eileen, America is still a land of possibility, of "miracles" even: "I believe in miracles, even if people call me naive. I know what my parents went through. It's been up, up, up for my family all these years [the 1980's], and I'm ready to work day and night to keep it that way. I know you can do better in other jobs. Maybe. But I love taking care of people, and when they're in trouble, they're hurting, and their health isn't so good, they'll show you a real good side of themselves. People can be cranky then, too. But I try to see the positive in people—in life. I try to find it in myself. If I see Mr. Blackmood coming on, I say no and find something to do that will help me get back in stride again.''

She has pointed out to us—in words that resonate as we think of the lives in this book, and our own—that "time disappears right before your eyes. . . . Life becomes one eye-blink and then another, and soon, it's more night than day.'' One woman, so singular and extraordinary to us, lives her ''ordinary'' life, is proudly of the working class, and hopes against hope that the arc of several generations in her family will tilt upward, that steps will be taken, a bit of social height achieved, and a bit more edge gained on life's hazards before that final blink of the eyes.

part seven

THE WAY WE WORK

Many readers and reviewers of *Women of Crisis* and *Women of Crisis II* have asked us how we go about doing our research and our writing. In January 1989 we sat down together and tried to answer their questions. We entered into a dialogue: about the differences in our training and our interests in the beginning, about "research" as against listening, about the hazards of tape recorders, and especially about how we found our teachers, the children and their parents all over America. The republication of both volumes of *Women of Crisis* seems a good occasion to record this dialogue and, in this way, to answer some of the questions about the way we work.

J.H.C. Perhaps we should start by remembering the way we used to work together when we first went South in 1960.

R.C. Yes, there certainly has been an "evolution" in our work.

J.H.C. In the beginning, you were trying hard to be a social scientist. We'd go to the homes of the children whom we wrote about in *Children of Crisis*, to Ruby's home, to Tessie's, and later to the Connors'.* You would have all those questions written out in advance. The psychiatric and psychoanalytic theory was uppermost on your mind, and you were trying to learn what the theory told you that you should learn.

R.C. And the tape recorder always came with us.

J.H.C. Everywhere we went, we would go through our tape-recorder ritual: all eyes and ears on it. We found ourselves talking *to* it, performing *for* it; we were losing our natural manner with one another because of the self-consciousness that machine causes in people. I was so glad to get away with Ruby's mother, or Mrs. Connor. We would just sit and gab, while you had to keep one eye and an ear on the machine and the other on all those "defense mechanisms." In the interviews, at first, we hung on for dear life to a kind of routine because we didn't quite know how else to go about it. We were learning not only what was happening to the kids, but something else: how to do the work we were hoping to do.

R.C. In those days we weren't working out of an office or a clinic or a hospital or a school. You were a high-school English teacher, and I was a child psychiatrist. And there we were, going to homes and asking parents and children to talk with us. These families had enough trouble on their hands without us! The black kids were going through mobs. Federal marshals took them to school. When the white kids finally went back to school, the mobs turned on them, too. It was hell—and there we were, trying to find out how the kids were managing. After a while, when we saw how strong the families were, and when the kids didn't develop symptoms—the symptoms I was trained to see and then treat—we had to stand back and figure out what was going on and how we could learn about it.

J.H.C. You described the shifts and turns that work took in the *Children of Crisis* books. For a year or two, we both floundered. You don't usually read about all the confusions that researchers

---

* The Connors are the white family who broke the boycott against desegregation and sent two of their sons to the Frantz School, where Ruby Bridges had been alone as a first-grade student.

experience, the shifts in thinking, the changes of tack. Maybe some research is different—a straight line from A to B. But we zigzagged. I remember a picture I took with that old Brownie camera, of you and Ruby sitting at the kitchen table. You're wearing a bow tie and a sports jacket on a hot, late summer day in New Orleans. You've asked Ruby to draw a picture—of the school, I think—and she's obliging you. You're looking at her as she draws. Somehow, for me, that picture tells the story of us at the start. You're a doctor, and you're asking a patient to work with you—the way you did at Children's Hospital in Boston. A year or two later, you'd be without that jacket and tie. You'd be sipping a Coke and maybe drawing a picture yourself. You'd be laughing or talking and not looking so austere. It took us time to get to know those children and their families. It took us time to feel our way, to relax a bit. We were white Yankees, and we'd gone to college, and you had all that training and all those ideas about what to look for.

R.C. I had to unlearn, as well as to learn. Instead of being a psychiatrist, I had to turn into an anthropologist, a journalist, a public health doctor, a documentary observer. Along the way, you reminded me we were *guests*, strangers and visitors and eventually friends; you stood up for common sense and common courtesy, *their* role in research.

J.H.C. After a while, we began to enjoy ourselves with the families. They fed us, and we brought soft drinks and food. We watched television with them and played with the kids, with their toys and games. We went on drives together, visiting their friends and relatives. Most important of all, I now realize, we went to church with them. Maybe we learned most from those long hours in church—the praying and singing, the shouting and crying, the intensity and passion of it all, the testifying and witnessing: people living tough lives and trying to figure out what mattered and what was silly or frivolous. At last we began to see and hear firsthand what *inspired* Ruby and her family! No wonder she prayed for those people who wanted to kill her! No wonder she was willing to forgive them! Her parents had taught her to remember the example of Jesus, and in church she and dozens of others spent a lot of time trying to "reach" Jesus. Their churchgoing wasn't the kind we had known up North.

R.C. We were learning to pay attention to the *lives* of people. I was moving away from an exclusive interest in symptoms and the unconscious, in the hidden meanings in children's words and drawings. I was now observing what pictures were on the walls, what programs the families watched, what music they played, what food they ate, and what they wore. I began to look for the rhythms and styles of a life, of the cultural inheritance of the children I'd set out to study.

J.H.C. We began to realize that if we wanted to understand the strengths and weaknesses of those kids, we had to see the world through *their* eyes, not keep on imposing our agendas on them. You didn't abandon your psychiatric and psychoanalytic curiosity, but we both tried to broaden it, so that it wasn't done in a social— or racial—vacuum.

R.C. By 1962 or so, Erik Erikson's work began to be very helpful to us. I remember buying *Childhood and Society* in that bookstore on Canal Street. I was trying to figure out how to connect my medical life—its knowledge and assumptions—to the "street life" you and I were living: going from home to home, to schools, talking with white hecklers on the sidewalk and with the federal marshals who escorted those children, and working with the civil rights student activists of SNCC and CORE, in their "freedom houses." One day I was a pediatrician, helping a child who had bronchitis or a stomach upset. The next day, I was back asking my psychiatric questions, though I was now getting better at putting them in plain, ordinary words and not rushing to ominous conclusions. Then there were days when I joined the student activists or became a journalist, doing a "story" for *New South*, a publication of the Southern Regional Council, our sponsor in those first years. But we were on our own in trying to learn how to do documentary work.

J.H.C. What we both wanted, I now realize, was to be "on our own." You wanted to get away from rigid professional thinking.

I loved living in the South, loved meeting those children and their families. I'd taught in a fancy private school, and I'd learned that people can be white and well-to-do and well educated and yet not necessarily live useful, stable lives. I'd had my fill of "the culture of narcissism." I was glad to be with people facing real, honest-to-goodness struggles and facing them with courage and even good humor. We both had our reasons to be happy down in Dixie! There's nothing like a little distance on your past when you're in your twenties and thirties.

R.C. Even though we were doing "research"—you talking with parents and teachers, me with kids—we were also exploring, trying to figure out how we were going to live our lives, what we believed to be important. During the 1950's, both of us had been "apolitical"—not really interested in social or racial questions. I was interested in literature, then in medicine and pediatrics, and then in psychoanalytic psychiatry. You taught history and English and have always been a great reader of novels and stories. Even before we got married, you were pulling me away from dogmatic, ideological psychoanalytic thinking and back to Dickens and George Eliot and Tolstoi and Chekhov. That "tension" was an important part of our lives then, and it had a lot to do with the work we eventually did together. You were pushing me, I now realize, to be an observer, a witness, and to link arms with the people we met, with the struggle they were waging. This move from "value-free" investigator to the participant-observer who learns from his subjectivity, from his personal involvements and commitments, rather than avoiding them, was a big shift for me.

J.H.C. We both loosened up a lot. In the early days of our work, as you tried to make conversation with those children, it was tough going. After all, they hadn't come to see you in a clinic. They were living their lives, and for some reason known only to you, they were seeing you a few times a week. They were as curious about you as you were about them. They must have had trouble knowing what to make of both of us. Who were we? We were wanderers; we'd said good-bye to a conventional middle-class life and to two professions—or at least to being the regular kind of doctor and teacher we'd once been. Besides, for those families in the Deep South of the early 1960's, we were the first whites who'd ever set foot in their homes. Maybe a white insurance man had come to the door—though there were black insurance agents, I remember, plenty of them—or maybe some town official. Only after months of meeting with us did they let us know that they'd been quite afraid, never mind curious, when we first showed up. Even though we were introduced by a person they knew and trusted, who explained to them who we were and that we were friends, the looks on their faces told us something else, how nervous they were. You and I were nervous, too, and maybe more scared than we realized. We didn't want to recognize how those people felt about us being with them because we didn't want to stop and think about how we felt being there. Though we can talk now about the work we were doing, we felt back then that we were on the brink of disaster. We seemed to be drifting; we had no financial support, and no institutional support; and there were lots of people back home who thought we had gone off the deep end!

R.C. It feels strange, thinking back to that time. Nowadays, the work we were doing seems so natural: an obviously sensible kind of study for someone to do. But it's almost thirty years ago that we began our work together, and *then* psychiatry was different, and so was psychoanalysis and medicine, not to mention the South. Segregation was the law. Resisting integration was respectable in universities and medical schools. Psychiatrists weren't involved in social and political issues the way some of them are today.

J.H.C. Being naive and maybe even a little simpleminded, we were ready to take a few risks; we were also so glad *not* to be "locked into" fifty-minute hours (you) and an uptight school regimen (me) that we felt excited and happy rather than frightened and anxious. You had plenty of reservations about the psychiatry you'd come to know in hospitals and clinics, and I was restless as a teacher.

R.C. . . . Restlessness as a reason for research?

J.H.C. By 1963, however, we knew we were scared. The high school kids we met in Atlanta, when school desegregation began there, persuaded us to join the civil rights movement. You kept asking them what they did after school, and they told you! Then Lawrence Jefferson, who was one of two black teenagers to desegregate Henry Grady High School, asked you if you wanted to come to the SNCC headquarters, and you went just to see how he spent his time. The next thing you knew, Jim Forman and Stokeley Carmichael were asking who *you* were and why *you* were there. You told them you wanted to be of help, and they put you to work sweeping the floor—one of your better moments in doing psychiatric research! They tested us both out—and why not? We hadn't been recruited on a campus. We were unknown whites who had suddenly showed up, and they had plenty of reasons to worry about who we were and what we had in mind.

R.C. We were "tested" for many weeks, and it was hard. I resented it more than you, because you accepted the desirability of that testing. I got on my high horse from the very beginning and felt after a while that I should pull back. We passed the tests—in the sense that we were "accepted," eventually—but in the interim I learned a lot about myself. I can now see the snobbishness, the sense of self-importance, the high-and-mighty attitude of the professional man: how *dare* they question my credentials and treat me with such continuing skepticism! A day or two of sweeping the floors was fine, but weeks and weeks of the same! Of course I fought back with the weapon I knew best—psychiatric reductionism! Why were they so suspicious, so "defensive," so "paranoid"? What "problems" did they have?

J.H.C. The civil rights movement helped us in ways we didn't anticipate. We were struggling against the segregation of blacks and whites, but with a little looking inward, we began to see other ways people have of keeping apart—by neighborhood and occupation, for example. As I look back to those days, I realize that we were learning not just about the South but also about ourselves. It was so easy for those of us from the North to "dump" on the South, to use it to stay blind about the arrogance and insensitivity and smugness in our own backyards. We didn't have to travel to Georgia or Louisiana to find all that. We were the lucky recipients of plenty of good teaching from the kids we were meeting, and their parents, and their teachers—both black and white.

R.C. After a year or two of important stumbling and floundering, we searched for ways to write about what we were hearing. Someday someone should write an essay on the importance of floundering and stumbling in "research"—but then, I'm afraid, we'll all be told that there's the Floundering and Stumbling stage and that, too, will become part of our dreary psychological self-consciousness. While we were learning how to get along with poor Southern black people, with white people who were being confronted by a major political change in their lives, and with civil rights activists, I was abandoning the language of the clinic (prodded by you).

J.H.C. Events, people, and experiences were prodding you, too, not only my preference for literature over psychology.

R.C. Right. But you were always there, laughing at all the pretentiousness and banality that gets called "social science." We were trying to learn how to tell stories—the stories of the people we were meeting.

J.H.C. Maggie Long was very helpful then, and Lillian Smith, those two Southern novelists.

R.C. Yes, they looked at some of my psychiatric reports and were aghast. They urged me to write in plain language, and as Lillian Smith put it, "Think of yourself as someone doing an *introduction* of someone else." A wonderful way of putting it. I'd sit in our home in Vinings [Georgia] and listen to our tapes, and read our notes, and remember scenes, comments, episodes, and accounts of this or that event. And I'd imagine someone in the room, standing and waiting to be told about them. I'd see myself as the introducer of one person to another, the person in the middle. And then I'd write. Those two novelists and you—the three of you—bore down hard on a jargon-filled professional man looking for "data"!

J.H.C. It was a big shift not only in the writing but in the way we did the work. By 1962, we weren't looking for psychological adjustment. We were listening to people give us accounts of what happened today or yesterday, or of what they hoped (or worried) would happen tomorrow. Then we tried to tell others what we'd heard, what we saw with our own eyes, or what we tried to see through the eyes of others.

R.C. We used the tape recorder less. I took more notes. I was carried back to my days with William Carlos Williams—all those notes he wrote to himself after he'd visited a patient, lines for future poems he'd heard from others, or lines they had stimulated in his mind.

J.H.C. In the first years, I used to think the transcripts were "overkill." Too much was being taped, not enough was being "extracted" by us as we listened, not enough going for the heart of things. That's what listening should be—close and careful attention paid on the spot. With the tape recorder present, you tend to sit back and be a piggy eater, indiscriminate—the machine slurping everything in. Without the machine, it's your ears and your eyes and your brain, and then your fingers holding the pen: it's *you*, working and noticing and keeping what you think is important, what you've noticed in your head, and remembering it while at the same time thinking about what it means, and then writing it down so it makes some sense and fits into what you've learned before and are now learning and hope to learn. *Context* is the word here; as a writer, you provide a context for what the researcher in you has heard.

R.C. You might say we've become "long-term listeners." In New Orleans, you started listening to the mothers and fathers, while I was with the kids. We then roamed through Appalachia and came back North. We went to the Southwest, and then back to New England. Your notebooks and journals gave us *Women of Crisis*, and mine turned into the *Children of Crisis* series and *The Moral Life of Children* and *The Political Life of Children*. Now that I think of it, all this writing seems a response to thirty years of experience, of being taught by kids and by their families, and by classes of schoolchildren and their teachers.

J.H.C. The school visits were always the high point for me, as a teacher. When I think back on our work, I sometimes remember the moments with the families in their homes, but mostly I remember the times in the schools, sitting on those low chairs, with the boys and girls in the first or second or third or fourth grades, hearing them ask questions or talk about what happened to them, watching while they drew pictures—or drawing pictures ourselves and then all showing them to each other. We were so lucky to be able to call all that *work!* It was a tremendous education for us. Some professors write textbooks, but I'd like to put in a word for some other "professors"—all the people willing to sit down with you and "profess," to tell you what's on their mind and what they've gone through in their lives, and in that way to provide you with plenty of knowledge or learning, whether colleges call it that or not.

R.C. After thirty years, you've won me over to that way of seeing things—after a long struggle. When we started out, my head was full of reductionist strivings. You kept smiling—and doubting; you listened to the people we met, and eventually I began listening in the way you did.

J.H.C. You were always attentive to the kids and their parents, but for a while you saw them as patients, or soon-to-be patients.

R.C. You saw many of the people we met in the civil rights struggle and afterward, as heroes.

J.H.C. Some of them were. In many of our lives there is trouble, but also great personal dignity in the face of that trouble: the patient and the hero. There's also the teacher in many of us, and it took us a long time to see those children and their parents as teachers. I wish our college teachers had helped us think of the other teachers we might find in the world. We had to go searching for the world of Ruby, to meet people like her, and when we came back, we found many right in Cambridge, though maybe not right in Harvard Square.

R.C. We've been well taught.

J.H.C. True, and thank God.

about the authors

ROBERT COLES, M.D., is a professor of psychiatry and medical humanities at Harvard Medical School and research psychiatrist for the Harvard University Health Services. Among his many books are biographies of Dorothy Day and Simone Weil and the five-volume *Children of Crisis* series, for which he won the Pulitzer Prize. A recipient of the MacArthur Prize Award, he is continuing the research he wrote about in the much-acclaimed works *The Moral Life of Children* and *The Political Life of Children*.

JANE HALLOWELL COLES graduated from Radcliffe College. She has taught English and history in public schools in Georgia, Louisiana, and, most recently, Massachusetts. She is also the co-author of *Women of Crisis: Lives of Struggle and Hope*. The Coleses live near Boston and are the parents of three sons.